Evil
in World Religions

Stephen J. Vicchio, Ph.D.

Wisdom
Editions
Minneapolis, Minnesota

Minneapolis
FIRST EDITION April 2021

Evil in World Religions
Copyright © 2021 by Stephen J. Vicchio.
All rights reserved.

Printed in the United States of America.
10 9 8 7 6 5 4 3 2 1

Cover and interior design: Gary Lindberg

ISBN: 978-1-950743-52-0

To Matthew Sayers, my fine student, scholar and friend, who also helped me with my Sanskrit for this book.

Contents

Evil
in World Religions

Introduction

The study to follow is an examination of what the religions of the world have had to say about the phenomena of evil and suffering. In other words, this is a work of the study of comparative religions of the world in terms of how they answer or respond to the issues of evil and suffering in the world.

This study may be conceived as having four parts. The first of these parts is an analysis and introduction of how to define "religion," "evil," and a variety of other religious concepts that will be of help in the remainder of this study. The first chapter is a kind of preamble on how to study the world's religions.

Part two of this study consists of Chapters Two, Three and Four, the oldest of the world's religious traditions in this study to follow. Hinduism is over four thousand years old; Judaism, at least three thousand years old, and the dualistic faiths of Zoroastrianism, Mithraism and Manichaeism, between two thousand and twenty-five hundred years old.

The third part of this study on evil and suffering in the religions of the world is about four Asian faiths of the Far East—Buddhism, Confucianism, Taoism and the Japanese religion called Shinto. For the most part, these faiths all have very long histories stretching back to what is known as the "Axial Age" of history—a time when many of the major faiths of the world first emerged. These four faiths of the Far East have also seen a good deal of intermingling and borrowing amongst each other, particularly the ones from China.

The fourth part of this study, Chapters Eight, Nine and Ten, include two religions, Christianity and Islam, which arose in the ancient Near East in Israel and on the Arabian Peninsula in the seventh century CE.

In these chapters, our approach is mostly a historical one. We begin with the foundational texts and then explore what medieval and modern thinkers have had to say about the issues of evil and suffering in their respective traditions. In Chapter Ten, the final chapter of part four of this study, we take up the question of how traditional African religions have responded to the phenomena of evil and suffering. Indeed, we will use the theological views of the Yoruba and the Igbo people as representative religions for how African has dealt with the issues of evil and suffering.

Finally, Chapter Eleven of this study serves as a catalog of the general conclusions we have made of the issues of evil and suffering in the religions of the world. It is a summary chapter that sets forth the major views to be found in this study.

We hope that this study will be valuable for scholars who study comparative religions, as well as those who study and write about the problem of evil and the issue of theodicy. We also hope this may be of some value to college and university students who are taking courses in those areas.

In my forty-three years of teaching, I have learned many languages, sometimes from teachers, sometimes from students, and sometimes from having four sabbaticals over the years. In this study, you will find words and phrases in Sanskrit, which I learned as a graduate student at Yale; classical Hebrew that I began studying in 1966 with the great scholar of Johns Hopkins University, William F. Albright; I learned 500 characters of Mandarin Chinese from one of my students in the 1980s, a woman named Bin Tu; I worked on Yoruba and Igbo while on a sabbatical in Nigeria in the late 1980s; I began learning Arabic during two sabbaticals in Damascus and Cairo in the early and late 1990s; and I studied Greek and Latin in college.

You will also find in this study the mention of words and phrases in Swahili, Old Egyptian, Urdu, Turkish, Muda, Japanese, and even, Old Saxon. All of these words and phrases appear in Appendices A through H at the end of Chapter Eleven.

We began collecting notes for this book at the beginning of our teaching career in the early 1970s when teaching Comparative Religions at the University of Maryland. It is only now, after our retirement from teaching in 2016, that we have gathered those notes together for the purposes of publication.

Over the years in our teaching and writing careers, we have been encouraged and aided by many mentors, colleagues, and, of course, more than ten thousand students we have encountered in the classroom.

SJV. July 2020

Chapter One:
On the Natures of Evil and Religion

The only thing necessary for the triumph of evil is for the good people to do nothing about it.

—Edmund Burke

There has to be evil so that the good may have its purity above it.

—Gautama Buddha

These words, it seems to me, give us a picture of the essence of human language… From this we learn that every word has a meaning and this meaning is correlated, it is the object for which the word stands.

—Ludwig Wittgenstein, *Philosophical Investigations*

Introduction

In this opening chapter, we have the following goals: First, to make some comments about the idea of a "definition" in Western culture. Secondly, to discuss the nature of "evil" in the world's religious traditions. Thirdly, we will describe and discuss several answers and responses as to why evil exists in the world. Fourthly, we will introduce several "supplementary" answers and responses as to the nature and the meanings of evil in the world.

These four goals will be followed in the first chapter with a discussion of the definition and extent of the category of "religion." As we shall see, this category is not always so easy to delineate in the religions of the world. We move first then to the idea of a definition in Western culture.

The Idea of a "Definition" in Western Culture

The first philosopher in the West to raise the question about the nature of a definition was the Macedonian, Aristotle. He discusses the idea of what a definition is in a number of his works, including *The Metaphysics*, *Posterior Analytics*, and *History of Animals*.[1] What all these works have in common on the issue at hand is that a definition of a thing is a "collection of necessary characteristics that together are sufficient" to call something what we call it.[2]

In *Posterior Analytics*, Aristotle, the pupil of Plato, sets out to define what a "human being" is. He goes on to suggests the following necessary conditions for a "human":

1. An animal.
2. That is mortal.
3. That is a biped.
4. That does not have wings.[3]

In *History of Animals*, Aristotle adds another characteristic for a human being—that he or she is "rational."[4] The Greek philosopher does this to make a distinction between humans and animals; the former has reason, while the latter does not. For many centuries in the history of Western philosophy, Aristotle's notion of a definition was the accepted one. Seven hundred years later, Augustine, the Bishop of Hippo, seems to hold the same view as Aristotle.

In his *Confessions*, Augustine sketches out how he first learned language. Augustine says, "When adults named some object by pointing to it and uttering a word, like 'book' or 'candle,'" he concluded that, "I perceived this and grasped that the thing was signified by the sound that they uttered, since they were trying to point it out."[5]

Later in Western philosophy, in the twentieth-century work of Ludwig Wittgenstein called *Philosophical Investigations*, the Austrian thinker gave the Aristotle-Augustine theory the name "picture theory." His idea is that there is an object, for example, a book, and there is a tag hanging from the object, which states the name of the object, such as "*buch*" or "book."[6] Wittgenstein says in *Philosophical Investigations* the following:

> These words, it seems to me, give us a picture of the essence of human language. It is this: that words in languages name objects... Sentences are the combination of such names... From all of this, we learn every word has a meaning, and this meaning is correlated; it is the object for which the word stands.[7]

Next, Wittgenstein argues against this common sense "picture theory" that is nothing more than Aristotle's necessary and sufficient conditions. He raises the question about what the necessary and sufficient conditions are for a "game." In other words, what is the picture that the tag "game" signifies? The Austrian philosopher goes on to say that there are no necessary and sufficient conditions for a "game," and he challenges his readers to come up with some with no success.[8]

Let us demonstrate this conclusion by speaking of a personal experience from the early 1980s. I was in Egypt with an Egyptian physician friend of mine, and we arrived at a village to find a group of young boys, about ten to twelve years old. The boys sat around a circle in the sand. The players moved their hands with a various number of fingers thrust out, and according to the results, pieces of colored glass were added or subtracted from the center of the circle.

As we watched, I said to my friend, "What is that game they are playing?" He responded by indicating it was not a game. Rather, it was a contest for who would lead a religious festival the following day. That day, I was convinced that the boys were playing a game. Indeed, I had the tag "game" hanging from the picture we were viewing. But it turns out my "tag" was wrong.

In *Philosophical Investigations*, Wittgenstein suggests that the "nature of language is to be found in its use." He calls his view of language the *Familienahnlichkeit* View, or Family Resemblance View. By this he means "There is a loose network of ideas" that go into the use of a certain word or words about our example, Wittgenstein would say, the activity of the boys had a number of traits that looked like what we normally would call a game. In other words, what I saw was the "family resemblance" of the boys' activity to other things I have seen called "game."

Next in this chapter, we will raise the question of whether there are necessary and sufficient conditions for calling something "evil" and a "religion." It is enough now, however, to point out that I will adopt Wittgenstein's Family Resemblance approach when examining what is an example of "evil," as well as what is a "religion."

The Nature of the "Evil" in Human Languages

There have been a number of attempts in contemporary philosophy to come up with necessary and sufficient conditions for calling something "evil." Going back to Immanuel Kant's *Religion Within the Limits of Reason Alone*, published in 1793, the German philosopher argues that there are three descending kinds of evil. He calls these "frailty, impurity, and perversity." A person with a frail will, Kant tells us, performs good actions because they are good, but he or she is too weak to carry through with his or her plans.[9]

Kant believes that at the second level of evil, the "impurity" level, a person does not attempt to do the morally right thing simply because it is morally right. Instead, he or she performs the action partially because it is morally right and partially for some other reason.[10] Kant says the impure person is worse than the frail person, even though the frail person does wrong while the perverse person does right.[11]

The final stage of evil for Kant is "corruption." Instead of prioritizing the moral law, he or she acts in his or her own self-interest and not for altruistic purposes. This view of evil is sometimes called "Philosophical Egoism."[12] Kant also makes the additional claim that human nature contains something he calls "Radical Evil." What he means by this term is that human beings have two separate moral natures: a capacity for moral goodness and what he calls Radical Evil, an inherent capacity to do Moral Evil.[13]

It is not entirely clear from his German text what Kant meant by Radical Evil. But it appears to be somewhat like the ancient Hebrew view that all human beings have two propensities, inclinations or imaginations, the *yetzer hara*, or "Evil Imagination," and the *yetzer tov*, or the "Good Imagination."[14]

Kant's theory of Radical Evil was adopted by German-born philosopher Hanna Arendt, who taught for many years in the United

States. Arendt's thoughts on the nature of evil stemmed from her attempt to understand and evaluate the evil of the Nazi concentration and death camps. She outlines her views on evil in two major books, *The Origins of Totalitarianism* published in 1951, and *Eichmann in Jerusalem: A Report on the Banality of Evil* published in 1963.[15]

In the former work, Arendt borrows Kant's view of Radical Evil, while in the latter work she concludes that Adolf Eichmann was a "terrifyingly normal human being, who simply did not think very deeply about what he was doing.[16] Other modern philosophers like Richard J. Bernstein, for example, have given careful analyses of Kant and Arendt's views.[17] Another contemporary scholar who writes about Radical Evil is Henry E. Allison of Fordham University.[18]

Very few contemporary philosophers, however, have attempted to come up with a set of necessary and sufficient conditions for calling something evil. Most writers who have tried such an exercise have not succeeded. Nevertheless, we will make another effort here. First, all examples of evil appear to cause harm. Second, evil is sometimes intentional and sometimes not. Third, evil is sometimes natural and sometimes not. Fourth, evil is sometimes a psychological phenomenon, and sometimes not. Fifth, evil often causes unnecessary suffering. That is, suffering that has no purpose.

These five characteristics outlined here are not necessary and sufficient conditions for evil. Rather, they should be seen as Family Resemblance characteristics for calling something evil. Any example of what may be an example of evil may not have all five characteristics. But it has enough of the five that it still may be called evil because it looks like other things we call evil.

For the purposes of this study, when we use the term "evil," we mean one of three separate phenomena. First, there is Moral Evil, acts of evil caused by moral agents, gods, angels, demons, or human beings. Murder, rape and stealing are all examples of Moral Evil. Second, there are Natural Evils. These evils are suffering caused by natural events such as floods, earthquakes or a toothache.

Thirdly, there are Metaphysical, or Psychological Evil. These are evils that are primarily in the mind, such as dread, anxiety or fear. When we speak of evil in the world's religious traditions in this study, we will be speaking of all three varieties outlined here—moral, natural and psychological. This brings us to the definition of the other concept in this opening chapter, the nature of a "Religion."

The Nature of a World "Religion"

When we will speak of a religion in this study, we will mean an entity that has a broad range of family resemblance characteristics for religion. We will list ten characteristics that religions have tended to have in common, and then we will discuss them one at a time. These ten elements of a religion are the following:

1. A conception of Ultimate Reality.
2. A collection of myths, symbols and rituals.
3. A distinction between sacred and profane.
4. Belief in religious heroes, places and things.
5. A system of ethics sanctioned by Ultimate Reality.
6. An explanation for, and meaning of, evil.
7. A view of the nature of the self.
8. A view of survival after death.
9. Holy writings or scriptures.
10. A view of eschatology or last things.[19]

A Conception of Ultimate Reality

By the concept of Ultimate Reality, we mean to speak of what a particular religion says about what is ultimately real—God, Allah, Brahma, yin and yang, the good god and bad god in dualistic religions, etc. Conceptions of Ultimate Reality in the world's religions have come in many varieties, including pantheism, polytheism, dualism, monotheism, deism and a variety of other views. Many conceptions of Ultimate Reality in the religions of the world may be seen as existing on a continuum that goes from monistic, or pantheistic views, to dualistic faiths, with monotheistic faiths in the middle between the two poles. Thus, we get something like this:

Monistic Faiths	Monotheistic Faiths	Dualistic Faiths
X_____	Y_____	Z _____

Figure IA.

At location X, we have monistic, or pantheistic religions, such as Vedantic Hinduism, Hinayana Buddhism, or the metaphysical view of several Western philosophers such as seventeenth-century Dutch philosopher Baruch Spinoza. By "monistic," we mean that when it comes to Ultimate Reality, believers in these faiths think that all of reality is made of a single substance and that substance is divine.

In traditional Hinduism, that substance is called *Brahman*. For Hindu believers, Brahman is the substance of which everything is made. In the ancient Indian language Sanskrit, there is the expression *Tat tvam asi*, or "That you are" in English. It means that ultimately all that exists in reality is related to this faceless, eternal and divine principle called Brahman.[20]

At point Z of our continuum, we have the dualistic faiths, such as the ancient Persian religion Zoroastrianism, or two Roman religions known as Mithraism and Manichaeism. In these faiths, there are two different sources for Good and Evil. Sometimes these sources are gods, sometimes they are principles, and sometimes they are a mix of a god and a principle, such as in the metaphysical view of Plato in his book the *Timaeus*.[21] In the Zoroastrian faith, there are beliefs in a good god and a bad god. The former is known as *Ahura Mazda*, the latter as *Angra Mainya*.[22]

In this view, all that is good comes from the good god Ahura Mazda. All that is evil comes from Angra Mainya. The word "Ahura" in the ancient Persian language is a cognate of the English "honorable." The word Angra, not surprisingly, is a cognate of the English "angry." Thus, we have the "Honorable god" and the "Angry god" in the ancient Persian faith Zoroastrianism.[23]

Mithraism was a Roman religion popular during the time of Jesus Christ. Worshippers of the Mithraic faith was centered on the god *Mithras*. This faith was very popular among soldiers in the Roman army in the first to third centuries CE. The followers of Mithraism had a complicated cosmology related to spiritual enlightenment. It consisted of seven stages of development, the seventh of which involves the vanquishing of a cosmic mythological bull by the god Mithras. Thus, ultimately in Mithraism, there are those who are associated with Mithras and the Good, and those associated with the bull and evil.[24]

The scene of Mithras killing the bull is known as *tauroctony*. In the killing of the bull, which is a symbol of strength and fertility, there springs a rebirth, or "new life." The sacrifice of the bull establishes a new cosmic order that was associated with the moon, another symbol of fertility.[25]

Manichaeism was another dualistic faith founded by a Persian philosopher named Mani in the third century CE. The Manicheans also had an elaborate cosmology, represented by Light and Darkness. In the Manichean faith, Light is associated with the Good and the spiritual world, while Darkness is the symbol of Evil and the material world. Through an on-going process, Light is gradually removed from the world of matter and returned to the world of Light from which it has come.[26]

Augustine, the Bishop of Hippo in North Africa, was a follower of the Manichean faith for nearly a decade. The followers of Manichaeism believed that Mani, their founder, was the final in a series of great prophets that included Zoroaster, the Buddha, and Jesus Christ.

Elsewhere, we have called the monistic faiths the "Religions of Dissolution" because, ultimately, everything in reality is made from one substance, and that substance is Good. It follows, then, that there is no such thing as evil. Thus, evil is dissolved.[27] The dualistic faiths we have labeled elsewhere as the "Religions of Solution" because there is a place to indicate the origin of evil, namely the Evil god or Evil principle.[28]

Between the two extremes of our continuum (X and Z), we may find the monotheistic faiths of Judaism, Christianity and Islam at location Y of the continuum. In these faiths, of course, God or Allah is said to be All-Good, All-Knowing and All-Powerful, as well as the Creator of the universe out of nothing. At the same time, the believers in these faiths assent to the existence of evil in moral, natural and metaphysical forms.

The religions at point Y of our continuum we have called elsewhere the "Religions of Paradox," for, at least at first blush, they seem to involve a paradox. That is, if God is All-Good, All-Knowing, and All-Powerful, then why is there so much evil and suffering in the world? Thus, we have the Religions of Dissolution, the Religions of Solution, and the Religions of Paradox, among the religions of the world. This brings us to an analysis of the second family resemblance characteristic of a world religion—myths, symbols and rituals related to conceptions of Ultimate Reality.

Myth, Symbol and Ritual as a Family Resemblance Trait of Religion

Our second family resemblance trait of a religion is that most of the world's faiths have a collection of myths, symbols and rituals that principally are connected with views of Ultimate Reality. By "myth," we mean "Sacred stories about the beginning of things."[29] The actors in myths are usually gods, agents of the gods or exemplary human beings. The first two chapters of the Book of Genesis are good examples of a myth. In these chapters, we find a sacred story about the beginning of the universe, in which God, or *Yahweh*, is the principal actor in the myth.[30]

Symbols are the accoutrements, or tools, of myth. They stand for representations of elements in a myth. In Manichean mythology, for example, fire is a symbol of the Light, while darkness is a symbol of ignorance. Rituals, for the most part, are reaffirmations that myths are true. In this sense, they are often a recreation of a myth. The myth of the first sin in Genesis 3, as well as how death entered the world, are reaffirmed in rituals in Judaism and Christianity.

Take, for example, the ritual of baptism in Roman Catholicism. Water is a symbol of the eradication of Original Sin that, in turn, is a myth to be found in the third chapter of Genesis. Most religious symbols in the religions of the world "participate in the things they symbolize." Let me illustrate this with an example. In many pre-literate societies, there is the belief that the Sun god awakens every morning and then travels across the sky to survey his kingdom. The Kotas of southern India have a ritual in which the chief priest builds a fire on a high hill and then thrusts a stick in the fire and moves the torch from east to west, whereupon he buries the torch.[31]

Thus, the Kota has a myth about why the Sun arrives every day, a ritual that recreates the myth, and the symbol of fire that stands for the Sun. The Kota have a similar myth about why the Moon appears at night, and a corresponding ritual and symbols, as well. In the Kota's Sun Myth, the symbol fire "participates in the thing it symbolizes," namely the Sun.

Most of the world's religious traditions have an abundance of myths supported by accompanying symbols and rituals. The story of the death and resurrection of Jesus Christ, for example, is reaffirmed by the symbols of bread and wine in the sacrament of the Eucharist, in a ritual similar to the Last Supper at the Gospel of Mark 26:17–30. The feast of *Eid Al-Adha* in the Muslim faith is a celebration of Ibrahim's (Abraham's) sacrifice of his son. This mythic tale is re-created in the Feast-Ritual, supported by certain symbols. [32]

As we have suggested earlier, most of the world's religious traditions have an abundance of myths, symbols and rituals where the symbol "participates in the thing it symbolizes." The symbols of Light and Darkness in Manichaeism participate in the dualistic distinction between the world of matter and the spiritual world. As we have suggested, the use of water in the Roman Catholic's baptism is an example of where the symbol participates in the thing that it symbolizes. Thus, there is the myth in Genesis 3 of the symbol of water and the ritual eradication of Original Sin.

This brings us to a third Family Resemblance characteristic of a world religion, the distinction between what is sacred on the one hand and what is believed to be profane on the other hand.

Distinction Between the Sacred and the Profane

In his book *The Sacred and the Profane*, scholar Mircea Eliade claims that all of the religions of the world make a fundamental distinction between those persons, places and things that are sacred and those that are "Profane."[33] Later in the book, Eliade says it is important to distinguish among three categories of religion. He calls these the "Sacred," "which are transcendent referents such as gods, God, or Nirvana," the "hierophany" which is a "breakthrough of the sacred into human experience, like Revelation," and "*homo religious*," where "the religious human appreciates the breakthrough."[34]

Eliade goes on in the same book to speak of sacred persons, places and things in the religions of the world. He tells us that Jerusalem, Mecca, Medina and Rome, for example, are sacred places, while New York, London and Damascus are not. Moses, Jesus and Muhammad are sacred personages, while you and I are probably not. The Ark of the Covenant and the Ka'bah in Saudi Arabia are sacred things, while the Trump Tower in New York City, or my place of residence in Baltimore, are not sacred things.[35]

Eliade thought that all the religions of the world have sacred persons, places and things. Sometimes these persons are individuals, and sometimes they are groups, such as the Prophet Muhammad and his *Sababah*, or "Companions," or Moses and the Israelites. Sacred places are most likely connected to myths related to sacred persons, like Bethlehem, the city of Jesus' birth, or the cathedral door in Wittenberg, where Martin Luther tacked his *Ninety-five Theses*, that started the Protestant Reformation.[36]

Eliade also maintained that all of the world's religious traditions have what he calls "Hierophanies," as well as acts of human appreciation in relation to what he calls "Religious Breakthroughs." In this latter category, Eliade places religious and mystical experiences that can be found among the Muslim Sufis, in thinkers of the Jewish Kabbalah, and in Christian thinkers like Theresa of Avila and John of the Cross.[37]

In addition to sacred persons, most of the world's religious traditions have what might be called "Sacred Heroes," the topic of the next section of the first chapter, and the next family resemblance characteristic of a world religion.

Belief in Religious Heroes

A fourth family resemblance characteristic of the world's religions is a belief in Sacred Heroes. For the most part, these are exemplary human beings that ought to be emulated by other believers. Abraham, Job, Jesus, the Buddha, Confucius, Zoroaster, and Mani, for example, were all believed to be heroic persons who had lives that other believers should replicate. These heroes are often seen as being sinless or without fault, such as the Old Testament Job, Jesus in the New Testament, and the Prophet Muhammad in the Islamic faith.

Eliade tells us that either explicitly or implicitly, the contemporary believer attempts to return to a mystical age or time when things were morally better, or ideal. He calls this the phenomenon of the "Myth of the Eternal Return." By this, he means an attempt to return to a time when the events in a myth are recreated in ritual and symbol. Eliade points out that these events are *ab origine* or *illo tempore*, or "at the beginning" or "outside of time."[38]

Genesis 1, 2 and 3 are "at the beginning" and "outside of time," in that God does not exist in time but is eternal. Many other creation myths of the world also suggest that things began at the beginning and/ or "outside of time." Indeed, myths about creation, or cosmogonic myths, are generally about how the world began and how humans began to inhabit it.

These stories mostly have developed and have been transmitted orally, and therefore there is often more than one version. The Pueblo people of the American Southwest have constructed ritual sites they call a *Kiva*, a circle of rocks in the center of which is a *Sipapu*, that is, a hole in the floor or ground through which the ancestors first emerged.[39]

The Pueblo also has a series of myths about the emergence of human beings on Earth, and that they first appeared in Pueblo villages and then spread throughout the rest of the world. This idea is what historians sometimes call the belief in the *Axis Mundi*, or the center of the Earth. Indeed, throughout history, many cultures and religions have described their homelands as the "Center of the World." For example, the Chinese word *China* means "Middle Kingdom."[40] The ancient Jews believed the center of the Earth is Mount Sinai, the place where Moses was given the Ten Commandments. In the Islamic tradition, the center of things changed from the Temple Mount in Jerusalem to the city of Mecca in the seventh century.

In the case of the Pueblo, the center of the Earth is in a certain Pueblo village that is now part of a national park in the American Southwest where the original *Sipapu* can still be seen. For the Pueblo, the names of the original ancestors are known, and have several rituals that recreate the emergence of these first ancestors from the Earth. This is accompanied by a symbolic hole in the ground and a representative man and woman who annually emerge from it.[41]

In this myth, the hole is sacred, while the earth or soil around it is profane. The humans who emerge are sacred. But the audience who watch the ritual are profane. The act of digging a tunnel so that the symbolic ancestors can emerge from the Earth is a recreation of the original myth about the *Axis Mundi*. The shovels and the removal of dirt are symbols of what they symbolize. This bring us to a fifth Family Resemblance characteristic—a system of ethics sanctioned by the Divine.

A System of Ethics Sanctioned by the Divine

A fifth Family Resemblance characteristic of the religions of the world is a system of ethics usually sanctioned or endorsed by the Divine. The Ten Commandments of the Hebrew Bible and the Golden Rule in the New Testament are prime examples of this characteristic.[42] Confucius sets out his rules of behavior in his *Analects*.[43] Zoroaster did the same thing in the *Zend Avesta*.[44] Sometimes these moral systems are related to universal moral principles, like "Thou Shat Not Kill," and sometimes, they are related to consequences, such as Harry Truman's decision to drop the atomic bomb on Hiroshima because it would save more lives than it destroyed.[45]

Moral systems based on universal moral duties are called "Deontological." Those based on consequences are called "Teleological" in modern Western philosophical language. Sometimes world religions have attempted to combine universal duties and consequences, and this has been the trend among philosophers from the late twentieth century to the present time.[46]

In Islam, its ethical system is displayed in certain passages of its Holy Book, *Al-Qur'an*, as well as in *Hadith* literature, the collection of the stories and activities of the life of the Prophet Muhammad, recorded by his followers. The closest that early Islam came to an ethical system can be found in Surah, or chapter 17 of *Al-Qur'an*, called "*al-Israa*," or "The Night Journey." From *ayat*, or verse 22 to ayat 37, we find the following prescriptions:

1. Worship only Allah (17:22).
2. Be kind, honorable and humble with one's parents (17:23).
3. Don't be miserly nor wasteful with one's expenditures (17:26).

4. Don't be a spendthrift (17:27).
5. Extend a helping hand to anyone who needs help (17:30).
6. Do not abandon your children (17:31).
7. Do not commit adultery (17:32).
8. Do not kill unjustly (17:33).
9. Care for orphaned children (17:34).
10. Keep one's promises (17:34).
11. Be honest and fair in one's interactions (17:35).
12. Do not be arrogant in one's claims or beliefs (17:37).[47]

Before the Islamic faith began in the seventh century, the Arabs existed in the period known as *Jahiliyyah*, or "Ignorance," where Arabs knew nothing of Islam. Thus, Muhammad and his followers had to dissuade people from five ideas that long had existed in the Arabian Peninsula. These ideas were the following:

1. The division of Arabs into tribes based on blood and kinship and replace it with the idea of the *Ummah*, or "world community."
2. Arab polytheism and its replacement with monotheism.
3. The rejection of *Muruwwa*, or "manliness," and its replacement with humility and piety.
4. The emphasis on achieving fame to be replaced with the idea of reckoning of Judgment Day.
5. The use of ancestor worship replaced by the submission to Allah.

In many other places in Al-Qur'an, as well as in Hadith literature, we find moral prescriptions for Muslim behavior. For example, in hadith number 1420, Sunni Asharite thinker and scholar Al-Bayhaqi sketches out three separate moral characteristics for all Muslim believers. These are dignity, justice and goodness.[48] Fourteenth-century collector of hadith Egyptian Ibn Hajar in his hadith number 7073, suggests that "Muhammad has given us a perfection of moral nobles and good deeds," that should be imitated. Hajar then goes on to speak of the Prophet Muhammad's honesty, truthfulness and justice to all those around him.[49]

In the religion of Jainism, we find five major moral duties. These can be summarized as:

1. *Ahimsa*, non-violence
2. *Satya*, truthfulness
3. *Asteya*, no stealing
4. *Brahmacharya*, celibacy
5. *Aparigrapha*, few possessions[50]

In the Hindu tradition, we find what is called the *Five Dharmas*, or "Moral Duties," These are:

1. Don't kill.
2. Don't lie.
3. Don't steal.
4. Don't practice adultery.
5. Don't hoard up treasures.[51]

These religious traditions show that each of them ties the nature and extent of the Moral Good to certain conceptions of Ultimate Reality, the Monotheism of Judaism, Christianity, and Islam, or the Pantheism of Vedantic Hinduism. In nearly all of the world's religious traditions, the ideas of the Sacred and of Ultimate Reality are attached to moral prescriptions outlined for human beings. This brings us to a sixth Family Resemblance trait of the world's religions related to the ideas of evil and suffering.

Definition and Meaning of Evil and Suffering

A sixth Family Resemblance trait of the religions of the world is the view that they all provide a definition of, as well as an origin, or origins of, and the meaning, or meanings of, evil. In other words, in all the faiths we shall explore in this study, each of them provides some clues about what evil is, where it comes from, and what meaning to make of it. Some religions say it is simply part of God's plan. Others that it is part of nature itself. Other religions simply say that evils are the opposites of what the moral duties prescribe.

In some faiths, like Judaism, Christianity and Islam, the idea of evil has many sources or origins, such as human free will, or the concept of the demonic. In other traditions, like Chinese Taoism, for example, evil is part of the overall nature of things, just as the Moral Good is. Thus, we have suggested so far in this chapter that the traits of a world religion, the family resemblance characteristics of a faith include:

1. A conception of Ultimate Reality.
2. A system of myths, symbols and rituals.
3. A distinction between the sacred and the profane.
4. Belief in religious heroes.
5. An ethical system sanctioned by Ultimate Reality.
6. A response to the phenomena of evil.

In addition to these six we will now add four more. These are:

7. A concept of the self.
8. A view of survival after death.
9. Sacred scripture.
10. A view of eschatology, or last things.

The idea of possessing a notion of the nature of the self is a seventh Family Resemblance characteristic of a world religion. Nearly all religions posit a view about what the self is and how it operates in the world. Some faiths believe the self and the soul, or spirit, are the same thing. Other traditions, like traditional Buddhism, the self is made up of what are called *Skandas*, a collection of memories, beliefs and experiences left over from an individual's previous lives.[52] In Zen Buddhism, as well, the *Skandas* are the aggregates of the self. In the Zen tradition, the five *Skandas* are the physical form, feelings, perceptions, volitions and consciousness.[53]

Other religions suggest that the self is nothing more than the material parts of the human body, most importantly, the heart and the brain. The Greeks thought the self resided in the liver, thus the origin of the organ's name. The ancient Jews believed the self resided in the heart. Modern medicine suggests the self is in the brain. This latter view is known as materialism. It suggests that the human being can only be a self if that person possesses a brain that works properly. The materialist thinks that when the body dies, the self dies with it.[54]

In the Hindu tradition, the self or soul is called the *atman*, an ancient Sanskrit word that is comparable to the English "soul," or "spirit." In many of the religions of India, when the body dies, the atman is reincarnated in a new body. This process continues until the atman is absorbed into a world-soul called Brahman.[55] This seventh Family Resemblance characteristic of a world religion leads to an eighth element—what the world religions believe happens to the self after death, the subject matter of this chapter's next section.

Survival after Death as a Trait of World Religion

Nearly all of the religions of the world give an analysis of what happens to the self after death. Some say the soul or spirit survives death, a view that is called Immortality of the Soul. Others say that at the end of time, the human body shall be resurrected, and the self will be reconstituted. This view is known as Resurrection of the Body.[56] In the Indian traditions—Hinduism, Buddhism and Jainism—for the most part, they posit a belief in reincarnation, or transmigration of the soul.[57]

There are a variety of names for what the religions of the world have called the soul. Some traditions even suggest that people possess multiple souls, such as the ancient Egyptians, whom employed the words *Ba*, *Ka*, and *Khet* to speak of different aspects of the self.[58] The Fang people, a Central African group found in Equatorial Guinea and northern Gabon, believe that human beings have seven souls. They are the *eba*, or vital principle; the *niem*, or conscience; the *edzil*, the soul that survives death; the *ki*, another name for the *edzil*; the *ngzel*, the active principle while in the body; the *nissim*, a word associated with human shadows; and the *khun*, a disincarnate spirit or ghost.[59]

The Mbua people of the Rio Branco territory of Brazil believe that there is both a "beneficial soul" and a "dangerous soul." They also believe in a third kind of soul called a *Nee*, which is the initial core of the human personality and plays the part of an enforcer, or protective power of the other souls.[60]

The Mossi tribes of Burkina Fasso of the Upper Volta believe that death comes from the disunion of the *sigla*, or soul, that has two separate elements. The first is called the *hirma*, or the "male soul." The other is known as *tule*, or the "female soul." In the views of the Mossi, human beings have different degrees of the two elements of the sigla. These determine how masculine or feminine one becomes.[61]

In other religious traditions, the soul is a unitary entity. The Greeks called it the *psyche*, the Romans, the *anima*. The ancient Jews used the words *nefesh* and *ruah* to stand for "soul" and "spirit."[62] The Qur'an uses cognates of these two Hebrew words. The *nafs* is the "soul," and the *ruh* is the "spirit."[63] In Jainism, the soul is known as the *jiva*.[64] In the Old Saxon language, the word for soul is the *seo*, and in Hinayana Buddhism, the soul is called the *anatta*.

Over and against these views, the materialists believe that the self is nothing more than the characteristics that the self acquires over time, or as David Hume puts the matter, "the continuity of memory over time."[65] In this view, when the body dies, the self dies with it. Most of the believers of the traditional monotheistic faiths believe in Immortality of the Soul, Resurrection of the Body, or some combination of the two. Many of the Indian religions have a belief in reincarnation after one has died.

This brings us to a ninth Family Resemblance trait of a world religion, the possession of a group of sacred scriptures or writing, the subject matter of the next section of this first chapter.

Sacred Scriptures or Writings

Nearly all the post-literate religious traditions have a body of sacred writings or religious texts. These texts often contain myths and stories of the lives of a tradition's moral heroes, like the Jewish Books of Moses, the Christian Gospels, or the Qur'an and Hadith literature in the Islamic faith.[66] The Shinto people call their scriptures the *Kojiki*.[67] Some Buddhist traditions read the *Tipitaka*, or the *Suttas*.[68] Jewish people have the *Tanakh* and the *Talmud*.[69] And Christianity has both the Old and the New Testaments. The Jains call their scripture the *Agamas*. Religions in Indonesia, Malaysia, Singapore and Brunei also sometimes use the word *agamas* to speak of sacred texts.[70]

The most authoritative texts in Hinduism are the Vedas and the Upanishads.[71] In Zoroastrianism, the sacred text is known as the *Zend Avesta*.[72] The sacred writings of the Taoists is called the I Ching.[73] And the followers of Confucius follow the precepts of their founder's *Analects*.[74] The members of the Sikh faith are devoted to the study of the Guru Granth Sahib. These texts were mostly composed by six Sikh gurus who are some of the religious heroes of the faith.[75]

In the Bahá'í faith, there are two collections of sacred writings. The first is known as the Seven Valleys. And the other is called the Four Valleys. The former describes the journey of a believer through seven stages of enlightenment, while the latter catalogs the four most important moral traits of a believer in the Bahá'í faith.[76]

Needless to say, pre-literate societies, or what are sometimes called "primitive societies," usually do not possess collections of sacred writings. There are, however, some societies, such as the Kota villages of southern India, who did collect written texts supposedly written by their ancestors.[77] This brings us to our final family resemblance trait of a world religion. It has to do with the area of theology known as "eschatology."

Eschatology or Last Things

Eschatology is a branch of systematic theology that deals with the doctrines of final things, or *ta eschata* in classical Greek. This is the name in religious literature for the study that examines, among other things, the end of the world, such as in portions of the biblical Book of Daniel or chapter twenty-one of the Book of Revelation in the New Testament. Among the Hopi Native Americans, the end of the world is associated with a spirit known as the "Spider Woman," who will appear at the end of time and weave her web across the landscape of the world, signifying that the end times is at hand.[78]

Scholars of the Muslim faith describe a series of events that must occur before the end of the world can happen. Natural disasters will increase, society will undergo a moral decline, and a false prophet known as *Al-Dajjal*, the Arabic word for the Antichrist, will appear and then attempt to convince believers into worshipping him rather than Allah.[79]

In Hindu mythology and eschatology, three separate gods will play a role in the end times. These are *Brahman*, *Vishnu* and *Shiva*. The world will come to an end, Hindu scholars say, when it has become sufficiently evil. Then an avatar of Vishnu called *Kalki* will appear on horseback and armed with a large sword, with which he will punish the most egregious wrong-doers before the world comes to an end.[80]

In some forms of Buddhism, it is believed that a sign of the end of the world will be the appearance of seven suns in the sky. They gradually will heat up the Earth, until finally, it will become one "mass of flame" that will become so consuming that it will not leave any ash.[81]

Both the Old and the New Testaments, of course, also provide descriptions and scenarios by which the world will come to an end. In the Old Testament, or Hebrew Bible, the Prophet Zechariah, in chapter 14:1–21 of his book, we may find an outline of events that will presage the end of the world.[82] The Old Testament's Book of Daniel also catalogs a collection of "signs" that will precede the end of the world. These come at Daniel 9:24–27.

In addition, there are a number of isolated verses of the Hebrew Bible that speak of the end times, like Isaiah 13:6, for example, that tells us, "Wait, for the Day of the Lord is near, and destruction from the Almighty will be upon the Earth." The minor prophet, Joel, in his book at 2:31, also relates events that will lead to the end of the world. Joel relates:

> The Sun shall be turned to darkness, and the Moon to blood,
> before the awesome Day of the Lord shall come.

In the New Testament, several chapters in the Book of Revelation describe what is to take place at the end of time. Among these passages are 1:1–20, 13:1–28 and 17:1–18, as well as the opening of chapter 21. References to the end of the world also may be found in the Gospels of Mark 13:32; Matthew 13:39–40, 24:5–28 and 36; Luke 21:25–26; and the John 3:16–17.

In the Letters of Paul, as well as in the Catholic Epistles, one may also find references to the end of the world. For example, Second Timothy 3:1–5, Hebrews 1:1–2 and 9:26, Galatians 1:4, First Thessalonians 4:14–17 and 5:1–5, Ephesians 1:21, First Corinthians

1:20–29 and 2:14, all at times have been interpreted that way in the history of Christian interpretation. At Second Peter 3:1–18 and 4:7–11, as well as at First John 2:18, are thought to refer to the end times, as well.

Several passages in the Acts of the Apostles also speak of the end of the world, including 2:17–21 that begins, "And in the Last Days it shall be," God declares, "that I will put out my Spirit on the flesh…" At Second Peter 3:13, we learn that:

According to His promises, we are waiting for the new
Heavens and the new Earth in which the righteous shall swell.

Thus, in the last ten sections of this opening chapter, we have argued that most of the world's religious traditions have a collection of ten Family Resemblance characteristics that each go into the making of a "world religion." As we have shown, those traits are the following:

1. A conception of ultimate reality.
2. A collection of myths, symbols and rituals.
3. A distinction between sacred and profane.
4. A belief in religious heroes.
5. A system of ethics sanctioned by the divine.
6. A definition and a meaning of evil.
7. A view of the nature of the self.
8. A view on survival after death.
9. A collection of sacred writings or scriptures.
10. A view on eschatology or last things.

Not each of the world's religious traditions must have all ten of these Family Resemblance traits. But each may have enough traits so that we know that something is a member of the family of religions. In the same way, not all members of a human family may not possess all of the characteristics that normally we associate with the family. Most may have blonde hair, but a few do not. Most family members may have blue eyes, but one has green.

Most family members are tall, except two of them are short. Most family members have a square jaw, but one does not. The members of this supposed family may still look very much alike, even though they do not all share exactly the same traits. This is what Ludwig Wittgenstein meant by "Family Resemblance."[83] This brings us to a discussion of a catalog of answers and responses to the phenomenon of evil, our next topic in Chapter One.

Traditional Answers and Responses to Evil

Among the religions of the world, there have been a number of answers and responses to the phenomena of evil and suffering that may be found across the different faiths of this study. Elsewhere, we have outlined a variety of explanations for evil in the Judeo-Christian-Islamic traditions.[84] After discussing those in this section, we will then turn to a group of supplementary responses that can frequently be found in the religions of the world.

In the traditions of Judaism, Christianity and Islam, the eight most popular answers and responses to the phenomena of evil are the following:

1. Retributive Justice Theory
2. The Free Will Defense
3. Original Sin Theory
4. The Influences of Demonic Forces View
5. The Contrast Perspective
6. The Test View
7. The Moral Qualities Perspective
8. Divine Plan Theory[85]

The first four of these answers/responses to the phenomena of evil are backward-looking in that they look to the past to discover the origin or meaning of evil and suffering. Positions five through eight, on the other hand, tend to look to the future to find the cause or meaning of evil and suffering.

Those who believe in Retributive Justice Theory hold that the reason an individual or group is suffering is that he or she or they have done something morally wrong. This is the view that lies beneath the sentence, "What have I done to deserve this?" The question implies a belief in Retributive Justice Theory. Several characters in the biblical Book of Job at 1:1 hold this perspective, while the omniscient narrator and God say that the patriarch is *tam va yashar*, or "blameless and upright."

The Free Will Defense is a theory that argues that much of human evil and suffering is caused by the use of human free will. God tells Adam and Eve not to eat from a certain tree in the midst of the Garden of Eden, and then they turn around using their free will and do precisely that. Since the time of Adam and Eve, many theologians and philosophers have relied on the Free Will Defense to explain the phenomenon of evil.[86]

Original Sin Theory is a view found primarily in the history of Christianity. The advocate of this theory says that Adam and Eve disobeyed God and sinned in the Garden of Eden, and all humans after them have inherited this original sin. C. S. Lewis believed that this is the only part of Christianity that is empirically verifiable.[87]

The assenter to the Influences of Demonic Forces Theory holds the view that Satan, the Devil, Iblis, or Shaytan, agents of the demonic, attempt to influence the behavior of human beings to perform evil acts. In Islam, the actions of the demonic are sometimes called *waswas*, the Arabic word for "whispering."[88]

In each of the four responses outlined so far, the believer looks to the past to discover the origin and meaning of evil and suffering in the world. This brings us to the four forward-looking answers/responses. The first of these is known as the Contrast View. It says that in order to know or understand the Moral Good, one also must have evil. One cannot have one without the other.[89]

A second forward-looking theory, theory number six in our list, is called the Test View. The advocate of the Test View maintains that God uses evil and suffering to "test" or to "try" the moral characters of human beings.[90] This position is sometimes tied to another view known as the Moral Qualities Perspective. This position says there are certain moral qualities like patience and fortitude, for example, that can only be developed by experiencing evil and suffering.[91]

Moral characteristics like perseverance, the advocates of this view believe it can only be developed if one has gone through moral strife and dread. In this view, one's moral character is not being "tested," rather, it is being improved.[92]

The fourth and final forward-looking theory of evil and suffering is the most popular of these views. It is known as the Divine Plan Theory. The assenters to this position suggest that something may appear to be evil in the short-run or present time, but in the long run, everything will work out for the Good.[93] This theory suggests that God has a divine plan by which, ultimately, the Moral Good shall triumph in the end.[94]

Those people in contemporary life who say, "Everything happens for a reason," are advocates of the Divine Plan Theory. Those who say, "What goes around comes around," or "Karma's a bitch," are believers in Retributive Justice Theory. This brings us to several supplemental explanations for evil and suffering often found in the religions of the world.

Supplemental Theories of Evil and Suffering in Religions of the World

In addition to the eight major theories on evil and suffering we already have discussed, there are also a number of supplementary views that are often found in the religions of the world. Among these theories are:

1. The Karma-Samsara Theory
2. The Deprivation of the Good View
3. The Permission Perspective
4. The Principle of Plenitude Position
5. The Best of All Possible Worlds Theory
6. Eschatological Verification Theory
7. Determinism
8. Ancestor Worship
9. Hidden God Theory[95]

The Karma-Samsara Theory is a view that suggests that evil and suffering experienced by human beings in the world is actually the by-products of bad moral behavior in an individual's previous lives.[96] Many of the Indian religions, as we shall see later in this study, believe that evil and suffering in the world is connected to the idea of reincarnation or transmigration of the soul.[97]

The Deprivation of the Good Perspective, or the *Privatio Boni* View in Latin, says that Evil is nothing more than a "deprivation" or absence of the Good. Thus, in this view, Evil has no positive existence. It is merely a kind of hole where Good should have been. The proponents of this perspective, such as Plotinus, Augustine and Thomas Aquinas, assert that Evil lacks any independent or ontological existence. Rather, only Good exists, and Evil is a deprivation of the Good.[98]

The gist of the Permission Theory maintains that God does not cause evil; he merely permits it. This theory has been employed by a host of Christian thinkers over the centuries. This theory most likely grew out of the Medieval Scholastic View of the distinction between the "Antecedent Will" and the "Consequent Will," in that God is the cause of everything (antecedent will), but humans are the consequent causes of their sins through the misuse of their free will.[99]

The Principle of Plenitude is a theory that asserts that the universe contains all possible forms of existence. The Historian of Ideas, Arthur Lovejoy, was the first modern thinker to introduce this view. Lovejoy distinguished between a "Static View," in which the universe "displays a constant fullness," and a "Temporary View," whereby fullness and diversity gradually decrease over time.[100]

The Best of All Possible Worlds Approach is an expression coined by German philosopher G. W. Leibniz in his 1710 book *Theodicy*.[101] Leibniz employed the expression when he suggests if God is truly All-Good, All-Knowing and All-Powerful, then it follows that this world, the one that He made, must be the best of all possible worlds.[102]

There is a theory known as the Eschatological Verification Approach. The name was devised by British philosopher John Hick in his book, *Evil and the God of Love*, published in 1966. In this work, Hick points out the Divine Plan Theory may be verifiable if true, but it cannot be falsifiable. If the Divine Plan approach turns out to be true, we will all know. But if it is false, no one will know, for we will all be dead.[103]

There is a supplemental explanation that is related to the philosophical view called Determinism. The best example from the world's religious traditions to explain this theory is an idea among the people of Tamil Nadu, the southern-most province of India. Hindu believers from this state explain misfortune in life in terms of Karma and Samsara, but they also attribute it to what they call headwriting.[104]

The believer in headwriting says that one's destiny is written on the forehead six days after the birth of a child. In this view, whatever experiences of Good and Evil that one has had were fatally written on his or her forehead long before they occurred. That all moral deeds, both Good and Evil, are inevitable.[105] This Indian idea of headwriting explains that it is a god who writes the destiny of the newborn on its forehead. The motif of headwriting in India expresses that the individual must bear one's fate since no amount of effort on the part of the individual can change it.

Many Western philosophers over the centuries have also believed in determinism. Karl Marx and Sigmund Freud are two thinkers who held a determinist view.[106] Both John B. Watson and B. F. Skinner developed nurture-based deterministic systems.[107] The Dutch philosopher Baruch Spinoza was also a determinist thinker. He thought that the idea of human freedom could only be understood by knowing the causes of our desires and affections. Spinoza's views on his brand of determinism are sketched out in the fourth and fifth volumes of his classic work *The Ethics*.[108]

The Hidden God Theory of response to evil and suffering primarily employed in the Judeo-Christian tradition. This perspective relates that the best way to respond to the phenomena of evil and suffering is to say that God is distant or is hidden.[109]

Finally, in many of the Far East religions in this study, a primary way of explaining the origins of evil and suffering in life is to suggest that it is sometimes caused by the actions or communications from ancestral spirits. As we shall see later in this study, this view appears in Buddhism, Confucian thought, Taoism, as well as in Japanese Shinto.[110]

This brings us to the major conclusions we have made in this first chapter. The principal goal of Chapter Two of this study is to examine and to discuss the phenomena of evil in the ancient Indian faith known as Hinduism, perhaps the oldest world religion in existence.

Conclusions to Chapter One

We began Chapter One by examining the concept of a "definition." In this section, we described Aristotle and Augustine's views of a definition, followed by Ludwig Wittgenstein's replacement of these views with his position that the meaning of words should be found in their use, and his idea of Family Resemblance characteristics to understand the meaning of words.

In the second section of this first chapter, we raised the question of whether there are necessary and sufficient conditions for calling something an evil. In the absence of these conditions, we have offered a set of Family Resemblance characteristics that examples of evil seem to have in common. Among these Family Resemblance characteristics for an evil, we have offered the following:

1. Evils cause harm.
2. Evil is sometimes intentional and sometimes not.
3. Evil is sometimes natural and sometimes not.
4. Evil is sometimes psychological and sometimes not.
5. Evil often causes unnecessary or meaningless suffering.

In the next several sections of this first chapter, we examined each of the Family Resemblance characteristics for a world religion. Those included sections on the concept of ultimate reality; myths, symbols, and rituals; a distinction between sacred and profane; religious heroes; an ethical system sanctioned by ultimate reality; a view of the nature of the self; a position on survival after death; a collection of holy writings or scriptures; and a perspective on eschatology.

In the next section of Chapter One, we cataloged and discussed eight traditional answers and responses to the phenomena of evil and suffering. Four of these answers—Retributive Justice, the Free Will Defense, Original Sin Theory, and the Influences of Demonic Forces Perspective, as we have shown, are backward-looking. The other four theories—the Contrast View, the Test Perspective, the Moral Qualities Theory, and the Divine Plan Perspective, as we have seen, are forward-looking.

In the final section of this first chapter, we introduced and discussed what we labeled Supplemental Theories of Evil and Suffering in Religions of the World. Among this group, we have seen the Karma-Samsara View, the Deprivation of the Good Theory, the Permission

Perspective, the Principle of Plenitude View, the Best of All Possible Worlds Theory, the Eschatological Verification Point of View, and Determinism.

In these seven supplemental theories about evil and suffering in the religions of the world, we have suggested that they all may be seen as assenting to many different traditions and figures in those traditions. This material in the final two sections of this chapter will be employed in a comparative way to examine the faiths we shall explore throughout this study.

We shall now turn out attention to the first world religion in this study, the Indian faith of Hinduism, quite likely the oldest world religion on Earth. As we shall see, Hinduism has a rich and long history, full of many of the Family Resemblance characteristics we introduced in this first chapter.

Chapter Two:
Evil and Suffering in Hinduism

The Sanskrit language, of which the Vedas are the oldest
surviving expression, became dominant in India.

—Joshua Mark, "Hinduism"

This Self is said to be "other than the known, as well as
other than the unknown."

—*Kena Upanishad*

In a strict sense, there was no "Hinduism" before modern
times, although the sources of the Hindu tradition are very
ancient.

—Gavin Flood, *The Oxford History of Hinduism*

Introduction

According to many scholars, Hinduism is the world's oldest faith, with
roots and customs dating back to the Iron Age (1200 to 600 BCE).
In the contemporary world, there are nearly a billion Hindus, behind
Christianity and Islam, among the world's religions. About 95 percent
of Hindus live in India. Because the religion has no specific founder, it
is difficult to trace the beginnings of Hinduism.

Our chief goal in this second chapter is to explore the religious faith
known as Hinduism and, more particularly, to sketch out and evaluate
what the ancient Indian faith has had to say about the phenomena of
evil and suffering. To that end, we shall begin Chapter Two by making

several preliminary remarks about the Hindu religion. This will be followed by the second section in this chapter about the origins and history of the faith of Hinduism.

These two sections of Chapter Two will be followed by a third part in which we shall describe and discuss the most fundamental concepts in Hinduism, including Brahman, atman, karma, samsara, maya, dharma, moksha, nirvana, as well as many other basic ideas in the oldest Indian faith.

Next, we will identify and discuss at some length the major religious texts, or scriptures, in Hinduism. These include, as we shall see, the Vedas, the Upanishads, the Brahmanas, the Puranas and the Hindu epics, the Mahabharata, the Ramayana and the Bhagavad Gita.[111]

These sections of Chapter Two will be followed by a section on the approaches and responses found in Hinduism regarding the phenomena of evil and suffering in the Indian religion. This is the most important section for the purposes of this study on evil and suffering in the world's religions and will be accomplished by looking at responses to evil and suffering in the Hindu tradition in the ancient, medieval, and modern periods. This brings us to some preliminary remarks about the faith of Hinduism, the subject matter of the second section of this chapter.

Some Preliminary Remarks About Studying Hinduism

The word "Hinduism" is a creation in modern times. The first mention of "Hindoo" in the *Oxford English Dictionary* comes in 1752. The word was not used to designate the follower of an Indian faith until the early nineteenth century. In the ancient world, the word "Hindu" came from the Old Persian *Sindus* that specified "those who lived across the Indus River."[112]

In the late eighteenth century, British Christian missionaries took aim at the idolatry of the Hindoos, often failing to understand some of the subtlety of their myths, symbols and rituals. Other eighteenth-century thinkers, such as William Jones (1746–1794), began to understand the wealth and sophistication of the faith.[113] Indian scholar Ram Mohan Roy (1772–1833), who was heavily influenced by Islam and by the British Unitarians, embraced the ancient texts of India. Roy was also a social reformer and was one of the first to employ the term "Hinduism." After the year 1816, the word began to refer to a coherent pan-Indian set of religious ideals and practices.[114]

Secondly, Hinduism is not a single religion. It embraces many traditions that went into the development of the earliest religious beliefs in India. Thirdly, Hinduism does not have an agreed upon starting point. The traditions that went into the making of Hinduism took several thousand years to develop. Fourth, the practitioners of the Hindu faith, even from the very beginning to the present day, believed/believe that the Hindu revelation is the oldest of human faiths and that its message is an eternal one.

A fifth preliminary remark for understanding Hinduism is that it is drastically different from faiths in the Western world, such as Judaism, Christianity and Islam. The ancient Indians had a vastly different notion of the self, as well as the concept of time. For them, time was a much more cyclical phenomenon than the past, present and future construct of linear time.

Sixth, the practitioners of Hinduism understand that there are many different ways of achieving salvation than going to the "Happy Hunting Grounds" of Heavenly bliss. The ancient Indians, as well as contemporary Hindus, have a drastically different understanding of what counts as enlightenment.

Seventh, although there are many gods in traditional Hinduism, their views of these gods are more like the notion of "henotheism" than they are like Western monotheism. Henotheism is a polytheistic belief that there are many gods, but your local god is the most important of those deities.[115] Eighth, the faith of Hinduism is extremely diverse and, as we have indicated earlier, was only recently conceived as a single, distinct faith. The written narratives of Hinduism span many eras of time, as well as many forms of existence.

We shall say more about these eight preliminary remarks throughout this chapter. We now move to the third section on the history of Indian religious thought. From the ancient world to the first appearance in India of the English word "Hinduism."

The History of Indian Religious Thought and Hinduism

The chronology below is a common way of summarizing the history of Hinduism:

> Before 2000 BCE, The Indus Valley Civilization.
>
> 1500 to 500 BCE, The Aryans and the Vedic Period.
>
> 500 BCE to 500 CE, The Epics, the Puranas and the Classical Age.
>
> 500 to 1500 CE, The Medieval Period.
>
> 1500 to 1755, The Pre-Modern Period.
>
> 1755 to 1947, The British Period.
> 1947 to the present, Independent India.[116]

In this section of Chapter Two, we shall make some comments on each of these seven periods of the history of Hinduism, beginning with the Indus Valley Civilization. Little is known of their early beliefs. There is some evidence from archeology, particularly at two sites known as Mohenjo-Daro and Harappa.[117]

We know from these two sites that the residents were involved in temple rituals, ritual bathing and animal sacrifice. Many terracotta figurines have been found there. Some of these are perhaps images of goddesses, and another figure depicts a seated man surrounded by animals that some scholars believe is a prototype of the god Shiva.[118] Other scholars believe the seals in the Indus Valley are very much like Elamite seals that represent seated bulls.[119] Another figure at Mohenjo-Daro, carved out of soapstone, shows a warrior battling with lions.[120]

From the finds at Harappa and Mohenjo-Daro, we may make three major conclusions. First, the residents appear to have been polytheists, with an emphasis on goddess worship. Second, animal sacrifice appears to have gone on regularly in the Indus Valley. And third, the archaeology research suggests they believed in the idea of ritual purity, and there was an emphasis on fertility, as well.[121] This brings us to the Aryan migration beginning around 1500 BCE.

In 1953, Sir Mortimer Wheeler proposed that the invasion of an Indo-European tribe from Central Asia, known as the Aryans, caused the decline of the Indus Valley Civilization. As evidence, he pointed to a group of thirty-seven skeletons found in various parts of Mohenjo-Daro, as well as passages in the Vedas that refer to forts and battles.[122] Not long after the introduction of Wheeler's theory, it began to be rejected by scholars of ancient India and Pakistan.

For example, in examining the skeletons in question, in 1994, Kenneth Kennedy showed that the marks on the skulls were not caused by violence and battle, but rather they are the products of erosion. Kennedy outlines his position on the skeleton remains in his essay, "Have Aryans Been Identified in the Prehistoric Skeletal Record from South Asia?"[123] The Aryan Migration thesis suggests that these Aryans, or "noble ones," migrated into the Indian sub-continent and became the dominant cultural force there.

In this view, Hinduism derives from the religion recorded in the oldest Indian scriptures, the Vedas, along with elements of the indigenous traditions that these Aryans found there. The indigenous people came to be known in scholarly circles as the "Dravidians." The language of the Vedic period was ancient Sanskrit and appears to be related to a large number of European languages.[124]

For example, the words for "mother" and "father" in Sanskrit are *mitar* and *pitar*, similar to the Latin mater and pater, the German, *mutter* and *fater*, and in English, "mother" and "father." This suggested to linguistic scholars that the Indo-Europeans had a common origin known as "Proto-Indo-European."[125]

There does seem to be an archaeological continuity in the Indian sub-continent in the Neolithic period. The history of this period is very complex. One of the key problems with the archaeological record is there have been no horse remains found in the Indus Valley, while in the Vedas themselves, horse sacrifice has a central place.[126] This ritual was known as the *Ashvamedha* and can be found in the Śrauta tradition of Vedic literature.[127]

The best-known text describing the horse sacrifice is the *Ashvamedha parva*, or "The Book of the Horse Sacrifice." In the fourteenth book of the Indian epic poem, the *Mahabharata*, the gods Krishna and Vyasa convince King Yudhishthira to conduct the sacrifice, the details of which are described at some length.[128] The *Ashvamedha* is recorded as being performed by many ancient Indian rulers. The Vedas also record the facts of many other animal sacrifices.

Among the passages of the Rig Veda that promote the practice of animal sacrifice are 10.86.14, in which the god Indra says, "They cook for me fifteen plus twenty oxen." At 8.43.11 of the Rig Veda, we find a description in which the fire god, *Agni*, devours "an ox and a barren cow." These verses suggest that the animals should be offered in *Yajna*, the Sanskrit term for "sacrifice."[129]

At any rate, we take the "Vedic period" to refer to the period when the Vedas were composed. It appears that the earliest Vedic religion centered on the sacrifice and sharing of sacrificial meals with fellow believers, as well as with what was referred to as the *Devas*, a Sanskrit word for "gods."[130] Another Sanskrit word for "sacrifice" is the noun *homa*. The words *homa* and *yajna* were used to refer to animal sacrifice, but they also referred more widely to any offering in "the Sacred Fire," such as milk and clarified butter.[131]

Many of the religious rituals described in the Vedas were elaborate and time-consuming events, some even continuing to the present-day. Sacrifices were offered to the various *Devas* who lived in different realms of a hierarchical universe divided into three separate realms. These realms were the Earth, the Atmosphere and the Sky.[132] The Earth contained the plant god, *Soma*; the fire god, *Agni*; and the god of Priestly Power, who was known as *Brhaspati*.[133]

The realm of the Atmosphere contained the warrior god, *Indra*, the wind deity, *Vayu*, and the storm gods called *Maruts*, such as the terrible deity known as *Rudra*.[134] Finally, the Sky realm contains the sky god, *Dyaus*, a cognate of the classical Greek and Latin, *Deus*. The Lord of "Cosmic Order," or *rta* in Sanskrit, was the god Varuna.[135] Varuna's companion was a deity known as *Mitra*, the god of the Night.[136] *Pushan* was the god of nourishment, and *Vishnu*, the Pervader God.[137]

The next period in the history of Hinduism was the time of the Epics and the Puranas. This period begins around the time of the Buddha, who lived and died from around 500 to 400 BCE. This period saw the addition of other texts into Hinduism called the Dharma Sutras and the Shastras, as well as the two epics, the Mahabharata and the Ramayana. The popular Bhagavad Gita is part of the Mahabharata.[138]

The idea of dharma (law, duty or truth), a concept we will discuss in the next section of this chapter, was developed in sections of a series of texts known as the Dharma Sutras. These texts recognize three sources of dharma—Revelation, such as in the Vedas and the Upanishads; Tradition, or Smrti; and Good Customs. In this period of the Epics and the Puranas, from around 500 BCE to 500 CE, the Vedic fire sacrifices became minimal, and the development of *bhakti*, or "devotion," became popular.

The rise of the Gupta Empire in India, from 320 to 500 CE, saw the development of schools devoted to particular deities, which the great tradition of *Vaishnavism*, that focused on the god *Vishnu*, and the *Shaivism*, which concentrated on the god *Shiva*.[139] Another Indian tradition was called *Shaktism,* which focused on the god *Devi*.[140]

One may see in the Epic and Purana period many of the ideas and traditions that go into the making of modern Hinduism, such as the idea of Bhakti and the activity of worship at Hindu temples. This period also saw the advancement of religious poetry, mostly in the Sanskrit language. This genre became the most important element in religious literature and in religious culture.[141] This brings us to the medieval period in this history of the faith of Hinduism, our next period, from 500 to 1500 CE.

In this medieval period, we see the continual rise of Bhakti, or devotion, to the major deities in the Hindu religion, particularly Vishnu, Shiva and Devi. With the collapse of the Gupta Dynasty, we continue to see the devotions to Vishnu, Shiva and Devi. During this time, we also see the development of regional temples and empires, such as the *Jagganatha* in Puri, the Shiva Temple in Chidambaram, and the Armarnath Shiva Temple in Kashmir.[142]

In this medieval period of Hindu history, Sanskrit devotional literature continues, but we also see the rise of vernacular languages in religious contexts, particularly Tamil and Hindi. In these languages, poets recorded their devotional sentiments. Most notable of these in the medieval period were what are known as the twelve *Vaishnava Alvars* produced from the sixth to the ninth centuries.[143] These were twelve poet-saints, principally from southern India. Some of these thinkers were orthodox in their beliefs, and some were not.

The most noted of the twelve is probably Sankara, who lived from 780 until 820. He traveled widely, often debating with other Indian poets and scholars, as well as some Buddhist and Jain thinkers. Sankara also re-established the authority of the Vedic canon, propagated *Advaita*, or monism, and laid the foundations for what will be called the *Vedanta*.[144] Other important philosophers in the medieval period were Ramanuja (1017–1137), as well as thirteenth-century Indian philosopher Madhva (1199–1278), a proponent of *Dvaita*, or "Dualism," with respect to Ultimate Reality.[145] This brings us to the pre-modern period in the history of Hinduism from 1500 to 1755.

In this period, the religion of Islam, which had arrived in India in the eighth century, was now competing with Hinduism, particularly in the northwest provinces of India. Muslim power in India began with the Turkish Sultanate around 1200 CE and ended in the Mughal Empire, beginning in 1526. Emperor Akhbar (1542–1605) was a liberal leader in the pre-modern period. He allowed Hindu people to freely practice their faith.[146] Akbar became the leader at the age of fourteen. He established a sprawling kingdom through military conquests and was known as Akbar the Great in India and beyond.[147]

In the pre-modern period in the history of Hinduism in India, we also see the continuation of the Bhakti, or worship tradition. The Sant tradition in the North, mainly in the Punjab, expressed devotion in their poetry to a god without "qualities," as well as a god "with qualities." The Sant tradition was later called Sikhism. It began in the Punjab region of India during the pre-modern period.[148] We will say more about Sikhism in a later chapter of this study. This brings us to the modern, or British period, in India from 1757 until 1947.

Robert Clive's victory at the Battle of Plassey in 1757 heralded the end of the Mughal Empire in India and the rise of the British presence there.[149] The battle was on June 23, 1757. Under the leadership of Clive, the British India Company defeated the Mughals under the command of Siraj-ud-Daulah. The battle took place north of Calcutta and south of Murshidabad, the then capital of Bengal.[150]

In terms of religion, the first thing that the British did was not to interfere with the religious and cultural beliefs and practices of the Indian people. They allowed the Hindus and other religious groups in

India to practice those religions unimpeded. Later, however, Christian visionaries began to arrive in India preaching the Gospel.

Shortly after that, the first scholars stepped on Indian shores, and though at first, they were initially sympathetic with the Indian religions, they also wanted to westernize Indian society. Chairs on Indology were established at British universities like Oxford, as well as other universities in Europe. The nineteenth-century saw the development of a "Hindu Renaissance," with reformers such as Ram Mohan Roy (1772–1833), who asserted that Hinduism is a rational, ethical religion. He founded the *Brahmo Samaj* to promote these religious views.[151]

Other reformers, such as Dayananda Saraswati (1824–1883), advocated a return to the religion of the Vedas and its emphasis on an eternal, omnipotent and personal Ultimate Reality of Brahman. Sarasvati wanted to return to what he called the *sanatana dharma*, or "Eternal Law," of Hinduism before the age of the Epics and the Puranas, beginning around 500 BCE.[152] He also wished to rid the practice of Hinduism from superstition and was an early figure in the Indian Nationalist Movement.[153]

Another important figure was Paramahansa Ramakrishna (1836–1886), who declared the unity of all religions in India. His disciple, Vivekananda (1863–1902), further developed his ideas and linked them to a political vision of a united India.[154] These ideas were further developed by Mahatma Gandhi (1869–1948), who also was instrumental in the establishment of an independent India. Although he helped to negotiate independence from Britain, he was deeply bitter and disappointed by the partition of his country. Gandhi was assassinated in 1948.[155] This brings us to Independent India.

The partition of India in August of 1947 into two countries, India and Pakistan, and the resultant bloodshed, reinforced nationalistic tendencies of both the Indian Hindus and the Pakistani Muslims. Since 1947, violence has frequently erupted. In 1992, Hindus were incited to tear down the Babri Mosque in Ayodhya, which they believed was intentionally built over the site of Rama's birthplace.[156]

From the mid-1960s on, many Indian Hindus imported themselves into the West, with wide-range migration to Britain and North America. Gurus traveled from the East to nurture fledgling Hindu communities, sometimes starting missionary movements that attracted Western youth. Transcendental Meditation, for example, achieved great popularity in America, attracting some Western celebrities like the Beetles' George Harrison.[157]

The Hare Krishna became conspicuous in many American cities. Their male followers sported shaved heads and saffron robes. By the turn of the millennium, many Hindu communities were well-established in Britain and North America. They built many impressive temples, such as the Swaminarayan Temple in London. At the same time, Hindu families became concerned that their children had become too secularized and were giving up Hindu customs. In many ways, young Hindus were turning their backs on the vast civilization that had brought them where they are.

This brings us to the next section of Chapter Two, in which we will identify and discuss the most important religious concepts and practices to be found in the faith of Hinduism, our next topic of this chapter.

Important Concepts and Practices in Hinduism

In this section of Chapter Two, we will introduce and discuss the ten most important religious concepts and practices in the religion of the Hindus. We will list these concepts here and then discuss them one at a time. These ten ideas are the following:

1. God and gods
2. Brahman
3. Atman
4. Karma
5. Samsara, Maya
6. Dharma
7. Bakhti
8. Moksha
9. Nirvana
10. The Caste System

Earlier in Chapter Two, we spoke of the notion of gods in the Hindu faith. In the Rig Veda alone, there are over fifty gods to be found.

The most prominent of these are Brahman, the Creator god; Vishnu, the Preserver god; Shiva, the Destroyer god; Ganapati, the Remover of Obstacles; the avatars of Vishnu, Rama and Krishna; Indra, the god of Heaven; Surya, the god of the Sun; Devi, a frightening deity; and Agni, the god of ritual fire.

The god Brahman is the first member of the Hindu trinity. He is called the "Creator" because periodically, he creates everything in the universe. In this sense, time in Hindu mythology is cyclical, as opposed to the West's idea of linear time. In some portions of the Vedas, the god Brahman is the monistic substance out of which everything comes. We will say more about this idea when we speak of atman, moksha and nirvana.

The atman in Hinduism is the principal word for the "Soul." It is also the eternal part of the Self. It is the true, or inner Self, as opposed to the Ego, or outer Self. In traditional Hinduism, the atman is the part of a human being that gets reincarnated after death. What determines the place of the next life is the law of *Karma*, the belief that one reaps what one sows. The Law of Karma is a natural law. One's life experiences—the good, the bad, the pleasant and the unpleasant in one's life determines the state of the next life.[158]

The Sanskrit word, *samsara*, appears in the Upanishads. It means "wandering." It refers to the process of deaths and rebirths of the atman that takes place in a cyclical process. It is sometimes related to the transmigration of the Soul, or it is called the "wheel of life." The word samsara is related to the Sanskrit root-word, *samsr*, which means "to go around," through a series of states.[159]

The word samsara is found in Buddhism, as well as in the religion of the Jains. The notion of samsara developed in the post-Vedic times. A similar idea can be found in ancient Greek thought in the writings of Pythagoras.[160] In the Upanishads, when the word samsara appears, it is often associated with the word moksha, which means "release." It is the word employed in Hinduism when one is "released" from the Karmic-Samsara Cycle.[161]

In some schools of Hinduism, as well as in Jainism, the atman is not always reincarnated in the body of another human. Sometimes the atman comes to reside in an animal or even insects. Good intentions and Good actions in one life lead to another good life. Bad actions and intentions lead to a bad future, whether in one's next life or some future lives.[162]

The Sanskrit word *maya* means "illusion." It also sometimes means "magic." The word was originally associated with the magical power of a god to make human beings believe in something that turns out to be an illusion. Later, the word became associated with the idea of seeing the phenomenal world as something that is real. Maya is sometimes associated with the expression *Tat tvam asi*, or "That you are," that is, that one's atman is really part of Brahman at the most basic level.[163]

The word maya also is sometimes associated with what is called *ajnana*, another Sanskrit word meaning "ignorance."[164] Usually, this is in the context where the true Self, the atman, is mistaken for the empirical Ego, when in fact it is identical with the notion of Ultimate Reality, or Brahman.[165] Earlier in this chapter, we discussed the idea of *Bhakti*, or "devotion," usually in the context of one of the Hindu gods discussed earlier. We have also spoken of the term *Dharma*, which in most Hindu schools is associated with "law" or "proper conduct."[166]

The word *nirvana* is also a term found in Hinduism, Buddhism, Jainism and in the Sikh religion. In Hinduism, the Sanskrit word *nirvana* is synonymous with the term *moksha*, as well as another term *mukti*. Nirvana is the state of quietude, freedom and perfect happiness, as well as the liberation from the Karmic-Samsara Cycle.[167] The idea of *nirvana* in traditional Buddhism has an entirely different connotation, as we shall see in Chapter Five of this study.

Achieving nirvana in Hinduism is at times associated with the word *armtan*, a Sanskrit word that means "immortality."[168] The word *nirvana* in Hinduism is the state of the atman when it flies off the cycle of rebirth, where *Tat tvam asi*, and the merging with *Brahman* occurs in a timeless state. The word *nirvana* exists in Bengali, Hindi, Sanskrit, Nepali, Punjabi, in Tamil, Javanese, in Odia, and in the Kannada language and Telugu.[169]

The word *nirvana* does not appear in the Vedas, nor in the earliest of the Upanishads. It does, however, appear in the Bhagavad Gita, where it indicates the paths to achieving nirvana. According to the Bhagavad

Gita, those two paths are karma, or action, and *jnana*, a Sanskrit word for "knowledge." Some scholars, like Shankaracharya, indicate that the followers of these two paths to nirvana are two separate groups of people with entirely different mind-sets.[170]

These two different paths to nirvana are also referred to as *Yoga* and *Sankya*. These paths are two stages that can be pursued by the same individual and are not exclusive of each other. Rather, they form a unitary path, where one path leads to the other. The supreme aim of human existence is the cessation of the cycle of birth, death and rebirth, or in other words, the cessation of samsara or nirvana. This is only possible through steady devotion to the knowledge of the Self, by the renunciation of all actions, following the path of jnana.[171]

Finally, there is the idea of the caste system, or *varnas*, in traditional Hinduism. The word *varna* is a Sanskrit word with several traditional meanings, including "type," "order" and "color." It was used to refer to social classes in Hindu texts, such as the Manusmriti that classified Hindu society into four *varnas*.[172]

These four castes, or varnas, were the following:

I.   The Brahmin
II. The Kshatriya
III. The Vaisya
IV. The Shudra[173]

The highest of these castes were the Brahmin. These were the cultic priests, the scholars and the teachers of Hinduism. Next were the Kshatriya. These were the ruling class, warriors and administrators. The Vaisya were the farmers and the merchants, and the Shudra were the laborers and the providers of services.[174] Hindu communities that belonged to one of these four Varnas, or classes, were called *Sarvana*, or Caste Hindus.[175]

The Dravidian tribes who did not belong to any of the four Varnas were known as the *Avarna*, that is "without a caste." This group is also sometimes referred to as the "Dark people," for they were much darker in color than the four Varnas. The English word "varnish," meaning to make a piece of furniture "dark," is a cognate of the Sanskrit word *Varna*.[176]

The first place where the Varna system is discussed in ancient Indian texts is the sections of the *Rig Veda* known as the *Purusha Sukta*, a description of the spiritual unity of the entire Universe. It presents this unity as being both imminent and transcendent. In the seventh verse of this text, it speaks of the organic connectedness of the traditional classes of Hindu society.[177]

The Purusha Sukta is a hymn that suggests that the world is created by and out of *Yajna*, or "Sacrifice." All forms of existence are held to be grounded in the primordial Yajna. In verse seventeen of the hymn, the concept of Yajna itself is held to have arisen out of this original sacrifice. In the final verse of the hymn, the Yajna is extolled as the primordial energy that is the ground of all existence.[178] This brings us to the central sections of this second chapter, what traditional Hinduism has had to say about the phenomena of evil and suffering. We will explore this material in a series of smaller sections, as we shall see next.

Evil and Suffering in Hinduism: The Vedic-Upanishadic Traditions

In its earliest recorded traditions, Hinduism appears to have assented to a view we have called a Religion of Dissolution in Chapter One of this study. Professor B. K. Matilal (1935–1991), the eminent Indian philosopher, tells us this:

> Theodicy is an old and worn out issue. Probably nothing new can be said about it. It is also believed that theodicy was not a problem for the Indians, specifically for the Hindus, because evil was, according to them, an illusion. Particularly, it is argued in Sankara's Advaita Vedanta, the whole world is an illusion along with its evils, and hence the problem of evil is resolved.[179]

The Katha Upanishad makes the same point about the monism of early Hinduism when it relates:

> As fire, which is one, entering the world becomes varied in shape according to the object it burns, so also the one Self [atman] within all beings becomes varied according to whatever it enters and also exists outside them all. As air, which is

one, entering this world, becomes varied in shape according
to whatever it enters and also exists outside them all. Just
as the Sun, the eye of the whole world, is not defiled by the
external faults seen by the eye, even so the one that is within
all beings is not tainted by the sorrow of the world, as he is
outside the world.[180]

The entity that is both inside and outside the world, of course,
in the Vedas and the Upanishads, is Brahman, the Ultimate Reality of
classical Hinduism. In his book *Problems of Suffering in the Religions
of the World*, scholar John Bowker writes about the ultimate monism of
Brahman in the oldest times of Hinduism. Bowker writes:

The individual who has an adequate grasp of Brahman will
find that suffering falls away in insignificance. Since everything that happens is a manifestation of Brahman, it follows
that true understanding only arises when the accidents of
time and space are penetrated and seen to reveal Brahman.
Brahman pervades all things without being exhausted in any
one of them, which means that suffering and sorrow cannot
be the final truth of existence.[181]

In another place in the same work, Bowker expresses the
relationship between the ultimate monism of *Brahman* and the classical
problem of evil. Bowker puts the matter this way:

Suffering occurs as a problem for Hinduism only when duality
in the universe, the contrast between pain and pleasure, is
seen as an abiding truth about existence. Then, inevitably, the
individual self spends itself in trying to find a solid and secure
home in objects that prove ephemeral and transitory. Suffering ceases to be a problem when it is realized that the individual self can transcend occurrences of suffering by finding its
identity in Brahman.[182]

If the phenomenal world and all that it contains is an illusion,
or *maya*, then there can be no individual personalities at the most
fundamental level of existence. Where there are no individual
personalities, of course, then there can be no individual suffering.

Where there is no individual suffering, there can be no problem of evil. The problem of evil is not solved in early Hinduism; it is dissolved. Thus, in our first view of Vedantic Hinduism, the Indian faith is seen as a Religion of Dissolution introduced in Chapter One.[183]

Another approach to evil and suffering in the Vedas and Upanishads is connected to the Karmic-Samsara understanding of the issue. Behind the idea of karma is the belief that beneficial effects in life are derived from past beneficial actions in previous lives and that harmful effects are principally caused by harmful or bad actions or decisions in previous lives. If one did good things in past lives, then those things have moral consequences in this life. If one did evil acts in past lives, then those actions have evil effects in this life.[184]

This point of view can be seen throughout the Vedas and the Upanishads. In the Svetasvatara Upanishad, for example, we find a reference to the law of karma. It informs us:

The vast Universe is a wheel. Upon it are all creatures that are subject to birth, death, and rebirth. Round and round it turns, and it never stops. It is the wheel of Brahman. It revolves upon the wheel in bondage to the laws of birth, death, and rebirth. But when, through the grace of Brahman, it realizes its identity with him, it revolves upon the wheel no longer, for it achieves immortality.[185]

In a chapter of the Brihadaranyaka Upanishad, the basic description of how the karmic law operates is revealed in the following passage:

Accordingly, as one behaves, so does he become. The doer of Good becomes Good. The doer of Evil becomes Evil. One becomes virtuous by virtuous actions. Others become bad by bad actions.[186]

In the Vedas and the Upanishads, it is not actions alone that determine one's condition in future lives. It is "actions" and "intentions"—the attitude with which we perform our moral deeds. The ancient Hindu sages warned against doing nothing at all in the hope of outsmarting karma, but inaction is not the same as good action. Inaction gets the individual nowhere on the karmic wheel.[187]

This importance of intentions in moral behavior in classical Hinduism may also be an indication that in some places, the Upanishads endorses what we have called the Free Will Defense back in the opening chapter of this study of evil and suffering in the religions of the world.

One realization of the Karma-Samsara explanation of evil and suffering in traditional Hinduism is that, as the Upanishads suggest, it is nothing more than what we have called Retributive Justice Theory back in Chapter One of this study. If "as one behaves, so one becomes," then this Hindu category appears to be little more than the reap what you sow view of Retributive Justice.[188]

Another point of view about evil and suffering to be found in the Vedas, the Upanishads, and particularly in the Puranas has to do with the roles of the gods in those texts in relationship to Good and Evil. For example, as described in what is known as the *Kali Purana*, the god Kali is described as:

A huge being, the color of soot, with a very large tongue and a terrible stench. From birth, he has carried an *Upasthi*, a "bone."[189]

In the same Purana, we learn that the god Kaki resides near places where there is gambling, the drinking of alcohol, houses of prostitution, places where animals are slaughtered, and people who are known for their greed.[190] In the Puranas related to Kali, we also find a group of other nouns related to the Demonic, such as *Asuras, Raksases*, and *Picacas*. These beings are types of demons and form different factions.[191] The god Kali in Hindu mythology is often depicted carrying a great sword, with which he vanquishes his many enemies.[192]

In some early traditions of Hinduism, Kali was believed to be the source of all evil among human beings. In the *Mahabharata*, one of the Hindi epics, Kali is a warrior god, and he created the wars between the *Pandavas* and the *Kauravas*.[193] This conflict arose from a struggle over the issue of dynastic succession over which group would take the throne of the *Hastinapura*. Several different ancient Indian kingdoms participated in the war.[194] The historicity of the war is still a matter of some dispute. In the *Mahabharata*, the war stretched out for a period of eighteen days.[195]

Another term for an evil humanoid demon in Hindu mythology is the *Rakshasas*, who are also called the "man-eaters," or *kravyads*. A female Rakshasa is known as a *Rakshasi*. These demons always take human forms. The Sanskrit word, *asura*, is often used interchangeably with the term Rakshasas. The word Rakshasas can be traced to the eighty-seventh hymn of the Rig Veda. The Rakshasas are classified among the *Yatudhanas* as mythological beings who consume raw flesh.[196]

The beings known as the *Picacas*, as well, are often referred to as the *Kravyad*, meaning "eaters of raw flesh." They are believed to infest homes and villages. There are many incantations against the Picacas. The god Agni is often invoked, for example, to restore the health of those attacked by the demons.[197]

The *Asuras* in traditional Hinduism are celestial demons. In some schools, the Asuras are considered the enemies of the gods. They only appear as enemies of human beings on rare occasions. In a number of the *Brahmanas*, the Asuras are associated with darkness. Thus, the day belongs to the gods and the realm of the night to the Asuras.[198]

The Sanskrit word *asura* appears to have changed its meaning over time in Indian culture. There are places in the Rig Veda, for example, where the term *asura* means "Lord," denoting a leader who is honored and respected and who commands some sort of military force. At times, the Asuras were also believed to possess magical powers called *Maya*. It was not until the development of the Atharva Veda that the word *sura* exclusively came to mean a "Demon."[199]

We mention these early Hindu demons because one explanation of evil and suffering in classical Hinduism is what we have called the Influences of Demonic Forces View, as introduced in Chapter One of this study. Thus, in the earliest traditions of the religion of Hinduism, advocates of this Indian faith appear to have supported the following views regarding evil and suffering:

I.   Monism and Hinduism as a Religion of Dissolution
II. Retributive Justice Theory (Karma-Samsara)
III. The Free Will Defense (The role of Intentions in Veda and Upanishads)

IV. The Influences of Demonic Forces Theory (Kali, Asuras,
     Rakshases and Picacas)

Evil and Suffering in the Medieval and Pre-Modern Periods

In the first section of this chapter, we suggested that the medieval period
of Hinduism lasted from approximately 500 CE to 1500 CE, much like
the dates for the medieval church in early Christianity or the Jewish
Middle Ages philosophical tradition from approximately the same time
period.

As we have suggested earlier in Chapter One, the medieval period
of Hinduism is known for the Muslim invasions of the sub-continent
that began in the eighth century and continued through the Turko-
Mongol Muslim empires that began to establish themselves in the
twelfth century, leading up to other Sultanates all the way until the
eighteenth century and the British occupation of India.

In this period, Persian and Arabic words began to enter local
languages in India, giving way to the formation of modern Indian
tongues like Bengali, Urdu, Hindi and Punjabi. The height of Islamic
rule in India was the reign of Mughal Emperor Aurangzeb.[200] Islamic
policies also were introduced in southern India by the Mysore King
Tipu Sultan.

During the medieval Hindu period, the two most prominent Hindu
philosophers to write about evil and suffering were eighth-century
thinker Adi Shankara and twelfth-century philosopher Ramanuja.
This section will begin with some biographical materials on the two
thinkers, followed by their views on evil and suffering. We will start
with Adi Shankara.

Adi Shankara (788–820) was born in southern India in the state
of Kerala in a village called Kaladi. He was born to Brahmin parents
who are said to have led devout Hindu lives in service to the poor.
Apparently, he was attracted to the mendicant life early as a child. His
father died when Shankara was very young. Various stories exist in the
many biographies available, most of which tell the tale of Shankara
surviving an attack from a crocodile.[201]

Shankara appears to have joined the life of a monk in early
adulthood. He traveled across India to propagate a philosophical view

with discussions with other thinkers throughout India. He established the importance of the monastic life as sanctioned in the Upanishads and the Brahma Sutras. In fact, he is reported to have founded four *Mathas*, or monasteries.[202] It is reported in his biographies that Shankara died at the age of thirty-two in the northern state of Uttarakhand.[203]

Over three hundred works are attributed to Shankara, including many commentaries on the Vedas and Upanishads, as well as poetry. His most famous work is a commentary on the Brahma Sutra and others on the ten most essential Upanishads. Shankara also wrote a commentary on the Bhagavad Gita and many other monographs and philosophical treatises. Hindu scholars disagree about which of his attributed works were actually written by him.[204]

Using ideas in the Vedas and Upanishads, Shankara systematized a Vedantic of the Advaita variety, one of the six major orthodox schools of Hinduism. Shankara made fundamental observations and discoveries in metaphysics, epistemology and in the area of Soteriology. He considered perception and inference to be primary tools, in fact, the most reliable of epistemic tools and ways to gain religious knowledge.[205]

The Advaita school, literally the "non-dualism" school of Hindu philosophy, is a classical system of spiritual realization. The term "Advaita" refers to its idea that the true self, or the atman, is the same as the highest metaphysical reality, *Brahman*. The followers of this view regard the phenomenal world as nothing more than *Maya*, or illusion. The Advaita school traces its roots to the oldest of the Upanishads. The philosophy of the Advaita school trace back to the first millennium BCE, but the most prominent thinker in the movement is Adi Shankara.

Perhaps the most stunning thing about Shankara is that unlike most major philosophers in the history of humankind who developed their major works after the age of forty, Adi Shakara developed his philosophical perspectives in his twenties and early thirties. This brings us to Shankara's views on evil and suffering.

Shankara on Evil and Suffering

In an article called "The System of Shankara," philosopher Will Durant tells us about Adi Shankara's written works:

There is much metaphysical wind in these discourses and arid deserts of textual exposition; but they may be forgiven in a man, who at the age of thirty, could be at once the Aquinas and the Kant of India.[206]

In his commentary on the Brahma Sutras, Adi Shankara sketches out four prerequisites for any Hindu philosopher:

1. First, logic is less important than insight in regard to Salvation.
2. One must be willing to observe, inquire, and think for understanding's sake.
3. The philosopher must acquire "Self-Constraint," patience, and tranquility while living above physical temptations and material needs.
4. Finally, there must burn deep within his soul the desire for blissful absorption in the infinite unity of all things.[207]

It should be clear from these observations of Adi Shankara that he was a devoted believer in the Hindu propositions that the atman is the true Self, distinct from the Ego; that Shankara was a believer in the Karma-Samsara process of birth, death and rebirth; and that the ultimate bliss for the Hindu philosopher is for him to realize *Tat tvam asi*. Thus, Shankara appears to assent to the Karmic-Samsara answer to the phenomena of evil and suffering, as well as to the belief that Hinduism is fundamentally a Religion of Dissolution.

Shankara distinguishes between two kinds of maya. He calls the first kind *avidya*, evil or ignorance, and the second variety *vidya*, or the Good. Avidya is that which causes us to move further away from the Real Self and "veils our knowledge of the truth." Vidya, on the other hand, is what enables us to come nearer to the Real Self by "removing the veil of ignorance."[208] For Shankara, both vidya and avidya are transcended when we pass "beyond maya into the consciousness of Ultimate Reality."[209]

However, in many other places of the corpus of his writings, Shankara often spoke freely about his belief in "God." For Adi Shankara, the word "God" is *Brahman*, in so far as *Brahman* refers to the world of existence. While God itself is "without cause or effect," God, or what he calls *Ishvara*, is the material cause, as well as the operative cause, of the world of existence. According to Shankara, being and non-being, life and death, existence and non-existence, "are not limiting conditions of the Universal Self."[210]

Shankara goes on in the same work to suggest that Ishvara is not the cause of the world because that would imply that God made a world full of evil and suffering. The eighth-century Hindu philosopher goes on to say:

> It is logical to say that the transmigratory existence has no beginning, for if it emerged capriciously all of a sudden, then there could have been the predicament of freed souls also being reborn here, as also the contingency of result accruing from non-existing causes, or the differences in happiness and misery would have no logical explanation.[211]

Near this same pronouncement in his commentary on the Brahman Sutras, referring to Section 10.190.3 of the *Rig Veda*, suggest that the conclusion made there about the cycles of creation is that "the past and future cycles of creation are numberless."[212]

Ultimately, when it comes to the phenomena of evil and suffering, Adi Shankara appears to fall back to the Vedic idea that Hinduism is a Religion of Dissolution through its numberless cycles of karmic birth, death and rebirth. This point of view may even be seen in his poem "Atma Shatkam," the opening two stanzas of which say this:

> I am Consciousness. I am bliss. I am Shiva. I am Shiva.
> Without hate, without infatuation, without craving, without
>   greed.
> Neither arrogance, nor conceit, never jealous am I.
> Adi Shankara ends the poem this way:
> Without form, without figure, without resemblance am I.
> Vitality of all senses, in everything I am.
> Neither attached, nor released am I.
> I am Consciousness, I am bliss, I am Shiva. I am Shiva.[213]

Another way to see Shankara's devotion to Hinduism as a Religion of Dissolution View is the fact that he defines Ishvara, or God, as "existence" and identifies the Real Being as God. This appears to be an early view of later Western philosophers like Anselm, who maintained that "God existence and His essence are one and the same thing."[214]

This brings us to the life and times of philosopher Ramanuja, followed by his views on evil and suffering, the next two sections of this chapter on evil and suffering in traditional Hinduism.

The Life and Times of Ramanuja

Another prominent Hindu philosopher in India during the medieval period is the South Indian Ramanuja (1017–1137). He was born in the village of Sriperumbudur in Tamil Nadu, a state in southern India. Several modern scholars have questioned his dates, who suggest the alternate dates of 1077 to 1157, for this South Indian thinker.[215] When Ramanuja reached the age of manhood, he married and moved to the adjacent village of Kanchipuram. He also began to study at a monastery there under the direction of Yadava Prakasa.[216]

Over the years, history tells us that teacher and pupil disagreed over several issues about how to interpret many Vedic passages. Eventually, the two split, and Ramanuja went to study on his own. He later became a priest at a temple to Vishnu, the Varadharaja Perumal, where he began to teach that the idea of *moksha*, liberation or release, is not to be achieved by metaphysical beliefs, but also with the *bhakti*, or devotion, to a single deity.[217]

There is also a collection of narratives in the hagiography of Ramanuja that, at times, makes claims that seem unlikely to be true. For example, one narrative says that Ramanuja began studying the Vedas when he was "an eight-day-old baby."[218] Another narrative maintains that Ramanuja first began speaking with Vishnu when he was five years old.[219]

Ramanuja grew up in the Tamil culture in a stable society during the Chola Dynasty, one of the longest-ruling dynasties in India, or the world, for that matter. It lasted from 848 until 1279.[220] There were many attempts in Ramanuja's life to assassinate him. One attempt was made by his teacher, Prakasa, and in a second, a rival teacher attempted to poison Ramanuja with no success.[221]

This brings us to a discussion of Ramanuja's views on evil and suffering, the topic of the next section of this second chapter on views in Hinduism regarding the phenomena of evil and suffering.

Ramanuja on Evil and Suffering

In contrast to the monistic views of Adi Shankara on evil and suffering, the ideas of Ramanuja are very much theistic, and specifically, monotheistic. For him, Brahman as atman, the highest Self of all, is the union of two deities, *Vishnu*, or *Narayana*, and His consort named *Sri*, or *Laksmi*. We will remember that in Hinduism, Vishnu is the God who preserves and upholds all things, while Laksmi is the goddess of prosperity.[222] For Ramanuja, the unity of the male Vishnu and the female Laksmi are two separate elements of Ultimate Reality, or Brahman.

The Sanskrit term that Ramanuja employs to speak of this unity is *ubhayalingam*, or "having both sexes."[223] In Ramanuja's view, Brahman as atman is antagonistic to all evils and faults and has enumerable and auspicious *kalanaguna*, or "qualities." These auspicious qualities are both moral and aesthetic in character. For Ramanuja, the greatest Good consists of being ever-aware of one's true nature of Brahman. When all the obstacles and impediments to this realization are removed, then the individual reaches moksha.[224]

The idea of morality in the thought of Ramanuja has two principal elements. The first of these is the keeping of a set of deontological duties. These are actions that ought to be done for their own sake and not for their consequences. This element is known as *Karma Yoga*. The second element of the ethics of Ramanuja is the constant worship of Brahman, particularly in the form of offering all the fruits of one's labor to the Divine. The keeping of these deontological duties involves the exercise of free will that includes proper intentions for the sake of moral duty itself, much like Immanuel Kant's moral theory in the West.[225]

The most important of Ramanuja's works is what is called in English, *A Summary of the Meaning of the Vedas*.[226] In this work, God is conceived as a personal being who has a will, agency and purposes for His actions. These are principally gratified through adoration or bhakti, and by rejecting and neglecting evil practices. God is a compassionate being who, above all, deserves our love and praise.[227]

For Ramanuja, God is a perfectly self-sustained being, who has no limitations, creates the cosmos as purely and as simply as possible, and He does this for the sake of *lila* or, "play." For Ramanuja, the cosmos is the arena in which the True Self may be rid of the burdens of its accumulated karma. The scriptures for Ramanuja are the *Agamas*, also called the *Samhitas*, believed to be the divine utterances of Vishnu and Laksmi. They are often chanted with the use of mantras, which are a kind of sonic form of the Deity.[228]

In Ramanuja's view, the body of God is made up of the cosmos of souls and matter. This understanding derives from a passage in the Upanishads. This passage relates the following:

> The Soul of yours is present within, but it is different from all beings, which all beings know not, whose body is all beings, and who guides all beings from within—he is the *Antar-yam-in*, the Immortal One.[229]

In other words, the idea is that the relation between God and the world is loosely analogous to the relationship of the individual soul, or *jiva*, for Ramanuja, to its material body. God ensouls the world as the jiva ensouls the body. For Ramanuja, he disagrees with views like the Advaita school because he disagrees with the overall monism of their position.[230] In its place, Ramanuja wishes to elevate his monotheism and its dedication to Vishnu.

In his view, Ramanuja elevates the moral duties to Vishnu and His consort that he outlines in his principal works. In acting on these deontological duties, the Hindu individual seeker uses his free will with accompanying intentions toward those duties. In essence, then, besides the Karma-Samsara response to evil and suffering, Ramanuja also puts emphasis on the Free Will Defense.

The brings us to the final section of this second chapter, in which we will describe and discuss more modern perspectives on the phenomena of evil and suffering in the faith of Hinduism.

Evil and Suffering in the Modern Period of Hinduism

In the modern Hindu period, various Hindu philosophers and theologians have commented in some depth on the phenomena of evil

and suffering from 1757 until the present time. Among these note-
worthy thinkers are the following: Rabindranath Tagore (1861–1941),
Swami Vivekananda (1863–1902), Mahatma Gandhi (1869–1948),
Aurobindo Ghose (1872–1950), Rama Krishna (1888–1975) and
Sarvepalli Radhakrishna (1888–1975.)

In the nineteenth and twentieth centuries, Hindu philosophy
was also sometimes known as the Neo-Hinduism Movement and
characterized by two elements. First, the belief that all of the religions
of the world lead to the same Divine Reality. As Swami Vivekananda
expresses this belief in his *Hinduism at a Glance* puts it:

> All true religions of the world lead us alike to the same goal,
> namely, to perfection if. of course, they are followed faithfully.
> Each of them is a correct path to Divinity. The Hindus have
> been taught to regard religion in this light.[231]

This first belief of neo-Hinduism often uses a metaphor that each
of the world's religions is like a stream or a river that leads to the
same goal, the ocean of Ultimate Reality. A second aspect of the Neo-
Hinduism Movement, at least among traditional Indian philosophers,
is the view that Vedantic Hinduism is not simply another of the many
faiths. It is the Universal Faith. Swami Vivekananda points to this
aspect of neo-Hinduism when he writes:

> Ours is the Universal Religion. It is inclusive enough, it is broad
> enough to include all major religious ideals.[232]

A similar conclusion may be found in the writings of
Radhakrishnan, where, for example, he concludes, "The Vedanta
is not a religion, but religion itself in its most universal and deepest
significance." Ramakrishna, a traditional nineteenth-century mystical
thinker, speaks of the world as God's "play."[233] He relates:

> Evil exists from a relative perspective, an unenlightened
> perspective, but also from an absolute perspective, there
> is no Evil.[234]

It should be clear that in this statement, Ramakrishnan is falling
back on the unreality view of what we have called the Religions of

Dissolution in our discussion of Chapter One. In his perspective on maya, as well, he maintains, "There is ignorance and knowledge. Darkness is needed too. It reveals all the more the glory of Light."[235] This appears to be an assent to what we have labeled the Contrast View in our explication in the opening chapter of this study of evil and suffering in the religions of the world.

The third aspect of neo-Hinduism in the nineteenth and twentieth centuries was the emphases in figures like Ram Mohan Roy and Mahatma Gandhi toward issues in social justice.[236] Gandhi set out a goal of the restoration of a just and equal society in the Indian sub-continent. He called for the dissolution of the caste system, as well as the universal following of the concept of *ahimsa*, or "non-violence" in the face of evil and suffering.

The two most complete philosophical views in the Neo-Hinduism Movement were those of Rabindranath Tagore and Sarvepalli Radhakrishnan. The former's most complete treatment of evil can be found in his *Sadhana*, which were lectures given at Harvard University.[237] In these lectures, Tagore points out that the existence of evil in the world is an indication of the incomplete nature of creation.[238] Tagore called for a greater awareness of the inner-self, or the atman, as opposed to the outer self, or the ego.

Sarvepalli Radhakrishnan (1888–1976) was born in a southern Indian Brahmin family but educated by Christian missionaries. Unlike many other Indian philosophers, Radhakrishnan holds a position on evil and suffering much like what we have called the Test View and the Moral Qualities Response as introduced in Chapter One of this study.

In one place, Radhakrishnan says, "Pain and trouble purify the soul. The metal shines the brightest when it passes through the furnace."[239] He continues in the same work:

The most poignant pain can be joyously accepted if it is recognized as contributing to the realization of one's ideas.[240]

About this passage, scholar William Cenkner says, "None of this is necessarily new or novel to traditional Indian understanding. What is new is the insertion of human freedom and its significance, an insight from the West, that he introduces into the discussion."[241] In Cenkner's view of Radhakrishnan on evil, the contemporary philosophers maintain that we should add the Free Will Defense to the Test View and the Moral Qualities Theory in the above analysis.

Thus, in the modern period of Hinduism, we have seen the endorsement of religion as a Religion of Dissolution View, Test Perspective, Moral Qualities Theory, Retributive Justice View through Karma-Samsara, Free Will Defense, and Contrast View.

This brings us to the major conclusions we have made in this second chapter. The topic of Chapter Three of this study is the phenomena of evil and suffering and responses to those phenomena to be found in the history of Judaism.

Conclusions to Chapter Two

We have divided this second chapter on evil and suffering in Hinduism into several parts. In the first of these parts, we have made some very general preliminary remarks about the nature of studying Hinduism. In these remarks, we pointed out that the Hindu faith is drastically different than the religions of the West in many different aspects on which we made comments.

In the second part of Chapter Two, we described and discussed the many periods of Hindu history, from the Indus Valley civilization to modern Hindu philosophers in the twentieth century. In each of these seven periods of Hindu history, we identified key thinkers, poets, philosophers and theologians who contributed to the history of Hinduism.

In the third section of Chapter Two of this study of evil and suffering in the religions of the world, we have identified and then discussed ten central concepts and practices in the Hindu religion, including views on the gods Brahman; atman; karma; moksha; samsara; maya; dharma; bakhti, or devotion; moksha, or release; the idea of nirvana; and the make-up of the Indian caste system. In this section, we have also shown that each of these ideas and practices in Hinduism have played important and central roles in the Hindu faith. In fact, we maintained that without any of these ideas, the faith of Hinduism would not be understandable.

In the fourth section of Chapter Two, we have examined the answers and responses to evil and suffering found in the Vedas and the Upanishads. Chief among these responses in the earliest portions of Hinduism, as we have shown, were the Karma-Samsara View, as well as the notion that early Hinduism was a monistic Religion of Dissolution.

In the fifth part of Chapter Two, we discussed the phenomena of evil and suffering found in the medieval period of the Hindu faith from 500 CE to 1500 CE. In this fifth section, we maintained that the two most significant medieval thinkers to write about evil and suffering were eighth-century philosopher Shankara and twelfth-century thinker Ramanuja. About the former, we have pointed out that much of what he said and wrote about evil and suffering was related to his metaphysical monism that we suggested is a version of the Religions of Dissolution.

In the case of South Indian philosopher Ramanuja, we suggested that he too endorses a version of Atman as Brahma Theory, as well as his employment of the Karma-Samsara Theory that is, as we pointed out earlier, really a version of Retributive Justice Theory as introduced in Chapter One. We also have maintained that given Ramanuja's ethics, he also appears to endorse the Free Will Defense because of his belief in the role of intentions in moral discourse.

In the final section of this chapter, we explored many views on evil and suffering in Hinduism found in the modern period, or what we have also called the Neo-Hindu Movement, mostly during the nineteenth and twentieth centuries. We began this final section with a description of several facets of the Neo-Hindu Movement, along with thinkers who held these beliefs.

Among the important thinkers of the Neo-Hindu Movement we suggested were Ram Mohan Roy, Mahatma Gandhi, Radhakrishnan, Aurobindo Ghose, Swami Vivekananda, and many others. Among these thinkers, we find more assent to monism and the Karma-Samsara View, but also saw among these modern thinkers some beliefs in what we have called the Free Will Defense, the Test View, the Contrast Perspective, and in Vivekananda, the Moral Qualities Perspective.

The bottom line on views on evil and suffering in the Hindu tradition we have seen belief in, or assent to, seven separate responses or answers. These were: monism, or the Religion of Dissolution View, the

Karma-Samsara approach to evil and suffering, a version of Retributive Justice Theory, the Free Will Defense, the Influences of Demonic Forces approach to evil and suffering, the Contrast Perspective, the Test View, as well as the Moral Qualities Theory.

We now turn to Chapter Three, a discussion of the phenomena of evil and suffering in the history of Judaism from biblical times to modern times.

Chapter Three:
Evil and Suffering in Judaism

The meaning of pain has never ceased to be plumbed
by man. How to avoid pain, or, when afflicted, how to
overcome it, would probably account for a good deal of
development in Civilization.

—H. Joel Laks, "The Enigma of Job: Maimonides and the
Moderns"

The most difficult matter, which is at the root of both faith
and apostasy is the problem of suffering, which all scholars of all ages agree, people and tongues have struggled.

—Nachmanides, "Commentary on Job"

No matter how good and concerned God might be, there
is always metaphysical evil to mark the fact that the universe is not God and God is not the universe.

—Nahum N. Glatzer, *The Dimensions of Job*

Introduction

The purpose of this third chapter is to explore the phenomena of evil
and suffering in the history of the religion of Judaism. We will open the
chapter with some preliminary remarks about how best to understand
Judaic responses to evil and suffering in their history. This will be
followed by sections on biblical materials, including ancient Judaism,
medieval perspectives, and answers and responses to evil and suffering
in the modern period, from the seventeenth century to the present. The

major tools for interpreting this material from Judaism are the concept of the *Berith*, or "Covenant," from the Hebrew Bible, and the many responses and answers to the existence of evil and suffering introduced in the opening chapter of this study. We move first to these preliminary remarks on evil and suffering in Judaism.

Preliminary Remarks on Evil and Suffering in Judaism

Before we catalog the history of responses to evil and suffering in Judaism, we will first comment on several ideas that need to be understood of what later in this chapter will follow. Among these are the nature of the texts in the Hebrew Bible, the idea of the *Berith*, or Covenant, as well as a summary of the answers and responses to evil and suffering that most often appear in the history of Judaism.

The ancient Jews understood their scriptures as having three principal parts. These are the Torah, the Nabim and the Kethuvim. The first of these parts, the Torah, are the first five books of the Hebrew Bible, or Old Testament. The second part is made up of the major prophets and the minor prophets. The three major prophets are Isaiah, Jeremiah and Ezekiel. There are twelve minor prophets in Judaism.[242]

The *Kethuvim*, or "the Writings," is the portion of the Hebrew Bible, or Old Testament, that comes at the end of the Hebrew scriptures. These books include Psalms, Proverbs, Ecclesiastes, the Book of Job, Lamentations, the Book of Daniel and many other books. We begin with this description because it is often the case that an answer to a theological question in the Torah may change in the prophets and the writings.

Another category, or concept of the ancient Jews, an over-arching idea for understanding evil and suffering in the earliest portions of Judaism, is the concept of a *Berith*, or "Covenant," among the ancient Jewish people. This word was most likely borrowed from a collection of people known as the Hittites. Their primary contribution to human civilization was the invention of the Contract. The Hittites occupied much of Anatolia, or Asia Minor, modern-day Turkey.[243]

Hittite history is divided by most modern scholars into two separate periods. The first is the "Old Kingdom," from approximately 1700 to 1500 BCE, and the "New Kingdom" from 1400 to 1200 BCE.[244]

The Hittites are important for our purposes because the ancient Jews adopted a version of the Hittite contract. Among the Hittites, those contracts had the following parts:

I.   Introduction: Identification of parties of the contract
II. History of their Relationship
III. New Agreement
IV. Blessings and the Curses
V.   Sealing Ceremony[245]

In part one of the Hittite contract, we see an introduction to the contractual parties. It might say, "I am King So and So, and you are my people," or "I am King So and So and you are King Such and Such." The contractual parties might have been between a king and his people, or a king and another king. In the case of the ancient Jews, they saw themselves as having a *Berith* with their God, *Yahweh*.[246]

The second part of the Hittite contract spoke of the history of the relationship between the two contractual parties. It might say, for example, "Last year we grew ____ cubits of wheat," followed by the "New Agreement," "And this year we will grow ____ cubits, plus ten more." The fourth part of the Hittite contract was called the "Blessings and Curses," because the ancient Jews would take their agricultural products, such as a sheep, for example, and cut the animal in half, so that the contractual parties could pass between the pieces with a lighted torch.[247]

The idea behind this ritual was that the light enables the god Yahweh to see more easily the agreement, and if one did not keep it, you would wind up like the dead animal. The Blessings and Curses also usually sketched out what benefits would follow if the agreement was kept and what evils would follow if it was not. The passing between the pieces was the "Sealing Ceremony," comparable to "singing on the dotted line" in contemporary life.[248] The first time the Hebrew Bible, or Old Testament, uses the word *Berith* is after the Flood, when Yahweh makes a "covenant" with Noah, to no longer treat His people, the Jews, as He has just done. A few chapters later, at Genesis 15, we find an exchange that looks very much like the Hittite contract. Verses seven to eleven are the introduction and the history. Verses twelve to sixteen is the "New Agreement." At verses seventeen to twenty-one, we find the Blessings and Curses, as well as the Sealing Ceremony.[249]

Some of the uses of *Berith* in the Hebrew Bible are between two kings, like David and Jonathan, at First Samuel 18:3, 20:8 and 23:18. Sometimes they are between two nations, like Isaac and Abimelech at Genesis 26:28. And sometimes the *Berith* is between a God and His people, as in Genesis 15.[250] We have introduced the idea of the *Berith* in this section because one way to understanding ancient Jewish views on the phenomena of evil is how well the nation of Israel has kept, or has broken, the Covenant. In fact, one way to understand the rise and fall of the fortunes of the Jews in the Hebrew Bible is by how well, or how not so well, they have kept the Covenant.

In addition to the idea of the parts of the Hebrew Bible and the notion of the *Berith*, or Covenant, many of the responses to evil and suffering that we have outlined in Chapter One of this study also can be seen in the Hebrew Bible. Indeed, over the course of this third chapter, we shall see many examples of both Collective and Individual Retributive Justice, the Free Will Defense, the Influences of Demonic Forces View, as well as a few examples of Original Sin Theory.

In the Hebrew Bible, we shall also see examples of the Test View, the Contrast Theory, the Moral Qualities View, and the Divine Plan Perspective. In the next section of this chapter we will see many of the supplemental theories we have provided back in Chapter One, as well as a few views we did not find there.

One final preliminary remark for ascertaining what the Jewish tradition believed about the phenomena of evil and suffering is what a movement or an individual thinker believe or wrote about the Book of Job. Since the central issue of that book of the Bible is about evil and suffering, that "litmus test" is often enlightening when it comes to making sense of the history of Jewish attitudes toward the phenomena.

As we shall see in this third chapter from biblical times until contemporary times, many major movements and thinkers in the History of Judaism have commented on Job, the Man From Uz, and his book, including prominent philosophical thinkers like Saadiah Gaon and Moses Maimonides, and biblical exegetes such as Gersonides and Nachmanides, and modern thinkers like the Jewish existentialists.

Evil and Suffering in the Hebrew Bible

For the most part, the earliest theological responses to the phenomena of evil and suffering in the Hebrew Bible are examples of the collective form of Retributive Justice Theory. At the Book of Numbers 16:26, for instance, God says to the Jewish people, "Turn away from the tents of wicked men, and touch nothing of theirs, or you will be swept away along with them."

At the Book of Deuteronomy 11:13–17 and 31:17–18, we see two more examples of Collective Retributive Justice. At Exodus 21:23–25, as well, we find some famous rules for dealing with those who cause evil and suffering:

> If any harm follows, then you shall give life for life, eye for an
> eye, and a tooth for a tooth, hand for hand and a foot for a
> foot; burn for a burn, and a wound for a wound.

Among the major prophets, Isaiah, Jeremiah and Ezekiel, we also find the Collective Retributive Justice View in the face of evil and suffering. In the opening of Jeremiah 12, for example, we find the prophet ask, "Why do the ways of the wicked prosper / Why do all who are treacherous thrive?[251] Similar questions arise in the prophecies of Isaiah and Ezekiel, as well.

In the Major Prophets, we also begin to see a rejection of the Collective Retribution View. Consider Jeremiah 31:29, Ezekiel 18:20, and Isaiah 45:15 for examples of this theological phenomenon. In the first of these, speaking about the future, Jeremiah relates:

> In those days they shall no longer say, "The parents have
> eaten sour grapes and the children's teeth are set on edge," a
> clear rejection of Familial Retribution.

At Ezekiel 18:20, we are told, "The person who sins shall die. A child shall not suffer for the iniquities of his parent, nor the parent suffer for the iniquity of the parent." At Isaiah 45:9 and 15, we see the prophet suggest two other responses to evil and suffering. In the former, Isaiah asked:

> Woe to you who strive with your Maker, earthen vessels
> with the potter. Does the clay say to the One who fashions it,
> "What are you making," or "Your work has no handles."

The clay, of course, is human beings and the potter is God. The prophet seems to be endorsing a version of the Divine Plan Theory in this passage. A few verses later, at 45:15, Isaiah introduces another theological response in Judaism. The prophet tells us, "Truly, you are a God who hides His face, O God of Israel, our Savior." This view, of course, is one of the supplemental responses as outlined in Chapter One of this study.

Another traditional response to the phenomena of evil and suffering in the Hebrew Bible is the ancient Jewish version of the Free Will Defense. It is the theory of the two "inclinations" or two "imaginations" in every human being. The ancient Jews called these the *yetzer hara* or the "evil imagination," and the *yetzer tov*, or the "good inclination."[252] These two *yetzerim* are employed throughout the Hebrew Bible. The first time the word is used comes at Genesis 6:5, where it relates, *Yetzer-lev ha adam 'ra*, or "The imagination (*yetzer*) of the heart (*leb*) of man (*adam*) is evil (*'ra*)."

The same expression is employed at Genesis 8: 21, where it tells us, "The imagination (*yetzer*) is evil (*'ra*) from his youth." The two Yetzerim Theory is also employed throughout the Old Testament, at places like Deuteronomy 31:21, First Chronicles 28:9 and 29:18, Psalm 103:14 and Isaiah 26:3, for examples.

So far in this section, we have shown that the writers of the Hebrew Bible have endorsed both the Collective and the Individual forms of Retributive Justice Theory, The Free Will Defense in the two *Yetzerim* Theory, the Divine Plan Point of View, in Isaiah's metaphor of the clay and the potter, as well as what we have labeled the "Hidden God" Approach in the opening chapter of this study.

We can also find several examples of the Influences of Demonic Forces View in the Hebrew Bible by its employment of the Hebrew word *Satan*. Sometimes this word is simply used to designate an "adversary" or an "accuser," such as at Psalms 71:3 and 109:6. Sometimes the word *Satan* is used to designate an "agent of God," such as at Numbers 21:22–24 and 22:21–32. And in the Book of Job, the word *Satan* is preceded by the definite article *ha*. Thus, the figure is called "The Satan" in English translations.

There are also many examples in the Hebrew Bible where Original Sin Theory seems the best explanation of a passage. Consider, for example, three passages in the Book of Job 5:7, 14:4 and 25:4. The first of these relates, "But human beings are born to trouble, as surely as sparks fly upward." At 14:4, the writer of the Book of Job asks, "Who can bring a clean thing out of an unclean? No one can."

At 25:4 of the Book of Job, the writer again asks a question:

> How then can a mortal be righteous before God? How can
> one born of a woman be pure?

Job 15:14 and 15 also suggests the idea of Original Sin to many exegetes. The text relates:

> What are mortals that they may be clean, or those born of a
> woman that they may be righteous. God puts no trust, even
> in His Holy Ones.

Many other passages in the Hebrew Bible are also interpreted as Original Sin Theory. Consider two places in the Psalms, at 14:2–3 and 51:5, for example. The former tells us this, "The Lord looks down from heaven on humankind to see if there are any who are wise, who seek after God. They have all gone astray, they are all alike perverse. There is no one who does good, no, not one."

At Psalm 51:5, the writer makes a declarative statement that also has the taste of Original Sin Theory. "Indeed, I was born guilty, a sinner when my mother conceived me." Several passages in the Book of Ecclesiastes, as well, may suggest Original Sin Theory. One of the principal ones is 9:4. That tells us, "... since the same fate comes to us all, to the righteous and to the wicked, to the good and to the evil, to the clean and to the unclean."

Two other Old Testament passages that appear to indicate Original Sin Theory are Jeremiah 17:9 and Psalm 58:3. In the former, the Prophet tells us, "The heart is deceitful above all things and desperately sick. Who can understand it?" The Psalmist, at 58:3, relates:

> The wicked are estranged from the womb. They go astray
> from birth, always speaking lies.

It is clear from passages like Genesis 3 that human beings often misuse their free will to commit evil acts. Thus, so far in this section of Chapter Three, we have suggested that the ancient Jews were advocates of:

1. The Free Will Defense
2. The Two Yetzerim Theory
3. Collective Retributive Justice Theory
4. The Individual Retribution View
5. The Hidden God View
6. The Divine Plan Theory

There are also a variety of passages in the Hebrew Bible that appear to assent to the Contrast View, the Test Perspective, the Moral Qualities Position, and the Divine Plan Theory. We now will establish these theories one at a time, beginning with the Contrast perspective. Many passages that appear to endorse this view are when Darkness, or Evil, is contrasted with Light, or the Good. Consider Isaiah 9:2, for example:

> The people who walk in darkness will see a great light. Those who live in a dark land, The light will shine on them.

At Second Samuel 22:29, we find another example of the Contrast View, "For You are my lamp, O Lord, and the Lord will lighten my darkness." The writer of the Book of Proverbs, at 20:20, tells us, "The way of the wicked is as darkness. They know not in what they stumble." At Isaiah 45:7, the prophet seems to endorse the Contrast View when he has God reveal:

> I form the light and create darkness. I make peace and create evil. I, the Lord, do all of these things.

Many other passages in the Torah, the Prophets, and the Writings ascribe to what only can be interpreted as what we have called the Contrast View back in the opening chapter of this study. What we have labeled the "Test View" can also be seen throughout the Hebrew Bible. The word *nacah*, which means to "test," "try" or "prove," often can be found in the Hebrew Bible. At Genesis 22:1, "God tested Abraham." At Exodus 16:4, the same word means "prove," while at Exodus 17:2, it implies "tempt."

Nacah is used in the past tense at Numbers 14:22 as "have tempted" and as an infinitive at Deuteronomy 8:2 as "to prove," as well as at Judges 3:1 and 4. At Psalm 26:2, the same word is employed as a verb as "prove," and at Psalm 78:18, 41, and 56, the psalmist uses the past tense, "tempted." The writer of the Book of Ecclesiastes also employed the word *nacah* throughout his book, such as at 2:1 (prove), 7:12 (tempt) and 7:23, where it used as the past tense "proved."

Another classical Hebrew term, *bachan*, is also used to indicate "to try" or "to test." It is employed at Genesis 42:15 and 16, First Chronicles 29:17, Psalm 7:9 and 11:4, as well as various passages in the Book of Job, such as 7:18, 12:11, 23:10, 34:3 and 36, for examples. At Job 12:11, *bachan* is used when the text asks, "Does not the ear try words, as the palate tastes food?" At Job 23:10, the writer uses the past tense of *bachan*. The line may be rendered:

> But He knows the way that I take, when He has tried me. And
> I shall come forth as gold.

From this discussion, we may add the Test View and the Contrast Theory to our Jewish responses to the phenomena of evil and suffering. This brings us to the Moral Qualities Theory, as the supplemental theories we have introduced back in the opening chapter of this study. The classical Hebrew word that indicates the Moral Qualities Theory is *Musar*, which is usually rendered "to chasten." It may be found at Job 5:17, 12:18, 20:3, 36:10, as well as Psalm 50:17, Proverbs 1:2, 3:11, and 4:13. At Psalm 50:17, for example, the word *musar* is often rendered as "discipline." In Proverbs, it usually is translated as "instruction." In both uses, of course, the verb is used to produce better behavior.

The Book of Job is also a good text to find the Divine Plan Theory, particularly in the Elihu and God speeches. When God asks, "Where were you when I laid down the foundations of the Earth?" He clearly was referring to his knowledge and power that human beings cannot understand.[253] A vast number of other passages in the Hebrew Bible also imply an assenting to Divine Plan Theory.[254]

From our analyses in this section of Chapter Three, we have established the Hebrew Bible's endorsements of the following responses to the phenomena of Evil and Suffering:

1. The Free Will Defense
2. Individual and Collective Retributive Justice

3. Original Sin Theory
4. The Influences of Demonic Forces View
5. The Contrast Theory
6. The Test View
7. The Moral Qualities Approach
8. Divine Plan Theory
9. The Hidden God Theory

This ninth theory, what we have called the Hidden God View, has been employed dozens of times in the Hebrew Bible. Often they occur when a text speaks of God "hiding His face," such as at Deuteronomy 31:17–18 and 32:20, Micah 3:4, Ezekiel 39:23 and 24, Psalm 10:11 and 30:7, for examples. At other times, it simply says that God has "forgotten His people." In other instances, we find that God "hides Himself," rather than "His face," such as at Isaiah 45:15, or at Psalm 10:1 when the Psalmist asks, "Why do you stand afar off?"

At any rate, what all these biblical passages have in common is that one response the ancient Jews had to the phenomena of evil and suffering is that the God of Israel, Yahweh, is a Hidden God. One final Jewish response to evil and suffering in the Hebrew Bible is the employments of two classical Hebrew terms, *Natash* and *rashyon*. These words usually are rendered into English as "Permits" and "Permission."

Sometimes when these words are used in the Hebrew Bible, it is to show that at times, although God does not commit evil, He sometimes allows it to occur. At Ezra 3:7, the writer uses the word *rashyon*, or "permission." *Natash*, on the other hand, can be seen at Genesis 31:28, Exodus 23:11, Numbers 11:31, Deuteronomy 32:15, Judges 15:9, Isaiah 21:15, and at many other passages.

At many of these, their purpose is to show that although God does not commit evil, he does, nevertheless, allow it to happen. As we shall see in Chapter Eight, this view was used extensively in medieval Christianity, but it is less often found in Judaism and in Islam.

To summarize what we have concluded so far in this third chapter, the Old Testament Jews demonstrated their employment of the following responses in the Hebrew Bible:

1. The Free Will Defense
2. Individual and Collective Retributive Justice
3. Original Sin Theory
4. The Influences of Demonic Forces View
5. The Contrast Theory
6. The Test View
7. The Moral Qualities Approach
8. Divine Plan Theory
9. The Hidden God View
10. The Permission Theory: That God Permits Evil

This brings us to the next section of this third chapter, in which we will examine Jewish responses to evil and suffering in the ancient world. This will be followed by sections on the medieval world and the modern world, as well.

Jewish Responses to Evil and Suffering in the Ancient World

The three most important sources for understanding Jewish theories on evil and suffering in the ancient world are the Talmud, the Midrash, and a body of early Jewish philosophy, such as Philo of Alexandria. Of these sources, the deepest and widest views are the rabbis of the Jerusalem and Babylonian versions of the Talmud.

In this Jewish material, we see the continuation of much of what we have seen in the biblical materials. For example, in the Genesis Rabbah, at tractate 33b, the rabbis tell us, "Man should bless God for the evil which occurs in the same way He is blessed for the Good." In the same work at tractate 7b, the rabbis appear to endorse a version of the Divine Plan Theory, when the text tells us that God says, "I will be gracious to whom I will be gracious, and will show mercy on those on whom I show mercy," an obvious statement on the ability of human beings to understand the ways of the Lord.

The Genesis Rabbah, at 6a, 7a, and 84, speaks of evil coming from or blamed on Satan or various other malicious demons. At tractate 11a of the Ta'an suggested that the world to come will be measures of compensations and punishments, a view that, ultimately, is a version of Retributive Justice Theory. In the Haggadah, at tractate 16a, the rabbis view evil as the product of, or is identical to, the *yetzer hara*, or "evil imagination." In fact, the Genesis Rabbah, at 9:9, relates that "The evil inclination is a necessary factor the in believer's existence in the world. The rabbis say, "Without it, a man could not marry, build a house, raise a family, or engage in trade."

Kedoshim 30b suggests that the reading of the Torah is an antidote to the *yetzer hara*. This enables the believer to serve God with his Good and his Evil imaginations. At Bereshith 60b, the rabbis advise people to accustom themselves to say, "All that the Merciful One does is for the Good." At Yoma 76a, the rabbis relate that "God's rewards will never exceed His punishments." And at Ta'an 21a, suggests that one Rabbi, Nahum of Gizmo, or *Ish Gamzu*, responded to every example of evil in the Talmud by proclaiming, "This too is for the best," another nod in the direction of Divine Plan Theory.

The Genesis Rabbah, at 9: 8, and well as at 5a, speak of developing moral virtues like patience and faith through the experience of evil and suffering. The rabbis quote Psalm 94:2, "Happy is the man whom You discipline, O Lord, and teach out the Law." This, of course, is a Talmudic example of the Moral Qualities Theory. The rabbis in the same tractate also quote Psalm 119:71:

> It is good for me that I have been afflicted, in order that I
> might learn Your statutes.

The Moral Qualities Perspective also can be seen in what the ancient rabbis sometimes call "afflictions of love," suffering that enables believers to develop virtues like patience, faith and courage. This view may be detected at Genesis Rabbah 9:8 and the Bereshith, tractate 5a, for examples.

In the Pirkei Avot 6:4, we learn that the "true student of the Torah carries on his studying despite whatever suffering or hardships have come to him." Scholars, Montefiore and Lowe, tells us this about this tractate:

> The Rabbinic attitude towards suffering is...one of
> humble resignation to the will of God, the convinced faith
> in the future life of happiness and blessedness enabled the
> Rabbis to face sufferings, not indeed, for the most part with

pleasure, but with fortitude, and even sometimes with joy,
because they were regarded as sure passports to Heaven.

In the Avot of Rabbi Natan 6:4, he also relates that a boy's evil
inclination is greater than his *yetzer tov* until he turns thirteen when "the
good inclination is born," and he becomes able to control his behavior.
Rabbi Natan also observes that "The greater the man, the greater his
Evil Inclination." In the Babylonian Talmud, at tractate 5a, Rabbi Resh
Laqish tells us, "The Evil Inclination and the Angel of Death are one
and the same thing."

In a comment from Abba Benjamin, we see the Talmud's belief in
demonic forces when he says, "If the eye were to be granted permission
to see, no creature would be able to stand in the face of the demons that
surround it." He continues:

We are all, apparently, constantly beset by invisible devils...
They are more numerous than us, and they stand around us
like a ditch around a mound of Earth.

Many portions of the Talmud speak of how to treat lepers and
other Jews suffering from disease. At Eruchin 16b, for example, the
rabbis discuss whether leprosy is a punishment for sin and what to do
if a leper approaches people who are healthy. In this tractate, the leper
was ostracized from the community, "alone and seemingly isolated."
Some of the rabbis used Retributive Justice Theory to explain that
leprosy was a "spiritual malady" and not a "physical one," caused by
"serious transgressions of the Jewish law." The leper was required to
announce his arrival.[255]

The Babylonian Talmud, at Baba Bathra 15b, tells us, "It is better
to remove the beam between our eyes before we point to the splinter
in the teeth of someone else." Shabbas 33a say we can never know the
true reason for suffering. "It may be that the suffering individual is so
great that God has punished him for the smallest infraction." At the
Babylonian Talmud's Metzia 85b, we see the following exchange about
suffering:

Shmuel was Rebbi's physician. One day the Rebbi was suffering from an eye ailment. And Shmuel said to him, "I will put

this medication into your eyes." The Rebbi told him, "I cannot
endure it." Then Shmuel said to him, "Then I will gently put
a salve on the surface of your eyes." The Rebbi replied, "I
cannot endure that either." So Shmuel put a tube of ointment
under Rebbi's pillow, and he was cured.

At times, the Talmud and Mishnah speak of what obligations the Jew has to alleviate poverty and the suffering from earthquakes and other disasters. In the Mishnah Berakot 9:2, for example, and the Mishnah Sanhedrin 4:5, the rabbis turn their attention to just such a problem. The Mishnah's Pirkei Avot at 6:5, or the "Chapters of the Fathers," is a compilation of the ethical teachings and maxims from the rabbinic period. It contains sayings attributed to various sages, like Rabbi Akiba, for example, who promulgated a maxim to "Love one's neighbor as oneself."

In the Mishnah's Berakot 7a, Moses asks God why suffering is so arbitrarily meted out. Why are the righteous brought suffering and the wicked prosperity? One rabbi answers, "Perhaps the righteous suffer for their sins here on Earth, while the wicked are rewarded here on Earth and they are deprived of bliss in the Hereafter." Indeed, many tractates in the Talmud and Mishnah, like Bereshith 4a, Ta'an 11a, and Kid. 39a, combine Retributive Justice Theory with punishment and rewards in the Afterlife.

So far, in these tractates from the Talmud and the Mishnah, we have seen mentions of:

1. The Divine Plan Theory
2. The *Yetzer Hara* View
3. Retributive Justice Theory in the Afterlife
4. The Moral Qualities View
5. Evil as Privation of the Good Theory
6. The Influences of Demonic Forces Theory[256]

Thus, the biblical themes on evil and suffering are carried over into the rabbinic period. Another way to see ancient Jewish remarks on the phenomena of evil and suffering are the many places in the Talmud, where the patriarch *Iyyov*, or Job, is mentioned. In that regard, four separate questions occupied the minds of the ancient rabbis when they referred to the Man From Uz and his book. These questions are the following:

1. When did Job live?
2. Was Job a Jew?
3. Is Job an Angry or a Patient figure?
4. What was the cause of Job's Suffering?[257]

In a variety of tractates, dozens of sages attempt to answer these four inquiries. In Berakot 5b, the problem of suffering is discussed at length in which several viewpoints are dismissed out of hand. The second-century teacher, Rabbi Simeon ben Yohai, remarks that, "Three precious gifts were given by God to Israel and they only were given through sufferings." These three gifts were: the Torah, the Land of Israel, and the World to Come.[258]

The Mishnah's Berakot 9:5 suggests that "A man is duty bound to utter a benediction for the bad person even as he utters one for the righteous person." The benediction on receiving good tidings is, "Blessed is He, the Good and the Doer of the Good."[259] On receiving bad tidings, the benediction should be, "Blessed is He, the True Judge."[260] The Talmud agrees. At Berakot 60b, the rabbis tell us, "The Benediction over the bad should be recited with the same joyfulness as that over the Good."

Another way to understand ancient Jewish responses to the phenomena of evil and suffering is in the comments of Jewish philosophers of the period, and chief among these was Philo of Alexandria, to whom we shall turn next.

Philo of Alexandria, also known as Judaeus Philo, was an important philosophical thinker who combines two cultures, the Hebraic and the Greek. He lived in Egypt from approximately 20 BCE until 40 CE. Philo was important for our purposes because he attempted to give a rational, philosophical justification for the beliefs of Judaism.[261] He is also important because he is the forerunner of an exegetical school of the Bible that primarily concentrated on the allegorical interpretation of Holy Scripture.

In this regard, Philo is the progenitor for views in Alexandria that will come after him, such as Clement of Alexandria, Tertullian, Justin Martyr, and Origen.[262] Among his principal works was his discourse, *On Providence*, a text provided by Eusebius in a Latin translation of Philo's Greek. Philo's *On Providence* is important for our purposes because he rehearses and assents to many of the responses to evil and suffering that we have seen in the biblical materials and in the rabbinic period.

In one section of his *Providence*, the philosopher suggests an analogy to God's creation of the world. Philo says it is like a Master Builder, where all the parts of a building fit together in a "Grand Design."[263] Philo observes:

> God took care at the Creation of the World that there should
> be an ample and most sufficient supply of matter, so exact
> that nothing may be wanting and nothing superfluous.[264]

Philo goes on to suggest that God had the exact materials necessary to make the universe He had in mind, and He had the exact plan necessary to bring about the creation of all that there is. Thus, it appears that the Greek philosopher was an advocate of what we have called the Divine Plan Theory.

In the same section of his *Providence*, Philo goes on to discuss the creation of human beings and what it means for them to be "in the image and likeness of God." The philosopher says of man, "God bestows on the race of mankind his special and exceedingly great gift, namely his Free Will."[265] Philo points out that without this liberty, Adam and Eve would not have been able to disobey God, and without that liberty, the first humans would not have been responsible for their disobedience.[266] Thus, Philo appears to be combining the Free Will Defense and Retributive Justice Theory.

A few paragraphs later, in the same work, Philo speaks of the "penalty which such evils inflict upon humans." Philo gives us the example of Polycrates, the sixth-century BCE tyrant on the island of Samos, whom Philo reveals:

> In retaliation for terrible acts of injustice and impiety which he
> committed, then it fell upon him great misery in his subsequent
> life as a terrible requital for his previous good fortune.[267]

Clearly, Philo is using here an example of the combining of the Free Will Defense with Individual Retributive Justice Theory. The philosopher continues his analysis of the life of Polycrates. He says:

> Add to this that he was chastised by a mighty sovereign, and was crucified by him, fulfilling the predictions of an Oracle.[268]

The philosopher Philo uses the Moral Qualities Theory with his use of "chastised," and he goes on to speak of a plan for Polycrates that was "anointed by the Sun and washed by the god Jupiter."[269] Thus, Philo appears to be asserting a version of the Divine Plan Theory with respect to the Samos Tyrant, as well.

In other places of his *Providence*, Philo assents to two other Jewish theological responses to the phenomena of evil and suffering, the Test Perspective and the Permission Theory. In the former, Philo says that God "sometimes sends hardships and sufferings to the Jews, solely for the purpose of 'testing' their moral character." The Greek philosopher makes this same claim in at least three places in his *Providence*.[270]

Oliver Leaman concurs that Philo endorses the Test View and Retributive Justice Theory when he writes, "What about all those instances in the Jewish Bible in which God is said to cause evil things to happen? These instances are doubtless explained by his motive in punishing and testing his creatures."[271] Leaman continues his analysis of Philo:

> Philo takes the line that if God does punish and test us, he does it through Intermediaries, and any text that suggests otherwise must be interpreted allegorically.[272]

In two other portions of the same text, Philo points out that because God is omnibenevolent, He is incapable of committing evil. He does, however, "Permit humans, in his infinite wisdom to do Evil acts with their own Free Will." This is a clear reference to the Supplemental Theory introduced in Chapter One that we have called the Permission View. That is that "God does not Cause Evil, He permits it."[273]

From our analyses of Philo's "Providence," we have suggested that the Greek philosopher, Philo has mentioned, or has endorsed, the following Jewish responses in regard to the phenomena of Evil and Suffering:

1. Divine Plan Theory (God as Master Builder)
2. The Free Will Defense
3. Retributive Justice Theory
4. The Moral Qualities View
5. The Test Perspective
6. The Permission Theory[274]

Thus, in the ancient period of Judaism, we have seen examples from the three sources alluded to at the beginning of this section of Chapter Three—The Talmud, the Mishnah, and Philo of Alexandria. In the next section of this third chapter, we shall speak of the responses to evil and suffering in the medieval Jewish period.

Responses to Evil and Suffering in the Jewish Middle Ages

By far, the most important treatments of Jewish views of evil and suffering in the Middle Ages come from prominent Jewish philosophers. In this section, we will examine the perspectives of six major Jewish philosophers, as well as other minor thinkers who have made important observations about the phenomena of evil and suffering in the medieval Jewish tradition.

Among the major Jewish philosophers we will examine are Saadiah Gaon, Rashi, Moses Maimonides and Gersonides.[275] Among the minor Jewish philosophers we shall discuss in this section are Joseph Al-Basir, Abraham ben Hiyya, Joseph Ibn Zaddik and Joseph Kara.[276] In most of these figures, we will discuss their philosophical views on theodicy, as well as what they have had to say about the biblical Book of Job. Indeed, all of the major Jewish philosophers listed here have written commentaries on the *Sefer Iyyov*, or "Book of Job."

The Egyptian Jewish philosopher Saadiah Gaon was born in Upper Egypt in 862. He died in Sura, about a hundred miles south of Baghdad, in 915. By the year 915, Saadiah had begun to teach as a rabbi in Palestine, moving in 928 to become the *Gaon*, or Head Teacher, at the ancient Jewish academy in Sura.[277] Saadiah's most important philosophical works for our purposes are his *Book of Beliefs and Opinions,* which was probably composed in 833. He also completed a commentary on the Book of Job. In this latter work, Saadiah suggests three different approaches to evil and suffering. He calls these "Discipline and Instruction," "Purgation and Punishment" and "Trial and Testing."[278]

The first of these explanations for evil and suffering is akin to what we have called the Moral Qualities View. It suggests, of course, that the purpose of evil and suffering is to allow one to develop certain moral traits, like patience and fortitude, that can only be developed in humankind through their suffering. The second of Saadiah's views, what he calls "Purgation and Punishment," is a version of what we have labeled Retributive Justice Theory. That suffering comes to those whose sins need to be purged or to be punished.[279]

Saadiah Gaon's third theological view of evil and suffering, the position called "Trial and Testing," is a version of the Test View or the Moral Qualities Theory. The first and third of Saadiah's positions on evil and suffering are teleological, or forward-looking. The second view is deontological and backward-looking.[280] Saadiah also makes a number of comments about evil and suffering in his *Iyyov* commentary that are supplemental comments to his three basic theological views.

Among these comments are the following. We may not understand in this life how we are to be compensated in the next life for the sins we commit in this life. He also says that we are ignorant of the plan that is in store for us because of God's superior wisdom to that of His creatures, and only He knows what is best.[281] This comment seems to be akin to the Divine Plan Point of View. Thus, we now have four theological responses to evil and suffering in the thought of Saadiah Gaon: the Moral Qualities View, Retributive Justice Theory, the Test View and Divine Plan Theory.

Saadiah also rejects Dualistic or Religions of Solution doctrines to explain evil and suffering. He also was decidedly against the idea that God was the creator of evil because, in his view, evil does not have a separate existence, but it is nothing more than "the absence of the Good." Thus, Saadiah Gaon had an early medieval Jewish theory of privation.[282]

From this analysis, we may conclude that ninth-century Egyptian philosopher, Saadiah Gaon, employed the following responses when discussing or writing about evil and suffering: The Moral Qualities

View, the Test Theory, Retributive Justice, Divine Plan Theory and the Theory of Evil as Privation of the Good.

Rabbi Solomon ben Isaac (Shlomo Yitzhaki), usually known by his acronym Rashi, was born in northern France near Troyes. At the age of seventeen, he began his education in the Yeshiva of Rabbi Yaakov of Worms. At the age of twenty-five, he returned to France, where he worked as a rabbi and as a laborer in a local vineyard.[283] In 1070, Rashi started his own Yeshiva, where he had many students, many of whom also became great Jewish scholars.

In the year 1096, Rashi saw the murders of many family members and friends at the hands of Christian crusaders while he was en route to the Holy Land. Rashi died in 1105 at his home in Troyes. Rashi's two major works are his commentary on the entire Bible and his commentary on the Babylonian Talmud. When Rashi writes or speaks about evil and suffering, it usually occurs in two different contexts. The first is when he makes very general remarks about the nature of evil and suffering. The other context is when Rashi speaks about the phenomena of evil and suffering in the context of particular biblical passages that he is commenting upon.[284]

On rare occasions, Rashi combines the two contexts, as in his discussion of the Suffering Servant passage in Isaiah 53. In his commentary, Rashi identifies the Suffering Servant as "the nation of Israel, who silently endures unimaginable suffering at the hands of its gentile oppressors." Rashi was the first to make such a claim. Since his time, it has become the standard Jewish view. One wonders, however, by how much he was influenced in this view of the Suffering Servant that was held by Christians of his day, that is the Suffering Servant is Jesus Christ, the Son of God.[285]

Another general comment that exegete Rashi makes about evil and suffering is related to Rashi's understanding of the Flood, as well as other passages like Deuteronomy 4:16. In commenting on Genesis 6:12, he suggests that the "corruption" in the verse refers to the "two greatest evils." Rashi calls these "illicit sex and idolatry." To support his reading of Genesis 6:12, Rashi offers two Talmudic passages as proofs of his view. Both of these are in the Sanhedrin, the first at tractate 57a and the second at 108a. About the former, Rashi observes, "Wherever corruption is mentioned, it must refer to illicit sex and idolatry."[286]

About the Sanhedrin 108a, Rashi comments, "Although the generation of the Flood transgressed all laws because they stretched out their hands here, it means illicit sex and idolatry."

The other contexts of Rashi's remarks on evil and suffering come in connection with times in which he was commenting upon biblical passages. For example, Rashi points out that the most important Hebrew term of the Akedah narrative was the word "Test," though Rashi calls it a "capricious request."[287] The Hebrew word is *nacah*, and Rashi points out that Genesis 22:1 was the word's first usage in the Hebrew Bible.

In addition to his use of the Test View regarding his commentary on Genesis 22:1, Rashi also points to another of our Jewish theological responses, when the French exegete calls 22:1 "The problem of Satan's accusation against Abraham." This is an obvious example of the Influences of Demonic Forces Theory. [288] In another comment about evil, in the context of Exodus 20:5, Rashi observes:

> The righteous person who prospers is a completely righteous person whose actions are entirely good, and whose reward is entirely good, both in this world and in the World to Come.

Rashi adds:

> The righteous person who suffers is one who is not completely righteous, because he has some transgressions, he is punished in this world so that he will receive a complete reward in the World to Come.

In each of these examples of Rashi's, the underlying theory that informs these comments is the Retributive Justice Theory, the Individual variety, as well as the Collective form. This brings us to Moses Maimonides and his theological responses to evil and suffering, the focus of our next figure in this section.

Moses Maimonides was born in Cordoba, Spain, in 1135 and died in Egypt in 1204. He spent most of his life in North Africa, in Egypt, his family being obliged to flee the Almohad in Spain. Maimonides was, however, a symbol of all that was remarkable in medieval Jewish Spain. During his time, Spain was dominated by Islam. It is customary to see the time of Maimonides as a golden age in the history of Judaism. It was also a period of inter-religious dialogue, harmony and coexistence.

The most important work of Moses Maimonides for our purposes is his *Guide for the Perplexed*.[289] In this work, the Spanish philosopher sketches out a distinctive philosophical position on a host of issues, including theodicy and the problem of evil. Citing the creation account of Genesis 1, Maimonides begins with the assumption that God created "World is Good" and humans are "very Good."[290]

In the *Guide*, Maimonides suggests that there are three separate varieties of evil. He enumerates these three types this way:

1. Evil that befalls people because they possess bodies.
2. Evil that people do to each other.
3. Evil that people do to themselves.[291]

These three types of evil in Maimonides' *Guide* are nothing more than what we have called Natural, Moral, and Metaphysical Evils back in the opening chapter of this study on evil in the world's religions. Indeed, of the first variety, Maimonides gives the examples of "landslides, earthquakes, and floods." Of his second type, Maimonides mentions "murder, rape, and stealing" as examples. And in his third kind of evil, he mentions "dread and fear."[292]

The Spanish philosopher observes that the third type of evil is "the largest and most frequent type." These are evils that a person brings upon himself or herself, mostly through "vices and excessive desires."[293] Another important aspect of Moses Maimonides' views on evil and suffering is that he was an advocate of what we have called the Deprivation of the Good View that we have described under the category of Supplemental Responses in our analysis in Chapter One.

As we have shown there, evil has no positive existence. Rather, it should be seen, Maimonides suggests, as a privation of the Good. At Book III, sections ten to twelve of the *Guide*, Maimonides explains his understanding of privation this way:

> Just as we say of him who puts out a lamp in the night that he has brought about darkness, we say of one who has destroyed sight that he has made blindness, even though darkness and blindness are privations and do not need an agent.[294]

For Moses Maimonides, darkness and evil are privations due to the absence of Light and the Good. And from this, it follows that God cannot be an Agent of Evil in any of its three kinds. Since it is a "consequent of the Good being absent, the agent can only be said to have produced the privation by accident."[295] This makes the Spanish philosopher one of the only advocates of the *Privatio Boni*, or the Deprivation of the Good Theory, outside of medieval Christian philosophy. Maimonides' theory that evil is nonexistent, or a privation, is also the aspect of his views on evil and suffering that is most criticized.

Indeed, Julius Guttmann, in his book *Philosophies of Judaism*, says this about Maimonides and Privation, "Maimonides' attempt to justify the existence of evil by defining it as a mere privation was a failure."[296]

In many places in his *Guide*, Moses Maimonides also discusses the idea of the two *Yetzerim*—the *yetzer hara* and the *yetzer tov*, as developed in the biblical and rabbinic periods of Judaism. He also makes observations on the *yetzer hara* in his *Commentary on the Mishnah* (9:5), as well as in his *Principles of Faith*.[297] Indeed, in the sixth of his *Shemonah Perakim*, Maimonides raises the question of whether the greatest believer, or *tsaddik*, is one who struggles and overcomes his *yetzer hara* or one who faces no challenge from his inclination.[298]

Maimonides' response appears to be that he believes that there is a "Yetzer Quotient." Some people have a weak *yetzer hara* and are able to achieve spiritual greatness. Others possess a strong *yetzer hara* and are overwhelmed by its demands, and are incapable of living up to religious demands. Maimonides does say, however, that a real *Tzaddik* is either someone who "does not possess a *yetzer hara*," or someone who is a "*shem hamushal*," or one "with a borrowed name," meaning one who pretends to be better than he or she actually is.[299]

At any rate, Moses Maimonides is of the belief that a great deal of evil and suffering that comes to human beings is the product of their two *Yetzerim*. Thus, we may add the Free Will Defense to our catalog of the views of Moses Maimonides. The Spanish philosopher also makes sporadic comments on the notion of Satan, as we shall see next.

Most of the comments to be found on the figure of Satan in the writings of Moses Maimonides are to be found in the parts of his *Guide for the Perplexed*, where he discusses the biblical Book of Job.

Maimonides points out in the opening of III, Chapter 22 of the *Guide*:

> The strange and wonderful book of Job treats the same
> subject as we are discussing. Its basis is a fiction, conceived
> for the purposes of explaining the different opinions, which
> people hold on Divine Providence.[300]

Not only does Maimonides claim that the Book of Job is fiction, but he also tells us this about *Ha Satan*, or the Adversary:

> The Adversary is then described as going to and fro on the
> Earth, and walking up and down thereon. He is in no relation
> to the beings above, and has no place among them.[301]

A few pages later in the *Guide*, Maimondes appears to agree with a judgment from Rabbi Simeon ben Lakish when the Spanish philosopher and exegete writes:

> The Adversary (Satan), the evil inclination (the *yetzer hara*),
> and the Angel of Death are one and the same being... The Ad-
> versary goes about and misleads, then he goes up and accus-
> es, obtains permission and takes the soul.[302]

At first blush, it would appear that Moses Maimonides is endorsing the Influences of Demonic Forces View, as well as the theory that God does not commit evil, but he does "permit it." But later in chapter 23 of the third book of the *Guide*, Maimonides implies that the Satan is a fictional character, like the rest of the book.[303]

On a second reading, however, it seems more likely that Maimonides is referring to Plato's notion of the "Emanations of the Divine," in which the Athenian philosopher suggests that at Creation the Demiurge, or God, "overflows into what has been fashioned."

In another section of the *Guide*, Maimonides appears to be borrowing a page or two from Plato's doctrine of creation in the *Timaeus*, when the Spaniard attributes evil in the world as the result of impurities in matter. In Plato's account, this is the chaotic stuff of the world that the Demiurge, his God, was not able to order perfectly. If this is the position that Maimonides is endorsing here, then the Spanish philosopher is also assenting to a "Religion of Solution," as outlined in Chapter One of this study.[304]

Another response to evil and suffering in the work of Moses Maimonides is what he has to say about Providence throughout his works, our next topic. In the *Guide* (III:17), Maimonides sketches out five different views of what he calls *Hashgahah*, or Divine Providence. The first four views he goes on to dismiss. The fifth opinion is the one that Maimonides favors. The Spanish philosopher says this about his view of Providence:

> Divine Providence, in my view, is the consequence of Divine emanation, the overflowing of the intellect and thereby becomes itself endowed with intellect through which it is made aware of all that the intellect can reveal.[305]

Maimonides then goes on to explain his view of Divine Providence:

> I do not believe that anything is hidden from God, nor do I ascribe to God any incapacity. Rather, I believe that Providence is a necessary consequence of intellect. For Providence can only flow from a mind of consummate perfection—and all who are touched by that outpouring sufficiently to be enlightened by it.[306]

What Maimonides seems to mean by this passage in the *Guide* is that Divine Providence only extends to those creatures endowed with intellect. In his view, human beings. He also, however, implies that God acts in history through his use and performance of miracles. This remark is directly connected to another observation that Maimonides makes about the patriarch Job. What Job lacks, Maimonides says, is not Moral Virtue, it is Intellectual Virtue.[307]

In another place in the *Guide*, Moses Maimonides shows his support of Retributive Justice Theory, the Intellectual Version, when he relates, "The reward given for fulfilling the commandments is nothing more than life in the world to come."[308] In many other places in the same work, the Spanish philosopher also speaks of rewards and punishment as species of the afterlife, in terms of those who keep the Commandments and those who do not.[309]

Indeed, in Maimonides description of the eleventh principle of the Jewish faith, he tells us this:

The 11th principle of the Faith, that He, the Exalted One, rewards
he who obeys the commands of the Torah and punishes he who
transgresses its prohibitions. God's greatest reward to man is the
World to Come and that His strongest punishment is *karet*.[310]

The Hebrew word, *karet*, as understood by Maimonides, means,
"The cutting off of the soul from eternal bliss in the Hereafter." Thus,
we may add Retributive Justice to our list of responses to evil and
suffering found in the philosophical views of Maimonides. Thus, we
have shown in this section that the Spanish philosopher either mentions
or directly assents to the following views:

1. Evil as Privation
2. The Free Will Defense (Two *Yetzerim* Theory)
3. The Influence of Demonic Forces View
4. The Permission Point of View
5. The Religion of Solution Theory
6. Divine Plan Theory (view on Providence)
7. The Retributive Justice Approach

This brings us to the final major Jewish philosopher in our
analysis, Gersonides (1288–1344), French mathematician, philosopher
and exegete. Rabbi Levi Ben Gershon was born in Bagnols but lived
most of his life in Orange and Avignon. Among his exegetical works,
he wrote commentaries on the Torah, Proverbs, Song of Songs,
Ecclesiastes, Ruth, Esther, Daniel, and the Book of Job. Gersonides
also completed a major treatise on astronomy. It is contained in the
second part of his *The Wars of the Lord*.[311]

Gersonides was also known by the acronym Ralbag. His comments
on evil and suffering come mostly in the *Wars* and his commentary
on the Book of Job. Any discussion of these views of Gersonides
must begin with his account of Divine Providence. He believed in a
strong version of Astral Determinism, in that he held that all terrestrial
phenomena—including human affairs—are ordered and determined by
the Heavenly Bodies. For him, God is never the source of Evil. Instead,
it either comes from "matter or chance." By matter, he means the
"mixture of elements in the material world." By "chance," he means

the unfortunate effects on human beings caused by natural events, such as earthquakes, land-upheavals or fire.[312]

In regard to the Torah's view of sin and its punishment, the French philosopher tells us this:

> When the Torah warns men of evil because of their
> great sin, it states clearly that the will be that God will
> not look upon them and He will abandon them to the
> contingencies of time. The punishment of sinners consists
> of God's hiding and indifference. God leaves them to the
> contingencies of time, and whatever happens to them is de-
> termined by the heavenly bodies. Nor does God save
> them from the Evil that is to befall them.[313]

From this passage from the *Wars*, we may make the following conclusions. First, evil occurs because of the deterministic scheme of astrology. Second, Gersonides employs what we have called the Hidden God Theory. And finally, God does not punish nor reward sinners and non-sinners. In another section of the *Wars*, Gersonides suggests that the ordinary events embedded in the general and providential laws of nature represent the "Best of All Possible Worlds" that God could have created. This, of course, is one of our Supplemental Theories described in Chapter One.[314]

Other aspects of Gersonides' understanding of evil and suffering can be found in his commentary on the Book of Job. For example, the French exegete believes that the speeches of Job's fourth friend, Elihu, are the most philosophically sound views of the patriarch's friends. More specifically, Gersonides suggests that Elihu's views are connected to what we have called the Test View, the Moral Qualities Perspective and the Divine Plan Theory.[315]

In his commentary on the Book of Job in commenting on the Satan passages in chapters one and two, Gersonides proffered the view that the Adversary's "purpose is simply to delude people," often by whispering to them.[316] From our analysis, we may conclude that the great French philosopher, Gersonides mentions, or assents to, the following theories in regard to the phenomena of evil and suffering:

I.   Determinism
II. The Hidden God Theory
III. The Test View
IV. The Moral Qualities Theory
V.   Divine Plan Perspective
VI. The Influence of Demonic Forces View

This brings us to a host of minor Jewish philosophers who made important observations about the phenomena of evil and suffering in the medieval period. These include Joseph Al-Basir, Abraham Ben Hiyya, Joseph Ibn Zaddik and Abraham Ibn Ezra. Each of these four Jewish thinkers developed important ideas about evil and suffering during this time.

Joseph al-Basir was an eleventh-century Karaite thinker. He suggested that the infliction of pain may, under certain circumstances, be examples of the moral Good, rather than 'Ra, or Evil. He says this because "ultimately an action may result in a greater advantage."[317]

Similarly, Spanish philosopher Abraham ben Hiyya (1070–1145) expressed the view that the righteous suffer in this world in order to "try them" and increase their ultimate reward.[318]

Rabbi Joseph Ibn Zaddik, who died in 1149, believed that the evil and suffering that affects the righteous is often simply natural occurrences, with no real relation to rewards and punishments. Rabbi Zaddik does add, however, that sometimes these evils are inflicted on good people for their sins, an example of Retributive Justice Theory, in this life.[319]

Abraham Ibn Ezra (1092–1164), a distinguished Spanish philosopher, suggested that the "whole world was made Good and that only Good may come from God." But he argues that evil sometimes comes as a defect of the object receiving Divine influence. Like Saadiah, Maimonides and Gersonides, Ibn Ezra employs the Evil as Privation Theory in his analysis of the matter.[320]

"Evil is not the major problem," said Ibn Ezra, "It is God's relationship to humans."[321] This brings us to the phenomena of evil and suffering in modern Judaism, from the sixteenth century to the present, the topic of the next section of this third chapter of the study of evil and suffering in the world's religions.

Evil and Suffering in Modern Jewish Thought: Sixteenth Century to the Present

The amount of materials for responses to evil and suffering in this period of Judaism is immense. Consequently, we will only examine five Jewish thinkers as a representative sample of this vast literature. These are Hermann Cohen, Martin Buber, Abraham Heschel, Mordecai Kaplan and Robert Gordis.

Hermann Cohen (1842–1918) was a German-Jewish philosopher, one of the founders of the Marburg School of Neo-Kantianism. Some say he was the most important Jewish philosopher of the nineteenth century. Cohen suggests that evil and suffering stir a person's conscience and prods him to ethical behavior.[322] Cohen identified the nation of Israel with the Prophet Isaiah's Suffering Servant.[323]

For Rabbi Cohen, the purpose of suffering is to arouse sympathy in human believers. He was not much interested in the traditional problem of evil and believed that discussions in Jewish philosophy on the matter were an attempt to cover or hide the many examples of evil in his society. In this sense, Rabbi Cohen was a forerunner who complained about evil in the German society long before the Nazi takeover. Cohen's most important work for our purposes is his *Religion of Reason*.[324]

Martin Buber (1878–1965) was an Austrian-born philosopher whose most important work is his *I and Thou*.[325] For Buber, the source of evil is a failure to enter into a relationship with the Divine, or *Thou*. In his posthumous work, *Between Man and Man*, published in 1966, he makes this remark about the nature of evil:

> Good and Evil, then, cannot be a pair of opposites like right and left or above and beneath. Good is the movement in the direction of home. Evil is the aimless whirl of human potentialities without which nothing can be achieved and by which, if they take no direction and remain trapped in themselves, everything goes awry.

For Buber, people are not evil by nature, but their misuse of their nature generates evil. In the same work, Buber relates:

> Some men carry Evil so far as to give it a kind of independent
> quality, but evil is never an independent entity. Such men
> crystallize it into a perverse resistance to the individual's
> self-fulfillment in relation.

After the Second World War, Buber began to raise the question about whether God is "kind and merciful" in light of what had happened to the Jews in Europe. Buber did retain, however, the possibility of humans redeeming evil. He also was forcefully against any Gnostic dualism, while humans have within their power the ability to "sanctify the world." In his book, *Images of Good and Evil*, Martin Buber suggests that "Man first became man when he was driven out of Paradise," an obvious reference to the Free Will Defense and to Retributive Justice Theory.[326]

In his *Imitatio Dei*, Buber says that Adam's fall consisted in his wanting to secure the "likeness of God" intended for him at the Creation.[327] Buber's *Right and Wrong* makes an important distinction between a "wicked man" and a "sinner." The sinner misses how to follow God's way, again and again, while the wicked man opposes it.

Beginning with his 1944 book, *Moses*, Martin Buber put a much greater emphasis on the Demonic. Buber ties the idea of the Demonic to those who refuse the Covenant between God and Israel. He indicates that the story of the Old Testament's *Korah's* rebellion is the archetypal example of the influences of the Demonic.

Thus, we see a range of responses to evil and suffering in the works of Martin Buber, including the Influences of Demonic Forces Theory, the Free Will Defense, Retributive Justice, as well as the Hidden God Point of View.

Abraham Heschel, a Jewish-American rabbi, scholar and philosopher, begins his analysis of evil in his 1961 *God in Search of Man* by quoting a midrash from the Genesis Rabbah (39:1) in which Abraham sees a castle in flames. Heschel asks, "The world is in flames consumed by Evil. Is it possible that no one cares?" Heschel tells us that after the Holocaust, "nothing in the world is wholly Good or wholly Evil. Everything is a mixture of the two." In his view, "Evil is not the ultimate problem, it is man's relationship to God." Heschel says the biblical answer to Evil is not the Good. It is the Holy.[328]

For Lithuanian-born Mordecai Kaplan (1881–1983), God is identical with certain principles in the universe whose analogs in human society lead to salvation, that is, the achievement of the good for all of Mankind. The existence of evil in the world, according to Kaplan, is due to the failure of people to act in accord with God's principles. The "function of conscience," Kaplan observes, is "not to philosophize or theologize the existence of evil in the world. It is to eliminate it." [329]

Finally, in the work of Robert Gordis (1908–1992), Bible scholar, teacher and rabbi, his two most important works for understanding his views on evil and suffering are *The Book of God and Man* (1965) and his *Commentary on the Book of Job* published in 1978. In these two texts, Gordis makes a number of observations about evil and suffering. Among these are the following.

In the former work, Gordis maintains that "Evil and suffering is the most agonizing issue concerning man." [330] In Gordis' view, the problem of evil and theodicy are at the "heart of Judaism," as well as several other world religions, as well.

Secondly, Gordis points out in his commentary that, "God does not deny that there is innocent suffering." In fact, Gordis says in some passages, such as Job 40:9–14, God comes close to saying as much.[331] Thirdly, regarding the comforters of Job, Gordis believes that Elihu identifies himself with Job. Gordis says, "He is a fellow sufferer and not an observer."[332]

In an essay entitled "Elihu the Intruder," Rabbi Gordis suggests that the "Elihu Speeches are a forerunner to the God Discourses, principally because they share the same three theological responses to suffering." More specifically, Gordis suggests that both Elihu and the Yahweh Speeches, we can find what we have called the Test View, the Moral Qualities Approach, and above all, the Divine Plan Theory.[333]

This brings us to the major conclusions we have made in this third chapter. The subject matter of Chapter Four of this study of evil and suffering in the religions of the world are the dualistic faiths, that is ancient Zoroastrianism, Roman Mithraism and Manichaeism.

Conclusions to Chapter Three

We began this third chapter on responses to evil and suffering in the history of Judaism by making a number of preliminary remarks in which we discussed the three parts of the Hebrew Bible, the idea of a *Berith*, or Covenant, in classical Hebrew, and the people known as the Hittites and what influence they may have had on the ancient Jews.

This material was followed in Chapter Three by a discussion of how the ancient Jews treated the phenomena of evil and suffering in their sacred scriptures. In this second section of the chapter, we have shown that the Jews were endorsers of most of the responses to evil and suffering that we cataloged back in Chapter One of this study. Altogether in this section, we demonstrated that the ancient Jews assented to the Free Will Defense; Individual and Collective Retribution Theories; possibly to the Original Sin View, the Influences of Demonic Forces Perspective; the Contrast View; the Moral Qualities Approach; Divine Plan Theory; the Permission View; and the Hidden God Perspective.

The remainder of Chapter Three was divided into three parts. These were evil and suffering in ancient Jewish perspectives, which included comments from the rabbinic period of the Talmud and Mishnah, and perspectives on evil and suffering from Jewish philosopher Philo of Alexandria.

This section of Chapter Three was followed by a discussion of major medieval Jewish thinkers who have commented on evil and suffering, including Saadiah Gaon, Rashi, Moses Maimonides and Gersonides. This discussion was followed by a number of views of four minor Jewish philosophers of the period. These were Joseph Al-Basir, Abraham Bar Hiyya, Joseph Ibn Zaddik and Abraham Ibn Ezra. We discovered that the same themes posited in biblical materials and in the rabbinic period and Philo are repeated in the Jewish thinkers from the Middle Ages.

Among these medieval Jewish thinkers, we have also seen some new and unique views, particularly Joseph Al-Basir's claim that some examples of pain are for the greater good here on Earth, and Abraham Ibn Ezra's views that Job was not a Jew and his weak endorsement of the Privation Theory.

In the final section of Chapter Three, we began by pointing out the voluminous amount of material on evil and suffering in the Jewish tradition of the modern period. Because of that fact, we chose to comment on only five modern Jewish thinkers in regard to their perspectives on the phenomena of evil and suffering in modern Judaism. These five modern Jewish perspectives were comments and writings by Hermann Cohen, Martin Buber, Abraham Heschel, Mordecai Kaplan and Robert Gordis.

In our analysis of these Jewish thinkers, we pointed out the range and depth of the five views and, at times, the uniqueness in their perspectives. Each of the five was considered a major Jewish observer of life in general and Jewish life in particular.

This brings us to Chapter Four. The major focus of this chapter shall be the chief versions of the dualistic faiths, or Religions of Solution, as we have called them back in the first chapter. At the heart of Chapter Four, then, will be ancient Persian Zoroastrianism, Roman Mithraism, and Manichaeism. However, we will also discuss other philosophical versions of dualism, lie Plato's account of Creation in his work the *Timaeus*.

We move next, then, to Chapter Four, a discussion of responses and attitudes toward the phenomena of evil and suffering in several dualistic faiths and philosophical views.

Chapter Four:
Evil and Suffering in Dualistic Faiths

If there is a good God, the only way to account for evil is to trace it, ultimately, to an eternally existing evil spirit, according to some great world religions. All religions that espouse this doctrine are forms of religious Dualism.

—John Kronen and Sandra Menssen, "The Defensibility of Zoroastrian Dualism"

Although the cosmic dualism of Manichaeism is not acceptable to believers in the existence of only one Supreme God of goodness, it does provide a good explanation of why evil in the world is substantial and virulent.

—Richard Foltz, *Religions of the Silk Road*

That Mithraism met in caves, which were distinctively designed and furnished, has had important consequences for the archeological record and thus for our ability to reconstruct the cult. In addition to the cave-like appearance, the Mithrae were designed with raised platforms on either side of a central aisle to serve at a banquet for the cult meal.

—M. L. White, *Building God's House in the Roman World*

Introduction

The purpose of this fourth chapter is to make some comment and evaluation of ancient dualistic faiths of the world. These include the account of Plato's view of Creation as outlined in his dialogue called the *Timaeus,* as well as the ancient Persian religion Zoroastrianism, and two Roman faiths known as Mithraism and Manichaeism. We will begin the chapter by describing Plato's view of how the world was created and why that view is a version of what we will call Dualism.

We will also indicate two other views of the origin of evil and suffering in two of Plato's major works, one in the *Republic* at 613a, and the other in the *Laws* in chapter X, 905b and c.

This section of Chapter Four will be followed by an introduction to Zoroastrianism and how that ancient faith responded to the phenomenon of evil and suffering in its ancient history, including portions of its sacred scriptures that confirm its Cosmic and its Moral Dualism. This section on Zoroastrianism will be followed by examining the two faiths of Mithraism and Manichaeism and how these religious systems were also forms of dualism, as well.

In another section of Chapter Four, we shall explore several examples from the modern period of philosophy, from the eighteenth to the twentieth centuries, who ascribe to what we shall call the Limited God Theory, beginning with David Hume in the eighteenth century, and continuing to other thinkers from the nineteenth, as well as the twentieth centuries.

Before we get to these parts of Chapter Four, however, we will first make some preliminary remarks about what we mean by a dualistic faith, at least in terms of the religions of the world, as well as what we mean by a Limited God Theory.

Preliminary Remarks on the Nature of Dualism

When we use the word "Dualism" in these remarks, we mean a philosophical or religious doctrine that holds that reality consists, or is the product of, two ultimate principles, and that cannot be reduced to a more ultimate First Cause. In other words, the necessary conditions for a "Dualistic Faith" is that they believe:

1. Reality consists of two ultimate principles.
2. They cannot be reduced to a single principle.

As we shall see, some dualistic systems, like Plato's Doctrine of Creation, for example, believes that one of the two principles is a god, which he calls the "Demiurge," and the other principle is a force that Plato refers to as the "Unordered parts of *Kaos*," or what Plato calls the "Given."[334] In some dualistic faiths, the two principles are gods, such as in Zoroastrianism. In these faiths, the universe or reality is the outcome of two ultimate and distinct first causes. In other religions, the dualism may be between a god and a principle or force.

Although some of the dualistic views mentioned here come from the ancient world, they still have appeared more recently in the modern period. Although Manichaeism originally developed in Roman times, it saw a resurgence in later centuries, as in the Cathars in medieval Christian times from the twelfth to the fourteenth centuries, and the philosophical work of Frenchman Pierre Bayle, in the seventeenth century.[335]

The Cathars believed in the existence of two cosmic principles, a good god and a bad god. The good god was the god of the New Testament, and the bad god was the god of the Old Testament. The Cathars identified the bad god with Satan. The Cathars endured persecutions during the Inquisition, as well as ex-communication from the Roman Church.[336]

The Paulicians were a medieval church sect that spread over Asia Minor, Armenia and Albania. They were particularly found in the Albanian church from the seventh to the ninth centuries. The Paulicians are important for our purposes because they were dualists with respect to the issues of evil and suffering. They affirmed two principles: the Heavenly Father who rules not this world but the world to come; and the other, an Evil Demiurge, Lord and God of this world who made all flesh.

Pierre Bayle, in his philosophical dictionary under the article on the Paulicians, tells us this about the Dualistic View:

> The hypothesis of two principles would likely have made greater progress if its details were given less crudely, and it had not been accompanied by several disgusting practices or if there had been as many disputes as there are today over

predestination, in which Christians accuse one another either of making God the author of sin or stripping him of the governance of the world.[337]

There also have been many versions of "Gnostic Dualism" going all the way back to early Christian times and continuing until the start of the High Middle Ages in the eleventh century.[338] Pierre Bayle points out that the Dualistic View of Manichaeism gives just as plausible an account of evil and suffering as does traditional Christianity.[339]

Another preliminary remark is in order about dualism. When we use the term dualism, we are referring to two cosmic realities. We are not referring to the Platonic belief and its followers that human beings are made up of two things—a body and a soul. Although this view is sometimes called Dualism in Plato and Rene Descartes, for examples, it is the cosmic variety about which we speak of in this fourth chapter.

Finally, when we speak of a "Limited God Theory," we mean by that term that the believer does not believe in a God who possesses the traditional omni-attributes in the West. That is that God is All-Good, All-Knowing and All-Powerful. Later in this chapter, we shall see that many thinkers in the West—from the eighteenth to the twentieth centuries—were advocates of the Limited God Perspective. This brings us to an analysis of Plato's version of Cosmic Dualism, the topic of the next section.

Plato and Cosmic Dualism

Several factors must be understood in comprehending Plato's account of the creation of the world. First, Plato's god, or the Demiurge, did not create the word out of nothing. Rather the Demiurge fashioned the world out of a pre-existent matter that the philosopher calls *Kaos*. This is an undifferentiated, chaotic matter out of which the world was made.[340]

Secondly, the Demiurge was not able to order all of the chaotic stuff. Thirdly, Plato's god used his theory of the eternal forms as a blueprint for the world. In this view, everything on earth is a replica, or an imitation of, the eternal form of the same entity. Thus, the Demiurge's model was the Eternal Forms. Fourthly, because the Demiurge was unable to order all of Kaos, there is some of the pre-existent "Stuff" that was not amenable to ordering. Plato calls this unordered part of chaos the "Given."[341]

In Plato's view, it is this unordered part of Kaos that are responsible for natural evils, like diseases, storms and other entities that cause evil and suffering. Plato explains moral evil, on the other hand, as by-products of the human will created by human souls. For Plato, the human soul is made up of three separate parts—the Appetites, the Spirit, and the Rational elements of the soul.[342]

The appetites for Plato are one's emotions, passions and feelings. The spirited elements are the rules of the Church and society. The Rational element of the soul is Reason, which should rule the other two elements. Plato gives an analogy to understand his view of the soul. It is like a chariot, a charioteer and two horses. One horse is feisty and difficult to control. The other is docile and usually follows the commands of the charioteer, who is the Rational element in the analogy.[343]

In Plato's view, it is the Rational element of the soul that is capable of surviving death. It is also the Rational element that is capable of discerning the Eternal Forms. The Appetitive element is tied to the body, and the Spirited element is tied to the Church and society, but the Rational element of the soul is the part that survives death. Connected to this point regarding the immortality of the soul is a series of arguments that the Athenian philosopher gives to establish his belief in immortality.

Among these arguments are the following: the Argument from Opposites; the Eternal Knows the Eternal Argument, the Doctrine of Recollection and the Argument from Simple and Compound. In the first of these, Plato points out that life is a series of opposites. We were not alive, then we were, and then we die. Given this series, the next part should be that we are alive again, and thus immortality.[344]

In the second argument, Plato says there must be something that is eternal in the soul because the soul is capable of knowing the Eternal Forms. That part of the soul, of course, is the Rational element. Thus, the Eternal knows the Eternal. In the Doctrine of Recollection, Plato suggests that if the soul is able to apprehend the Eternal Forms, and we did not learn this theory in this life, then we must be remembering it from a previous life, perhaps a version of the Karma View from Chapter One.[345]

In the Argument from Simple and Compound, Plato points out that everything in reality is either simple or compound, either made of parts or not. Now the soul is made of three parts, Appetitive, Spirited and Rational. And the first two elements of the soul are also compound, for the former includes emotions, passions and feelings, and the Spirited is made of rules. But the rational part of the soul is pure reason. This part is simple and not compound. Now, if the Rational part of the soul is simple, then it cannot change, so it must survive death.[346]

In reviewing Plato's view of evil, then Moral Evils are caused by the rational part of the soul because that is the part that should rule the soul and the part that knows the Eternal Forms, including the Eternal Form of the Good. For Plato, this is the highest of the Eternal Forms.

Natural Evils, on the other hand, are caused by the unordered parts of Kaos. In terms of Plato's Cosmic Dualism, then, there are two eternal principles in the universe that cannot be reduced to One First Cause. These are the Demiurge who is All Good and the unordered parts of chaos that are the cause of Natural Evil.

Plato also suggested two other responses to the origins of evil and suffering, one in *The Republic* and the other in the *Laws*. In the former, at 613a, Plato suggests that the evil in life may be a punishment for sin in a previous life, or, if not that, "then it may be a good that we cannot recognize."[347] The first alternative offered in *The Republic* may be a version of the Karmic View and, thus, ultimately an example of Retributive Justice.

In Section X of the *Laws* (903b and c), Plato suggests a solution regarding evil and suffering that later would be adopted by the Stoic philosophers. There Plato observes that "Evil and Suffering of the past may be conducive to the good of the whole, and thus, is not really Evil." This view, of course, is nothing more than what we have labeled the Divine Plan Theory—something may appear to be evil, but it goes to the making of the Good of the Whole.[348] In the same section of the *Laws*, at 906 b and c, Plato again suggests "that small examples of evil may contribute to the completeness of the whole of things, which in its completeness is Good."[349]

Thus, we have seen in the works of Plato, the unordered "Given," as the cause of Natural Evil, human Free Will as the cause of Moral Evil, and the Retributive Justice Theory in the form of karma, and the Divine Plan Perspective, where examples of Evil are part of the Greater Good, where everything works out for the Good in the End.

This brings us to the second kind of Cosmic Dualism, the one expressed in the ancient Persian faith Zoroastrianism.

Evil and Suffering in Zoroastrianism

Zoroastrianism was an ancient Persian religion founded by a man named Zoroaster, or Zarathustra, who most likely lived in the late seventh or early sixth century BCE. He apparently was from an aristocratic family from Rhages, Media or Persia. Although he was from the priestly class, he became disillusioned with his Persian ancestral religion. Instead, he decided to travel and search for inspiration and religious wisdom. After ten years of traveling, he finally realized that he had been called to be a prophet to a god called Ahura Mazda, the Lord of Light.[350]

Zoroaster received his revelation in the form of a sacred scripture, the *Zend Avesta*, the Holy Book of his religion, and he was commissioned to preach to all of mankind.[351] He also was to preach something called the *Gathas,* a series of hymns to the gods.[352] The central claim of the Zoroastrian faith is that there are two equally powerful and intelligent gods who controlled the universe.[353] Their names were *Ahura Mazda* and *Angra Mainya*, the Lord of Light and the Lord of Darkness. These gods represented an extreme form of Cosmic Dualism, in which followers, who are endowed with free will, are given the option to choose which god to worship. Believers of the faith would be rewarded or punished based on how they choose to behave and which god to follow.

If the believer followed the "good words, good thoughts, and good deeds," then they would be able to appreciate all the pleasures that Ahura Mazda had in store for them. Followers of Zoroaster believed that Ahura Mazda created the World of Thought and then gave birth to the World of Living Things. The god Angra Mainya challenged this pre-creation with its own counter-creation and to destroy whatever Ahura Mazda will create.[354]

The Lord of Darkness wished to destroy the World of Living Things with darkness, sickness and death. Before Angra Mainya could attack, Ahura Mazda forced him to retreat into the darkness. The evil god was stunned into a kind of unconsciousness for three thousand years, according to the tradition. The Zoroastrian faith became the religion of the ancient Persian Empire under Cyrus the Great, the leader of the Achaemenid Empire. The emperor appeared to be a devout Zoroastrian, and he was a tolerant monarch who allowed his non-Persian subjects to practice their own religions.[355]

Cyrus ruled his kingdom under the Zoroastrian idea of *Asha*, a Persian word for Truth and Justice. This Persian faith was spread across Asia mostly by the Silk Road, a network of trade routes that spread from western China to the Middle East and Eastern Europe. The major tenets of Zoroastrianism helped to shape important ideas in the three Abrahamic religions—Judaism, Christianity and Islam.

Among these ideas of Zoroaster's faith were Heaven and Hell, a Day of Judgment, Immortality of the Soul, and Resurrection of the Body. Many of these ideas may first have entered Judaism during the Babylonian captivity, where the people of Judea had been living for decades. When Cyrus conquered the Babylonians, they allowed the Jews to return to Israel.[356] Over the next millennia, Zoroastrianism dominated two subsequent Persian dynasties, the Parthian and the Sassanian empires, until the Muslim conquest, beginning in the seventh century.

The Muslim conquest of Persia occurred between 633 and 651 CE, which finally led to the fall of the Sassanians. It also led to the decline of the Zoroastrian faith in Iran and the ascendency of the faith of Islam there. The Arab invaders charged Zoroastrians higher taxes if they wished to retain their faith, and they made life difficult for them. Over time, most members of the Zoroastrian faith converted to Islam. [357]

Some Zoroastrians left Iran, traveled across the Arabian Sea and landed in the city of Gujarat, a state in western India, sometime between 785 and 936 CE. In India, they called themselves "Parsis" or "Parsees."[358] Today, there are between 60,000 and 100,000 Parsis in India and another 2,000 in Pakistan.[359] Among the most important religious symbols in Zoroastrianism is the *Faravahar*, an ancient symbol of the faith of Zoroaster. It depicts a bearded man with one hand reaching forward. He stands above a pair of wings that are outstretched from a circle that stands for eternity.[360]

Fire and water are two other important religious symbols in Zoroastrianism. They are seen as representations of purity. The earliest places of worship in the faith were known as "Fire Temples." In each of these, there burned an eternal flame. It burns forever and is never put out. These original temples often were in caves.[361] The followers of Zoroaster conducted what they called "Sky Burials." They built high, flat on the top towers called *dakmahs*, or "Towers of Silence." Bodies were placed atop these towers, and vultures picked clean the bones. Then they were collected and placed in lime pits or "ossuaries."[362]

The dakmah became illegal in Iran in the early 1970s before the Iranian Revolution. Today, many Zoroastrians bury their dead beneath concrete slabs, though some Parsees in India still practice Sky Burial. There is, for example, one *dakhma* in Mumbai, India. The ritual of the Sky Burial is attested to by Herodotus in his *Histories*.[363]

Many Europeans first became aware of the Zoroastrian founder when German philosopher Friedrich Nietzsche wrote a novel called *Thus Spoke Zarathustra*.[364] Nietzsche follows the travels of the prophet, though Nietzsche himself was an atheist and the inventor of the phrase *Gott ist tod,* or "God is dead."[365]

The Zoroastrian scriptures are usually divided into the following parts:

The Yasnas-Gathas
The Visperad
The Yashts
The Vendidad
The Minor Texts
The Fragments[366]

Zoroastrian tradition holds that the original work of twenty-one books, known as the *Nasts*, was revealed to Ahura Mazda, the One True God, who recited them to his benefactor King Vishtaspa who had them inscribed on sheets of gold. These original texts were then memorized, recited at services called *Yasnas*, and passed down through generations of Zoroastrians. They were finally committed to writing during the Sassanian Empire. At this time, they began to be accompanied by commentaries called the *Zend*. Thus, they are now known as the *Zend-Avesta*.[367]

This brings us to an analysis of what the Zoroastrian faith has had to say about the phenomena of evil and suffering, the topic of the next section of this fourth chapter.

Evil and Suffering in Zoroastrianism

Needless to say, the most fundamental response to the phenomena of evil and suffering in the Zoroastrian faith is that its believers are engaged in a Religion of Solution, as outlined in Chapter One. The earliest statement of dualism in the *Avesta* is in the "Gathas" at Yasna XXX. This text relates:

> Thus are the Spirits primeval,
> Who, as Twain, by their deeds are famed.
> In thought, and word, and deed,
> A better, they two, and an Evil.
> Of these, let the Wise choose aright,
> And not as the Evil minded.[368]
> This portion of the Yasna continues:
> Then these spirits created.
> At first the two came together,
> Life and our death decreeing
> How all at the last shall be ordered;
> For Evil men, Hell, the worst life.
> For the righteous, the Best Mind, Heaven.[369]
> At another section of the Yasna, at XLV, 2. The text relates:
> Announce the two spirits at the beginning of the world
> Of them spoke the blissful also unto the destructive
> Neither our thoughts, nor our commends, nor our intelligence
> Nor our beliefs nor our speeches, nor our deeds
> Nor our doctrines, nor our souls correspond.[370]

Zoroaster, the prophet, tells us this in another section of the *Avesta:*

> I will speak out concerning the two spirits of whom at the
> beginning of existence the holier spoke to him who is evil,
> Neither our thoughts, nor our teachings, nor wills, nor our
> choices, nor our words, nor our deeds, nor our convictions,
> nor yet our souls agree.[371]

Zoroaster is quite clear about this fundamental split of reality. He observes:

> In the beginning the two spirits who are well endowed twins
> were known as the one good and the other evil in thought,
> word, and deed. Between them, the wise choose the good
> not so the fools. And when these spirits meet they estab-
> lished in the beginning life and death that in the end the evil
> should meet with the worst existence, but the just with the
> best mind. Of these two spirits, he who was of the lie chose to
> do the worst things, but the most holy spirit, clothed in righ-
> teousness (or truth)...as did all of those who sought with zeal
> to do the pleasure of the wise Lord by doing good works.[372]

In these final two passages, Zoroaster implies the metaphysical dualism that underlies his faith by suggesting that Ahura Mazda and Angra Mainya are twins, eternal, and presumably equal in power and strength. This ontological dualism is the key to understanding the duality of human life. In Zoroastrianism, evil comes from the bad god, Angra Mainya. Human beings, through their volitions, can choose to ally themselves with "he who is the lie," or with Ahura Mazda. The problem of evil is solved in this view, and not dissolved, by turning to and obeying the good god.[373]

In this Yasna 30:1–6 and 8–9, tells us this:

> Truly for seekers I shall speak of those things to be pondered,
> even by one who already knows, with praise and worship for
> the Lord of Good Purpose, the excellent Wise One and the
> Truth... Hear with your ears the best things. Reflect with clear
> Purpose, each man for himself, on the two choices for deci-
> sions, being alert indeed to declare yourselves For Him before
> the Great Requital.

In this passage, we find the combination of several of our responses to evil and suffering. The language about "Good Purpose" is an indication of Divine Plan Theory. The "Great Requital" is the final culmination in Zoroastrianism when one's moral actions finally will be evaluated, a version of Retributive Justice at the End of Time. The mention of choice and the "decision" are an indication of the Free Will Defense.[374]

Another passage in the same section speaks of those "who act well and have chosen wisely between the two, and not so the evil-doers." A few lines later, "The house of Just Purpose shall be for the Just man." The same section of the Yasna refers to the "daevas who did not choose wisely between these two, for the Deceiver approached them as they conferred. But they chose the wrong Purpose."

The "Deceiver," of course, is a reference to Angra Mainya. The word *Daevas* is an Avestan term that means "Devils." It refers to the followers of Angra Mainya. In the *Younger Avesta*, around the fifth century BCE, the Daevas are divinities that promote chaos and disorder.[375] In later Zoroastrian folklore, the *divs* are personifications of every imaginable evil.[376] The Persian words *Deva, Daevus, Divs* are cognates of the Greek *Deus,* the Georgian *Devi*, the Urdu *Deo*, the Turkish *Div* and the Latin *Deus*.[377]

This passage from the Yasna, chapter 30, seems to combine Divine Plan language with Retributive Justice Theory at the End of Time that will come about by the use of human Free Will. At 30:8–9, the Yasna reveals, "Then, when the Retribution comes for these sinners, then Mazda the Good Power shall be present for He with Good Purpose." Again, we see the combining of the Free Will Defense, Retributive Justice Theory and the Divine Plan Perspective, not to mention the Influence of the Demonic Forces Theory in regard to Anga Mainya attempting to dissuade the believer to Darkness and Evil.

So far in our analysis, we have suggested the employment of the Divine Plan Theory, the Free Will Defense, Retributive Justice Theory at the End of Time, and the Influence of Demonic Forces Theory in the Dualism of Ahura Mazda and Angra Mainya. Indeed, throughout the Yasna, Zoroaster calls upon people to use their Free Will to choose the good god. "The good choose wisely," says Zoroaster, "while the evil chose wickedly."[378]

Albert Bailey, in an essay entitled "Zarathushtrian Theodicy," adds another approach that he finds in the ancient Persian faith. Bailey observes:

> Zervanism carried this development one step further, seeing the existence of the world, good and evil as an act of Divine Purgation. The Godhead becomes perfect by purging itself of Evil. In doing so, it temporarily loses its omnipotence but will regain it at the end of days. This Divine Purgation is the reason for the existence of the universe.[379]

Bailey's reference to Zervanism is a modified version of Zoroastrianism that appeared during the Sassanian Empire, from the third to the seventh century CE. It was opposed to orthodox Zoroastrianism that by that time had become completely dualistic in doctrine. According to Zervanism, Ahura Mazda alone is limitless, eternal and uncreated. Thus, Zervanism is a monotheistic version of the Zoroastrian faith.[380]

Bailey goes on in his article to tie the Purgation View to a perspective in contemporary, Western philosophy, one of our supplementary perspectives outlined in the first chapter of this study. Bailey remarks:

> This is also in line with what is now known as Process Theology, the understanding of the Divine not as a state of perfection, but as a growing, active Reality. All is not yet well, but all will be well in the fullness of time. The *Frashkereti* is not yet here, but it will come. This, for me, has proven to be the most reasonable understanding of this age-old theological problem.[381]

In order to unpack Albert Bailey's view of the Zoroastrian perspective of the problem of evil, we must say something about Process Theology, as well as something about the Frashokereti. This latter idea is an Avestan term to refer to the End of the World when evil is destroyed, and everything will then exist in perfect unity with Ahura Mazda. According to the doctrine of the Frashokereti, Good will prevail over Evil. Creation, which was originally perfect, will revert back to that perfect state. The state of an individual's fate will be determined by the sum of that person's thoughts, words and deeds.[382]

The idea of Process Theology or Process Philosophy is derived from the philosophical view of Alfred North Whitehead, whose Gifford Lectures were published as *Process and Reality* in 1929. In his view, God is seen as a participant in the larger creative process.[383] David Ray Griffin, a member of the youngest generation of Process thinkers, tells us this about their view of God:

> God does not refrain from controlling creatures simply because it is better for God to use persuasion, but it is because it is necessarily the case that God cannot completely control his creatures.[384]

In practical terms, this means that in the Process View, God is understood to be participating in a larger, creative process so that He influences and is influenced by other entities in his creation. God participates in a changing universe. This limitation of God's power resolves questions about God's responsibility for evil in the world.[385] Albert Bailey sees the process of purgation to be tied to the Process Theology's idea of God being limited in His, and in the universe's, development.

Ultimately, of course, in the Zoroastrian view, at the time of the Frashokereti, people ultimately will be judged in a version of Collective Retributive Justice. And at that time, in Bailey's view, Ahura Mazda will have completed the process of purgation, or emptying out.

Thus far in this section of Chapter Four, we have suggested that contemporary Zoroastrian thinkers, like Albert Bailey, for example, appear to have assented to the following theories or responses to evil and suffering:

1. The Free Will Defense
2. Retributive Justice Theory
3. Zoroastrianism as a Religion of Solution
4. The Influences of Demonic Forces View
5. Divine Plan Theory
6. The Process Theology Perspective

This brings us to a discussion of Mithraism and its responses to evil and suffering, the next topic in this fourth chapter of this study of evil and suffering in the religions of the world.

Mithraism on Evil and Suffering

Our third dualistic metaphysical view in this fourth chapter is the faith of Mithraism, a mystery-cult in the Roman world. Followers of this faith followed the worship of Indo-Aryan deity *Mithras*, originally an Akkadian word for "Contract."[386] The cult of Mithras first appeared in the late first century CE, and it spread from the Italian peninsula and border regions across the whole of the Roman Empire.[387]

Like many other mystery cults of the day, the Mithraic faith was a secret one. Originally, followers of the cult often worshipped in temples built inside caves and hidden away from the world. This was done so the followers felt of sense of belonging to a special movement. At first, the Roman authorities tolerated the secrecy of the cult, particularly the Roman emperors.

In the extant archeological record, over 200 Mithras temples have been discovered stretching from Syria to Great Britain, but are mostly concentrated in Italy, on the Rhine River, and on the Danube River, as well.[388] After the establishment of the Christian Church in the third and fourth centuries, the practice of the Mithras cult diminished, and temples were walled off or destroyed. Some of the Mithraic temples, however, remained in use until the fifth century.[389]

The most important element of the faith of Mithraism is the god Mithras' killing of a sacrificial bull. This scene is also known as *Tauoctony*. This was an ancient ritual associated with the cult of Cybele. The myth is associated with the "Cult of the Great Mother," the *Magna Mater*. The new follower had to be baptized in the shower of the blood from the sacrificed bull.[390]

The followers of the faith of Mithraism believed in a seven-degree process of spiritual enlightenment, which ultimately led to a "Ritual Suicide," in which the initiate was killed with a non-lethal sword so that he might be reborn again.[391] These seven stages of initiation were known as the following names:

1. The *Corax*, or "Raven"
2. The *Nymphus*, or "Bride Groom"
3. The *Miles*, or "Soldier"
4. The *Leo*, or "Lion"

5.   The *Peres*, or "Persian"
6.   The *Heliodromus*, or "Sun-Runner"
7.   The *Pater*, or "Father"[392]

Each of these successive stages is protected by a heavenly body: Mercury, Venus, Mars, Jupiter, the Moon, the Sun and Saturn.[393] At the lowest degree of initiation into the grade of *Corax* symbolized the death of a new member from which he would arise reborn as a "New Man." Some suggest the Raven level originated with the Zoroastrian custom of the "Sky Burial" we have spoken of earlier in this fourth chapter.[394]

Other Mithraic rituals accompanied the other six stages of initiation. Some of these involve the clashing of cymbals, the beating of drums and the unveiling of a statue of Mithras. The initiate drank wine to recognize it as a sign of ritual purity. In another ritual, the initiate ate a small morsel of bread that had been exposed to the rays of the Sun. By eating the bread, it was believed, the believer was partaking in the Divine essence of the Sun itself.[395]

When the initiate reached the degree of Soldier, he was offered a crown that he had to reject by saying, "Only Mithras is my crown." At this stage, the initiate was also given an indelible mark on his forehead to symbolize the fact that the soldier is "owned by a God."[396] The followers of the Mithras cult also professed a number of other fundamental beliefs. Among these were the following:

1.   Mithras had a miraculous birth that he was born from a rock.
2.   His birthday was celebrated on December 25.
3.   Water had a symbolic role in the Mithras cult.
4.   The belief in the immortality of the soul.
5.   A final judgment of the soul.
6.   A doctrine of resurrection of the body.[397]

When it came to the phenomena of evil and suffering, the cult of Mithras mostly relied on a doctrine of dualism. This doctrine held the view that the world was a battleground between a Good Principle and an Evil Principle. The Evil Principle in the Mithras cult was associated with light and the day, while the Evil Principle was associated with night and evil. In some traditions of the Mithras cult, these two principles are associated with the Persian gods, Ahura Mazda and Angra Mainya.[398]

These two powers are thought to be in a state of constant warfare against each other. It was Mithras, a Spirit of Light and Truth, who became quite naturally a celestial warrior on the side of Ahura Mazda.[399]

The most fundamental thing to say about the cult of Mithras' view on the phenomena of evil and suffering is that it was a Religion of Solution, where evil was believed to arise with the Evil Principle, or Evil God, Angra Mainya. With the cult's belief in a final judgment, we also may add the Free Will Defense and the Retributive Justice View to our list of Mithraic responses to evil and suffering.

This brings us to an analysis of what the faith of Manichaeism, another Roman metaphysical system, has had to say about the phenomena of evil and suffering, the topic of the next section of this fourth chapter of this study of evil and suffering in the religions of the world.

Evil and Suffering in Manichaeism

Much of what we know about Manichaeism comes from Christian sources like Augustine of Hippo. The movement was founded by a Persian man named Mani in the third century CE. Mani (ca. 216 to 274) and his faith originated in Babylon, not far from present-day Baghdad. The Prophet Mani considered himself to be the final in a series of prophets that included Zoroaster, the Gautama Buddha and Jesus Christ.

According to what is known as the *Cologne Mani-Codex*, Mani's parents were members of a Jewish Christian, Gnostic sect known as the *Elcesaites*. This was an Aramaic-speaking sect. As a child, Mani is said to have received his first revelation from the Divine. In his early twenties, he felt compelled to announce himself as a prophet, and he began to preach. He gathered a following and organized a church when his existence became known to the Zoroastrians. However, they declared him a heretic and banished him from the Persian Empire.[400]

Mani is said to have wandered as a mendicant for eighteen years, reportedly in central Asia, Tibet and northern India. He is said to have adopted a number of religious beliefs that he had learned in those years.

Mani appears to have returned to the Persian Empire at the age of sixty. At first, he was accepted by the emperors, but in a short while, the Zoroastrian priests plotted against Mani, and they induced the emperor to order that he be executed.[401]

According to tradition, Mani was executed in the most horrible of fashions, and his carcass was stuffed with straw and then publicly displayed to deter any who followed him.[402] Mani's death did not end the Manichaein faith, but it did drive it underground. It penetrated the West as far as North Africa and Rome and as far east as western China.[403]

The Uighur, a tribe in Turkey, converted to Manichaeism, as did the Bogomils in Bulgaria and the Cathars from northern Italy and southern France, who we mentioned earlier in this chapter. There is some evidence that the Manicheans survived in Europe until the fifteenth century.[404]

The principal doctrines of the Manicheans are somewhat obscure. According to the *Gospel of the Prophet Mani*, a Supreme God created two separate worlds of light and darkness. The world of darkness, in the distant past, has penetrated the world of light, and this was the origin of evil. The co-mingling of the light and the darkness is the material world as we know it. Human beings, too, are seen as the co-mingling of light and darkness, the darkness of matter and the light of the spirit.[405]

According to Mani, human beings should help promote the eventual separation back to the Realm of Light and the Realm of Darkness, and he believed that in the end, the light would conquer the darkness.[406]

The Manichean faith was divided into two parts: the Elect and the Hearers. The Elect were the select few who lead a life of austerity, devotion, celibacy, vegetarianism and poverty, much like the life of Mani in his wanderings. The Hearers' position was to revere and care for the Elect, and if they could, aspire to become one of the Elect.[407]

The Manichean myth of Creation tells the tale of the God of Light sending an "Original Man" to battle with the attacking powers of Darkness, including a figure called the "Demon of Greed." The Original Man was armed with five separate shields of light, which he lost to the powers of Darkness.[408] The myth continued about how the Light was captured into the world of matter and eventually was liberated by entrapping a group of large demons and causing them to become sexually aroused by "Twelve Virgins of Light."[409]

Originally, in the Manichean cosmology, Good and Evil existed as two completely separate realms. At some point, the king of Darkness notices that the followers of Light have become greedy, and so he attacks them. This is the first of three separate creations in the Manichean faith.[410] The Manicheans believed in two co-equal substances, Light and Darkness, and their mixture is responsible for the physical universe. Augustine of Hippo describes this process in a succinct way:

> Then they [the Manicheans] declare that the world has been made by the nature of the good, that is by the nature of God, but yet that it was formed of a mixture of Good and Evil that resulted when these two natures fought against themselves.[411]

What Augustine means by this mixture and fight is that the Manichean saw evil as an active substance waging war against the light, and that ordinary evil in the physical world correlates to the metaphysical evil that had existed from eternity. The Manicheans understood sin as evil. Thus, they were advocates of the Free Will Defense in that they thought that human beings are responsible for their own sins.[412]

Among the scriptures of Manichaeism, seven are noteworthy. These are:

1. The Book of Secrets
2. The Book of Giants
3. The Book of the Precepts of the hearers
4. The Book of Shahpurakan
5. The Book of Quickening
6. The Book
7. The Fihrist[413]

The first of these works is a commentary on Judeo-Christian scriptures; the second is about Demons; the third, regulations for the Hearers; the fourth is a long letter to a king named Shapur; the Book of Quickening is about eschatology; and the *Fihrist* is also called the "Gospel of Mani."[414]

Among the other ideas in Manichaeism were the following: they had a version of the Fallen Angels story, which they relate to the Watchers Story in the Book of Enoch.[415] Secondly, the faith requires its believers to pray four times a day.[416] Thirdly, the Manicheans had a very large number of "Fasts," that for them was determined by the movements of the Heavenly Bodies.[417]

Like the Mithraites, the Manicheans considered the death date of their leader, Mani, to be a sacred day. It comes in the month of March. The faithful prostrate themselves before an empty chair that was raised above the podium with five steps. Long fasts accompany feasts in Manichaeism.[418] The Manicheans also ascribed to a litany of both Evil, or Fallen Angels, as well as good angels.[419] The good angels in Manichaeism include Raphael, Michael, Gabriel and Sariel, who collectively "protect the believers from all adversity."[420]

And its most fundamental level, like the other dualistic faiths discussed in this fourth chapter, the primary way that the Manicheans dealt with the issues of evil and suffering was as a Religion of Solution. Earlier, we also spoke of a belief in the Free Will Defense as an explanation for Moral Evil. This brings us to the final section of this fourth chapter, in which we will describe and discuss a number of more modern attempts at dualistic responses to the phenomena of evil and suffering.

Modern Dualistic Responses to Evil and Suffering

The oldest version of a Limited God Theory in Western philosophy comes from Scottish philosopher David Hume. He sketches out his view in one of the sections of his *Natural History of Religion*. In the book, Hume suggests the possibility of a kind of Monotheism, a form that would be adopted by many of the subsequent thinkers we shall see below.

In several of Hume's other works, like the *Dialogues Concerning Natural Religion*, for example, he suggests several possible causes for the existence of evil. In addition to the Limited God View, he also points out that there may be several deities who all contribute to the existence of evil.[421] In section X of his *Enquiry Concerning Human Understanding*, Hume again suggests the possibility that

God is either not All-Powerful, not All-Knowing, or both, as we have indicated earlier.[422]

Among philosophical circles since the nineteenth century to the present era, there have also been a number of more modern, philosophical and theological responses to the phenomena of evil and suffering in the West. Among these thinkers are Scottish philosopher David Hume in the eighteenth century, John Stuart Mill and William James in the nineteenth century, the process theologians we already have discussed in this chapter, British philosopher and Anglican priest Hastings Rashdall, and Charles Hartshorne, E. S. Brightman, and Rabbi Harold Kushner in the twentieth century.[423]

For Hartshorne, who is another of the process theology thinkers, God is as good as it now is possible for Him to be. For him, God, in effect, is developing and improving, even though He has not yet managed to alleviate the world of suffering. As human beings struggle against Natural, Moral and Metaphysical Evils, they can assist God in His own development.[424] In Hartshorne's version of his Finite God Theory, God cannot know the future; hence He cannot be absolutely certain about how the details of history will be worked out.[425]

According to Hartshorne, this fact is due both to the randomness of nature and because He has endowed human beings with free will. Because God is situated in time, in Hartshorne's view, and was not the Creator of the universe, he both suffers and rejoices with human beings, but He cannot control them. God and humans may enter into a partnership in a project designed to reduce or to eradicate evil, but the Divine cannot force them to cooperate. Any cooperation comes from persuasion, not coercion.[426]

For Hartshorne, if God is subject to the limitations of the basic structure of the universe that He did not create, then the laws of that universe are eternal and immutable, not matters that could be changed by Divine decision. Thus, Hartshorne has a ready-made answer to the origin and existence of evil.[427]

E. S. Brightman finds the roots of his views on God and the problem of evil to be found in the dialogues of Plato. The Boston philosopher says about the Athenian philosopher, "Plato puts into the mouth of Socrates the principle that God is not the cause of all things, but only the Good things."[428] Brightman goes on to explain that in the *Timaeus*, where divinity is represented not as the omnipotent Creator of the universe, but rather a "good god who desires that as far as possible, all things should be good and not evil."[429]

Here Brightman alludes to the fact that for Plato, the Demiurge, or god, was not omnipotent because He could not completely order all of the chaotic material out of which the universe was fashioned.[430] In Brightman's sense, then, God is not all-powerful, so the Boston philosopher may be numbered among the Limited God theorists and the assenters to the Religions of Solution View, as well.[431]

Brightman also found another source for his views on God and Evil in the philosophical writings of John Stuart Mill, particularly his *Three Essays on Religion*. Brightman relates this about Mills' essays:

> John Stuart Mill was the first among the Moderns to suggest the idea of a Finite God... If the Maker of the world can do all that He wills, then He wills misery, and there is no escape from the conclusion.[432]

Brightman goes on to maintain that God cannot do all that He wills because of His incapacity to order all of chaos to which he had alluded earlier. In addition to Brightman's view of God and his limited God, the Boston philosopher also introduces a philosophical category he calls "Surd Evil." For Brightman, Surd Evil is the most severe form of evil. He goes on to give several examples of this category of Surd Evil, included imbecility.[433]

Brightman observes about the imbecile:

> Let us grant that the imbecile may encourage Psychiatry and arouse pity, yet it is an incurable condition. There remains in it a Surd Evil embodied in the intrinsic worthlessness of the imbecile's existence and suffering which his existence imposes on others.[434]

In his entire corpus, E. S. Brightman never quite gets around to defining Surd Evil. Rather, he seems to imply that it is simply part of the fabric of the way things are. Again, this conclusion is most likely related to the Boston philosopher's debt to Plato's *Timaeus*, in that the

Surd Evils are connected in Brightman's view to the unordered parts of chaos. Like Plato, Brightman is a subscriber to the Limited God Theory, as well as an assenter to a Religion of Solution.[435]

Another philosopher, who is a believer in a Finite God Theory, is American pragmatist William James. James discusses the issues of evil and suffering in a number of his works, including:

"The Will to Believe" (1897)
Human Immortality (1897)
The Varieties of Religious Experiences (1907)
The Dilemma of Determinism (1910)[436]

From these works, two separate theological responses to evil and suffering may be found. The first of these two views can be seen in three representative quotations from the American philosopher. In the first of these, James observes, "Since you make evil or good in your own thoughts, it is your ruling of your thoughts that proves to be your principal concern."[437] In a second passage about evil and suffering, William James observes:

> We are spinning out our own fates, good or evil, and never
> to be undone. Every smallest stroke of virtue or vice leaves
> its never so little scar... Nothing we ever do is, in strict
> scientific literalness, wiped out.[438]

In the third and final passage from William James about good and evil, the philosopher simply remarks, "We are spinning our own fates, good or evil, never to be undone."[439] From these three quotations, it should be clear that James was a believer in what we have called the Free Will Defense.[440] The other theological response on evil and suffering found in his work is more specifically about his limited conception of God.

In his *The Varieties of Religious Experiences*, James tells us this about his view of God:

> The practical needs and experiences of religion seems to
> me sufficiently met by the belief that beyond each man
> and in a fashion continuous with him there exists a large

> power which is friendly to him and his ideals. All the facts
> require is that the power should be both other and larger
> than our conscious selves. Anything larger would do, if
> only it be large enough to trust for the next step. It need
> not be infinite, it need not be solitary.[441]

In these remarks, James suggests that there may be more than one God, and if there is only one, then He only needs to be more powerful than human beings. In his essay, "The Will to Believe," James argues for a God who is not all-powerful, for if He were, then He should be able to do something about evil.[442] In *A Pluralistic Universe*, James suggests that God does not know the future and says that human freedom is "incompatible with God knowing the future."[443]

We already have shown in this analysis of James that he is a true believer in human free will, so it follows that God does not know the future. And if God is neither All-Knowing nor All-Powerful in the traditional meanings of those terms, then it follows that William James was another believer in a Limited God Theory, as well as an assenter to a Religion of Solution.

In the major work of British philosopher, theologian and Anglican priest Hastings Rashdall (1858–1924), *The Theory of Good and Evil*, published in 1907, we may see our final advocate of a Limited God Theory and an assenter to a Religion of Solution.[444] Hasting's book ostensibly was an attempt to define the nature of Moral Goodness, and in the process of the book, he also makes some observations on the concept of God and His attributes.

Hastings escaped having to hold God responsible for evil in the world because he had doubts that God was, strictly speaking, omnipotent. Rather, Hastings suggests, God is "limited by those eternal necessities that are part of His own nature."[445] In other words, Hastings and his book, *The Theory of Good and Evil*, was a proponent of what we have called a "Limited God Theory," as well as an assenter to a Religion of Solution.[446]

In *The Theory of Good and Evil*, Hastings also develops a version of nineteenth-century Utilitarianism. He also constructed a type of Moral Argument for the existence of God, similar to that of Thomas

Aquinas in his *Summa Theologica*.[447] Hasting's reasoning in his Moral Argument goes something like this:

> If there is a Moral Law, then it must exist some place.
> Since this place is clearly not the world and not completely
> with any particular mind, then the Moral Law must reside
> in the Mind of God. From this, Rashdall suggests, there
> must be an epistemic function in God as the source
> for human moral judgments.[448]

In his Moral Argument, God becomes the Great Law Giver. Rashdall's central feature of his argument is its attention to God as Thomas Aquinas' "Efficient Cause" of the Moral Argument, and Rashdall posits God as an efficient cause of such knowledge. The British philosopher called his moral theory "Ideal Utilitarianism" to distinguish it from Act and Rule Utilitarianism.[449]

Rashdall criticizes the moral theories of Immanuel Kant, Jeremy Bentham's Act Utilitarianism and John Stuart Mill's Rule Utilitarianism. He does, however, agree with Mill's notion of a Limited God.[450]

When Bad Things Happen to Good People by Rabbi Harold Kushner is our most recent version of a Limited God Theory. In his book, which he began writing after the death of his son at the age of fourteen, Rabbi Kushner finally decides that it is best to believe in a Limited God than to believe in one who is All-Good, all-Knowing and All-Powerful. Kushner relates that "God does his best for people and is present in their suffering, but He is not fully able to prevent it."[451] Kushner's beliefs, which seem to question God's omnipotence, have been criticized mostly by conservative scholars associated either with Orthodox Judaism or evangelicals in the Christian faith.[452]

This brings us to a summary of the major conclusions of this fourth chapter on dualistic religions. The primary focus of Chapter Five of this study of evil and suffering in the religions of the world is the history of Buddhism.

Conclusions to Chapter Four

We began this fourth chapter on evil in dualistic faiths by making some preliminary remarks on the nature of dualism. In the first section, we suggested two necessary conditions for a dualistic faith and introduced a number of dualistic faiths in Western history, such as the advocates of Gnosticism, the Cathars and the Paulicians, as well as Plato's version of dualism.

This section of Chapter Four was followed by a section dedicated to the view of metaphysics sketched out by Plato in his dialogue, the *Timaeus*, where the Athenian suggests that the Demiurge attempts to fashion a universe out of a pre-existent, chaotic matter, but he was not able to complete the task, in that some of the pre-existent stuff was unamenable to ordering.

We also pointed out in this section of Chapter Four, dedicated to Plato's views, that the Athenian philosopher also suggested a version of the Karmic Perspective in *The Republic*, as well as a type of the Divine Plan Theory in Section X of Plato's *Laws*.

In the next section of Chapter Four on dualism, we described and discussed the ancient Persian religion of Zoroastrianism, which most likely began in the sixth century BCE. In that section, we indicated the Cosmic Dualism between Ahura Mazda and Angra Mainya, and we sketched out a history of Zoroastrianism from its beginning until the Muslim conquest of Persia. Along the way in this section, we also gave a summary of the Zoroastrian scriptures.

We have dedicated the next section of Chapter Four to a description and discussion of the many theological responses to evil and suffering in the Zoroastrian faith. In that section, we suggested that, at one time or another of its history, the believers in Zoroastrianism have assented to the Free Will Defense, Retributive Justice Theory, to the Influences of Demonic Forces View, to the Divine Plan Theory, as well as the Process Theology Perspective. We also concluded in this section that Zoroastrianism had been a Religion of Solution for most of its history.

In the next section of Chapter Four, we described and discussed the religion of Mithraism, a mystery cult in the Roman Empire. We began the section by describing the major beliefs of the Mithras cult, including its seven levels of spiritual development. We then have shown the answers and responses to the phenomena of evil and suffering to be found in that faith. The most important of those responses was the conclusion that Mithraism, too, was a dualistic faith, or a Religion of Solution, through its cosmic dualism.

These sections of Chapter Four were followed by an introduction to the faith of the Manicheans, popular in the Roman Empire from the third to the fifth centuries. We also gave a summary of the Manichean scriptures, as well as the answers and responses to the phenomena of evil and suffering in the Manichean faith.

In the final section of Chapter Four on religious dualism, we provided a summary of the major modern thinkers from the eighteenth to the twentieth centuries of philosophers and theologians who have subscribed to a Limited God Theory, and thus to a Religion of Solution. Among the thinkers in this section, we included David Hume, John Stuart Mill, William James, Charles Hartshorne, Hastings Rashdall, Boston philosopher E. S. Brightman and Rabbi Harold Kushner.

In each of these seven modern thinkers, we concluded that they all assented to a Limited God Theory and thus to a Religion of Solution. This brings us to Chapter Five. The major focus of this chapter shall be on the answers and responses in the history of Buddhism to the issues of evil and suffering.

Chapter Five:
Evil and Suffering in Buddhism

Ancestors may linger on, holding on to their identities for
a long time before returning to the cycle of causality and,
eventually, rebirth.

—Kohei Kikhuchi, "Buddhist Ancestor Worship"

Now while the demonic specifies the vague category
of Divine absence, for the purposes of our analysis, the
demonic is also a soteriological category in so far as it
calls attention to the forces that resist the achievement of
human freedom.

—Daniel Olivaw, "Buddhist Traditions of the Demonic"

What gets reborn in Buddhism is our peculiar neurosis.

—Chogyam Rinpoche, "Kamma"

Introduction

The main focus of this fifth chapter is to give a description and evaluation
of what the Buddhist faith has had to say over its history on the issues of
evil and suffering. We will begin the chapter with some general remarks
about Buddhism, including its founder, Gautama Buddha, as well as the
faith's principal ideas, beliefs and practices. This introductory section
will be followed by a description and evaluation of how the Buddhist
faith's view of categories like the self, the law of karma, and moksha or
nirvana, are radically different than the view on these same matters in
traditional Hinduism.

These two sections of Chapter Five will be followed by what the Buddhist faith has had to say about responding to or answering questions related to evil and suffering. We begin this chapter, then, with a short introduction to Buddhism.

A Short Introduction to Buddhism

The religious tradition known as Buddhism was founded by a spiritual leader known as Gautama Buddha, a Nepalese man who lived from around 563 to 483 BCE. His teachings and life have served as the foundations of the Buddhist faith. For most of his life, the Buddha taught in and around the region of the world between the modern-day border of Nepal and India in southern Asia. The name "Buddha" means "one who is awakened," or the "Enlightened One."[453]

According to the most widely distributed narrative of his life, after leaving his home, the Buddha began experimenting with different teachings for years, finding none of them completely acceptable. Afterward, the Buddha is said to have spent a woeful night in deep meditation under what is called a *Bodhi Tree*.[454] During this meditation, all of the answers he had been seeking were dispersed, and he came upon what may be called "full awareness of reality."[455]

By all accounts, the Buddha grew up near the town of Lumbini in present-day Nepal. He belonged to a class known as the *Shakyas*. Archeological remains found in 2013 near Lumbini suggests that a "Tree Shrine" predated the traditional dates for early Buddhism.[456] These archeological finds suggest that the Buddhist faith may be far older than the tradition asserts.

Another story about Gautama tells us that when his mother was pregnant with him, she was visited by a holy man who prophesized great things about the child. He would either be a great king or a great military leader.[457] The Buddha's parents were said to have sheltered the child from the world. At the age of sixteen, however, he left his home and wandered into the world.

The first three things the Buddha encountered in the outside world were an old man, a sick man and a corpse. Until this time, these were elements of life Gautama was unaware of.[458] From these experiences, the tradition tells us, Gautama was convinced that suffering is at the heart of all existence. Indeed, the Buddha realized that religious enlightenment is nothing more than the extinguishing of suffering.[459]

The Buddhist faith is based on what it calls Three Universal Truths. These are claims about reality and the nature of things. The first of these is this: Everything in life is impermanent and always changing. The second universal truth in Buddhism tells us: Because nothing is permanent, a life based on the possession of things or people cannot make one happy. The third universal truth is this: There is no eternal, unchanging atman, or Self. In Buddhism, the Self is a collection of changing characteristics or attributes that move from one life to the next.[460]

These three universal truths gave rise to what has come to be known as the Four Noble Truths, the central religious category in Buddhism. These may be summarized in the following way:

1. The key to life is suffering, or *Dukkha*.
2. The cause of suffering, or *Samudaya*.
3. The end of suffering, or *Nirhodha*.
4. The path that frees us from suffering, or *Magga*.[461]

The first truth identifies the most fundamental problem of life—evil and suffering. The second truth identifies attempts to discern the cause of evil and suffering—desire and ignorance. The third truth pertains to the end of evil and suffering—to extinguish desire. And the fourth truth charts the method for the accomplishment of the eradication of desire.[462]

The Buddha made sure that his followers were not to treat him as a god. Rather than that, Gautama said that people should take responsibility for their own lives and actions. He taught what he called a Middle Way, a path to salvation between luxury and its opposite, too much fasting and hardship.[463]

The Buddha believed that these four principles explain a great deal about the nature of evil and suffering, as well as how it may be overcome or to which one may respond, in the Buddhist faith. Gautama taught his followers that the end of suffering, as described in the fourth Noble Truth, could be achieved by following what is called the Eight-Fold Path.[464] More than anything else, the Eight-Fold Path is a group of ideas, both moral and secular, that the Buddhist should follow. They may be summarized this way:

1. Right View, or Right Understanding.
2. Right Thought.
3. Right Speech.
4. Right Action.
5. Right Livelihood.
6. Right Effort.
7. Right Mindfulness.
8. Right Concentration.[465]

The Eight-Fold Path is a set of ideals for ethical conduct, mental discipline, and the achieving of wisdom. They are a means by which the Buddhist may achieve enlightenment. Some divide the Eight-Fold Path into three types:

I.   Wisdom (numbers 1, 2 and 3)
II.   Moral Conduct (numbers 4 to 6)
III. Mental Discipline (numbers 7 and 8)[466]

In addition to the Eight-Fold Path, the Buddhist tradition also ascribes to five precepts that must be followed by all Buddhists in regard to ethics. These are:

1. Don't kill any living thing.
2. Don't steal what is not yours.
3. Refrain from sexual misconduct.
4. Don't lie, use abusive speech, or engage in useless chatter.
5. Refrain from alcohol and drugs.[467]

In terms of its Holy Scriptures or Writings, the Buddhist tradition reveres the following:

I.   The *Tipitaka*, or the "Three Baskets."
II.   The Suttas.
III. The Book of the Dead.[468]

The Three Baskets in early Buddhist thought—that is in Hinayana or Theravada Buddhism, were the following:

A. The *Vinaya Vaibasha*, or "Rules for monks and nuns."
B. The *Sutra Vaibasha*, or the "Five Dharmas." Rules for the people.
C. The *Abhidharma Vaisbasha*. The analyses of the scholars.[469]

The original version of the Three Baskets was written in Sanskrit, for Buddhism originally was a heresy of Hinduism. Later, the Three Baskets were translated into Pali, Chinese, Japanese, Tibetan, Japanese and other languages.[470] The Gautama Buddha's teachings were in oral form. However, after his death around the age of eighty, a series of Buddhist councils were held. By the fourth of these councils held in India in the first century CE, the Buddha's teachings finally were written down. This was the beginning of the Sanskrit canon.[471]

With the beginning of Mahayana Buddhism around 150 BCE, a group of new *Sutras* was written, and the Sanskrit canon was incorporated into the new faith. These new sutras were based on existing texts, but new material was added to incorporate into the new form of Buddhism. Of these new Sutras, four became the most popular in Mahayana Buddhism. These were:

1. *Prajnaparamita Sutras* (The Sutra of Wisdom and Perfection)
2. *Saddharma Pundarika Sutra* (The Lotus Sutra)
3. *Vimalakirtinirdesa Sutra* (The Layman's Sutra)
4. *Sukhavati Sutra* (The Land Sutra)[472]

The first of these four new Sutras set out the teachings of "Emptiness," which we will discuss in the next section of this fifth chapter. The Lotus Sutra explains the monistic character of Buddhism. The third of these new Sutras in Mahayana Buddhism explains that even an average person may become a Bodhisattva as the Buddha had done at the Bodhi Tree. The Sukhavati Sutra teaches that the Buddha's land was open to all who were believers.[473]

By 150 BCE, Buddhism consisted of these two basic types—
Hinayana, or Theravada, and Mahayana. The third type of Buddhism,
called the *Nikaya* School, is a term associated with the form of Buddhism
practiced by many Buddhist monks and nuns. It is a contemplative form
of Buddhism. Indeed, the word *Nikaya* is sometimes translated as the
"Fraternal Order" of Buddhism.[474]

There is also a fourth school of Buddhism known as the Vajrayana.
It is a form of Buddhism that probably arose from the Mahayana
School. It is better known now as Tibetan Buddhism. It is a complex,
philosophical school, complete with a number of important rituals.
The word, *Rajrayana* means "The Way of the Diamond." It refers to a
diamond-hard thunderbolt that was used as a weapon by the Hindu god
of thunder and rain. This is the god Indra.[475]

The Vajrayana School began in India between the sixth and seventh
centuries CE. This system relies on what are known as "Tantric" ideas
and practices. The word "tantric" means a "loom of thread." It implies
the interweaving of traditions and practices such as rituals leading to
altered states of consciousness through chanting and the recitation of
certain prayers.[476] Thus, we have introduced four types of Buddhism—
Hinayana, Mahayana, Nikaya and Vajrayana.

The Buddhists all observe several holidays in the faith. These
include Chinese New Year, a three-day event, and Nirvana Day
celebrated on February 28. It is a celebration of the death of Gautama
Buddha, a festival called *Wesak* that celebrates the birth, enlightenment
and death of the Buddha. *Wassana* is a celebration of the Buddha's first
teachings.[477] Some Buddhist traditions also celebrate *Dhamma Day*
that commemorates the time when the "Wheel of Dharma" is set in
motion.[478] Another holiday is known as *Kathina Day* when donations—
especially robes—are given to monks to express their gratitude.[479]
Finally, most forms of Buddhism practice known as *Bodhi* Day that
marks the day under the tree when Gautama first became the historical
Buddha.[480]

This brings us to the second section of Chapter Five, in which we
speak of how Buddhism differs from traditional Hinduism regarding the
nature of the Self, Karma and Samsara, as well as Moksha and Nirvana.
As we shall see, many of these beliefs are drastically different from

views in Hinduism. We will remember that in traditional Hinduism, the *Self* is referred to as the "atman," the element that gets reincarnated at death.

In this section, we will also explore how Buddhism adopted and changed four other principal ideas of Hinduism. These were the views of the concept of *Dharma*, their understanding of *Maya*, the Buddhist reworking of the demonic, and finally, a revamping of the category of *Khansha*, the Sanskrit word for *Skandas*.

Buddhist Reworkings of Ideas in Hinduism

In Hinayana Buddhism, what gets reincarnated are called the *Skandas*. These are five aggregates or "heaps." They are form, feeling, perception, mental formation and consciousness. These are a collection of memories, perceptions, feelings, bodily attributes and thoughts left over from a previous life. In traditional Buddhism, what gets reincarnated is not the atman; rather, it is this collection of traits known as the *Skandas*.[481]

The word *Skanda* is originally a Sanskrit term that can also be found in the Buddha's Pali, where it is spelled *Khansha*. After the advent of Buddhism, the word *Skanda* is no longer employed in Hinduism. It was a strictly Buddhist term that now meant "collection," or "aggregate."

The "form" Skanda are bodily traits left over from a previous life. This Skanda is mostly connected to the five senses. The "feeling" Skanda are experiences, often of pleasure and pain, inherited from a previous life. The perception Skanda is believed to consist of memories of perception from past lives. The mental formation are related to memories from the organs of the senses—nose, mouth, eyes, touch, tongue.[482]

The fifth and final Skanda, consciousness, is different from the other four in that the fifth Skanda realizes that these aggregates, or heaps left over from a past life, are fleeting and ephemeral. The fifth Skanda is aware that the other four are subject to change and decay. When one becomes at peace with this realization, then one can begin to be free from suffering.[483]

Thus, in traditional Buddhism, what passes from one life to the next is this aggregate of Skandas: memories, perceptions, feelings, thoughts, body attributes, and even intuitions left over from a previous life or lives. Different Skandas are transferred from one life to another. This view is different from the idea of a Soul, or an atman. But it is what moves from one life to the next—Skandas.[484]

From our chapter on Hinduism, we will remember that what determines one's condition from one life to the next is the Law of Karma. The atman moves from one life to the next in a cause and effect relation, such that what the atman reaps it later sows. We also find the use of the word *karma* in early Buddhism, but the term has a radically different understanding in Hinayana Buddhists.

In early Buddhism, the word for karma is the Pali term *Kamma*. This word is used, contrary to the Hindus, to speak of actions, rather than results. In Buddhism, the process of karma is non-linear, as well as complex. Although the past has some role and influence on the present, it does not determine the present. For Buddhists, the present is also shaped by the present.

In his book *What the Buddha Taught*, Buddhist scholar Walpola Rahula gives us this observation about the use of karma in Buddhism:

> Instead of promoting resigned powerlessness, the early Buddhist notion of Karma focused on the liberating potential of what the mind is doing with every moment. Who are you?—what have you come from—is not anywhere near as important as the mind's motives for what it is doing right now. Even though the past may account for many of the inequalities we see in life, our measures as human beings is not the hand we have been dealt. For that hand may change at any moment. We take our own measure by how well we play the hand we've got.[485]

Zen Buddhist teacher John Daido Loori also speaks of the role of karma in his faith. He tells us, "Cause and effect are one thing. And what is that one thing? You. That is why what you do and what happens to you are the same thing."[486] Some Buddhist thinkers prefer using the terms "wholesome" and "unwholesome" rather than "Good" and "Bad" karma. Wholesome actions spring from selfless compassion, loving-kindness and wisdom. Unwholesome actions spring from greed, hate and ignorance.[487] Some Buddhist teachers prefer terms like "helpful" and "unhelpful" in discussing the nature of karma, or *Kamma*, in Buddhism.

The Buddha taught a doctrine known as the *Anatman*, or *Anatta*, that means "no soul," or "no self." In this view, there is no permanent self, or autonomous being, within the individual. What we think of as our personality or ego are temporary creations that do not survive death. What survives death, as we have suggested earlier in this section, is the aggregate of Skandas.

Renowned Tibetan teacher Chogyam Rinpoche—borrowing a page right out of Sigmund Freud—tells us that "What gets reborn is our peculiar neuroses."[488] By this, he means our bad habits and ignorance that gets reborn.

Now we must remember that in the Four Nobel Truths of Buddhism, it is posited that evil and suffering are at the core of human life. The cause of evil and suffering is desire, and the way to eliminate evil and suffering is to eliminate desire. Thus, the goal of the Buddhist believer is to attempt to eliminate desire as far as possible. This brings us to annoyer big difference between Hinduism and Buddhism. It has to do with the idea of nirvana.

In the Hindu faith, we will recall, the believer wishes to experience *moksha*, or a release from the Karma-Samsara cycle of rebirth, so that one's atman becomes merged with Ultimate Reality, or *Brahman*. The emphasis in Hindu accounts of nirvana is to experience moksha. In traditional Buddhism, however, the emphasis is on the elimination of desire, or the elimination of the Skandas.

For the Buddhist, the key to nirvana is the *Nir* part of the word, meaning "nothingness." So the ultimate goal in traditional Buddhism is to achieve a state of nothingness. In early Hinduism, on the other hand, particularly in the Theravada tradition, the emphasis was on the *Vana* part of the word nirvana. This part means "way," referring to the different "ways" in which salvation may be reached.

Thus, salvation is reached through moksha in classical Hinduism and in classical Buddhism by achieving a state of nothingness. A number of other ideas from Hinduism also survive in Buddhism. The Sanskrit/Pali word *dharma*, for example, is another category carried over from Hinduism to Buddhism, as is the idea of *maya*, or "illusion" in Sanskrit. We now will compare the two traditions on dharma and maya.

In Vedic times, the word *dharma* was thought of as an "unchanging universal law," similar to what we would call "Laws of Nature." Later, with the development of what we called the *Dharma Sutras*, the use of the word dharma had changed. It now implied the idea that dharma was a "duty," according to Vedic law.[489] The word appears simply to mean, "One's duty in Vedic society."[490]

The Pali word, *Dhamma*, or Dharma, has two distinct meanings in Buddhism. The first of these is that the word is synonymous with the teachings of the Buddha. In this respect, the word Dhamma may mean "Teachings," referring to the teachings of the religion's founder, Gautama Buddha. When this meaning of the word Dhamma is used, it is usually capitalized.[491]

The second meaning of the word dhamma in Pali is most often expressed in the lower case. It might be translated, "the way things are." In the Thailand version of Buddhism, the Thai expression, *thamma chart* is used. It comes from the words *dharma* and *charti*, which imply "nature," or "environment."[492]

In the Bhagavad Gita, or "The Song of God," there are several passages about the nature and extent of dharma. Krishna explains the idea of dharma means something like "the way of righteousness in sustaining the order of the universe." It implies that everyone has a path that they must follow. Of the three paths to salvation in early Hinduism, that is *yoga*, or ascetic practices; *bhakti*, or devotion; and *dharma*, or wholesome activities, the latter of the three is the most important.[493]

In Buddhism, the idea of dhamma was the main focus of the Buddha's meditations, beginning at the Bodhi Tree. The Buddhists believe that the Dhamma has five characteristics.

These may be summarized this way:

1. It is infinite and can be found in the material and spiritual worlds.
2. It should be thought of as a "mental sense." It is related to the mind.
3. It is a carrier of goodness.
4. It is a person's duty.
5. It is a permanent universal truth.[494]

It was through the Buddha's early meditations that he sought to understand the true meaning of Dhamma. It was from his teachings that Gautama thought the common man could know the Dhamma.[495]

As we have shown in the chapter on Hinduism, the Sanskrit word *maya* was employed to describe anything that was illusory or false. In most forms of Buddhism, like in Tibetan Buddhism, for example, the word for maya is *Sgyu*, a word that implies "deceit."[496] In Mahayana Buddhism, as well, the word is used to describe anyone who pretends to be something he or she is not.

In Hinduism, then, *maya* is anything that is illusory, like an oar that looks bent in a lake. In Buddhism, *Sagu* is always a term that refers to humans and to their characters. In Pali, *Sagu* is a noun. In Sanskrit, on the other hand, *Maya* is only used as an adjective, always modifying a human being.

One final idea in the faith of Hinduism that carries over into Buddhism is the notion of the personification of evil and death. In traditional Hinduism, this figure is known as *Namuci*. In the Vedas, Namuci is synonymous with "Destroyer," and "Death."[497] There is an *Asura Namuci*. In Indian mythology, Namuci is a friend of the god Indra, who "remains unsubdued and indomitable after Indra has fought with his fellows. So great is his bond between Indra and Namuci that Indra promises never to kill him."[498]

Despite the pact between the two, Indra twists off the head of Namuci with "the foam of the waters at the half-light of dawn." Indra had promised Namuci that he would not be subject to death in the day, nor at night.[499] From that point on, Namuci becomes the personification of death and destruction in Vedic Hinduism.

The figure of Namuci in classical Hinduism has an analog in a demon named *Mara*. He, too, is a mythological figure responsible for death and destruction. Most of the Buddhist traditions contain a tale in which the demon Mara attempts to dissuade the Buddha from reaching Enlightenment. In most of these, Mara attempts to dissuade Gautama with three of his beautiful daughters, with no success. We will say more about this tale of the Buddha and the demon Mara, in the next section of this chapter. It is enough now, however, to point out that Buddhism adopted the Hindu idea of a personification of death and destruction.

This brings us to the central section of this fifth chapter on Buddhism, in which we will introduce and discuss many of the answers and responses to the phenomena of evil and suffering to be found in the Buddhist faith.

Evil and Suffering in the Buddhist Faith

Before we begin our analysis of evil and suffering in the history of Buddhism, we must make some preliminary remarks. First, unlike many of the other traditions in this study, Buddhism's answers and responses to evil and suffering cannot be expressed in terms of the categories we have introduced back in Chapter One. Secondly, unlike the other faiths, for the most part, Buddhism does not make a distinction between the sacred and the profane.

For the Buddhists, the world is not divided into sacred and profane. Everything is composed of, and consequently interdependent upon, everything else. Therefore, there is nothing that exists outside the "all of it." In Buddhist cosmology, evil and good are always co-dependent. They are conjoined, and they inform each other. In this sense, we might say that early Buddhism assented to what we have labeled the "Contrast View" back in the opening chapter of this study.

Thirdly, in the Buddhist faith—particularly among the Mahayana tradition—there is far more emphasis on the place of ancestor and ancestor worship than in any faith we have explored so far. Indeed, the lives of the ancestors in Buddhism often have repercussions for the life of the living.

With these preliminary remarks in mind, there are, nevertheless, some general judgments in the Buddhist faith about the origins of evil and suffering. First, the negative actions and beliefs of human beings such as greed, anger, and ignorance, are the major causes of evil and suffering in the world. It is these three things that keep the Buddhist believer from reaching Enlightenment.

The Buddhist believes that greed, anger and ignorance in the world often lead to more greed, anger and ignorance. Suffering is a natural part of life. When the Buddha left his family's palace to see the world, the three things he encountered next were an old man, a very sick man and a dead person. This was the first time in Gautama's life that he had seen suffering. The first of the "Three Sights," as they are known, taught the Buddha that many painful experiences are the result of unsatisfied desires.[500]

The second of the three sights taught Gautama that suffering is often caused by constant change.[501] Even when people are not immediately suffering, they often are unsatisfied because they are not yet Enlightened. For the Buddha, this is the most fundamental truth about evil and suffering.

The Buddha taught that the immediate roots of all evil and suffering is desire. In Buddhist art, greed is often represented by a rooster. Ignorance is often shown as a pig. The snake in Buddhist art is often depicted as a snake.[502]

The Buddha believed that it is possible to bring an end to suffering. In fact, Gautama was a living example that it is possible in one human lifetime, and this is, ultimately, what all Buddhists strive for. Someone who reaches Enlightenment is full of compassion and love for all living things. In this state, desire has disappeared.[503] The *Ayacanna Sutra*, or "The Request," sums up much of these fundamental beliefs of Buddhism. It tells us:

> This Truth that I have realized is profound, hard to see, hard
> to realize, harmless sophisticated, more than just specula-
> tion, subtle, and only really understood by the wise. But this
> present generation takes delight in attachment, is excited by
> it, enjoys it. For a generation like this, it is really hard to un-
> derstand how things arise in attachment and dependence of
> each other. It is also really hard to understand the calming of
> all fabrications, the rejection of all attachments to rebirth, the
> destruction of craving, dispassion, cessation, nirvana.[504]

In Buddhism, because *kamma*, the Pali word for karma, is inextricable from the categories of good and evil. Many Buddhist scholars prefer to replace the words good and evil with *Kusala* and *akusala*, or "healthy," and "unhealthy." Things that are Kusala are not always considered things to be good. Something that is akusala may not always be understood as evil things. For example, depression, melancholy, sloth and distraction, are akusala, but they exist in the mind. In this sense, the Buddhist tradition recognizes the three-part distinctions among natural, moral, and metaphysical evils introduced back in Chapter One of this study.

Among most schools of Buddhism, scholars point to four separate connotations for the word *Kusala*, derived from the Commentaries. These are known as:

1. Arogya
2. Anavajja
3. Kosalasambhuta
4. Sukhavipaka[505]

The first of these indicates that the Buddhist wishes to be free of sickness and to maintain physical and mental health. The word *Anavajja* means "unstained." This means the mind must be freed from things that may sully it. The third connotation mentioned above for the word Kusala pertains to the fact that Kusala thoughts must be intelligent and wise.[506] And Sukhavipaka might be called the "reward of well-being" that leads to a state of contentment and the possibility of Enlightenment.[507]

On the other hand, the conditions of the Akusala often arise in particular human situations. These are sexual desire, ill will toward others, sloth and torpor, restlessness and anxiety, doubt, anger, jealousy, and avarice. These attributes make the mind spiteful, oppressive and damage the quality of the mind. Anger stirs up the mind in such a way that it may affect physical health.[508]

In regard to the ideas of Kusala and Akusala, Buddhist scholars point out the role of intentions in moral discourse in Buddhism. Gautama spoke of the idea of making sure that one's moral intentions are in line with one's true moral values. In fact, Buddhist scholar Sylvia Boorstein remarks that "Right intentions is the key to the Buddha's Eight-Fold Path."[509] In Western philosophy, the importance of intentions in moral discourse goes all the way back to Aristotle and his *Nicomachean Ethics*.[510] Precisely the same idea, however, was suggested by the Buddha two hundred years before the Athenian philosopher.

Renowned Tibetan teacher Nyoshul Khenpo Rinpoche also wrote about the importance of intentions in moral discourse. He relates, "nothing happens without intentions. They are so crucial."[511] Rinpoche (1932–1999) was a revered Tibetan master who wrote extensively on matters connected to Buddhist ethics.[512]

Three other places where the Buddhist tradition has said something about the causes and meanings of evil and suffering are in relationships to the demonic in Buddhism, to ancestor worship, and to the connection to Karma-Samsara in Buddhism. We now turn to these three phenomena and their relation to evil and suffering in Buddhism.

Ancestor Worship in Buddhism

In the Far East, ancestor worship or ancestor veneration has been practiced for thousands of years. It most likely began in China and then spread to Japan, Vietnam, Laos, Thailand, Cambodia and much of the Far East. In many contemporary Chinese homes, they participate in family traditions elated to funeral rites and survival after death rituals. Often on the 49th or 100th day after the passing of the Chinese individual, grave-cleaning and annual death celebrations are still conducted in China.[513]

Often in Chinese homes, there are ancestral tablets engraved with the names of dead ancestors. Every day, many Chinese children offer a bowl of rice, fruit and cups of tea in honor of their ancestors.

In contemporary Japan, similar rituals may be found. In most Japanese homes, it is common to see a *Butsudan*, a Japanese Buddhist altar, in a corner of the house. A cup of tea often can be found on the altar, as well as a bowl of rice and some fruit. Japanese Buddhists believe that when death occurs, the person takes on the form of a *Hotoke*, an ancestor worthy of worship.[514]

The Japanese also conduct what is known as the *Bon* Festival, an annual ritual to commemorate the dead ancestors, usually in July or August. It is now a kind of family reunion holiday during which people return to ancestral family graves and clean them so that the ancestors will continue to visit the household altars mentioned earlier. The Japanese call an ancestral spirit a *Kami*, a being that could protect one's descendants in the same way that parents protect their children.

We introduce these Chinese and Japanese practices because believers in both places maintain that the ancestors may bring defilement and curses to the living descendants. Thus, worshipping the dead to guard against these spirit curses is a common practice in both China and Japan, even today.[515] In some parts of Japanese culture, the word *Kiryo* is employed to refer to a spirit that leaves the body of a living person and subsequently haunts other people or places, often some distance away.[516]

The Kiryo is also sometimes called a *Shoryo* and is believed to have the capacity to bring sickness, death or disability to the living, sometimes to their own descendants. This category is important for our purposes because many Chinese and Japanese people believe that these ancestors who are worshipped may be the cause of natural disasters, like floods and landslides, as well as metaphysical evils like dread and anxiety.[517]

During the Edo period of Japan, there was a belief in a condition called *Rikonbyo*, or in Japanese, "soul-separation," in which it was believed that the soul separated from the body and then could assume the shape and appearance of an animal.[518] Another condition in the period was known as *Kage no yamai*, or "shadow sickness," in which, because of curses from the ancestors, a person may become seriously ill.[519] Sometimes these curses last generations, a kind of familial Retributive Justice, which we have described back in Chapter One of this study.

In more modern times, the practice of ancestor worship is on the decline in China and Japan. Many modern believers have given up the importance of these rituals. Funerals in China and Japan are given far less attention to funeral rites than was given in earlier ages. Nevertheless, one way to explain the origins of certain forms of evil in the Far East is related to the idea of ancestor worship.

The Korean version of the Bon Festival is known as *Baekjung*. Participants present offerings at Buddhist shrines and temples, and often masked dances are performed to ward off the effects and curses of the ancestors.[520]

In Vietnam, there is a great separation between the worlds of the living and the dead. When a person dies, his soul will be led to the realm called *Yin*, which is invisible to those in the land of the living. It is believed, however, that the soul lingers for a while at the grave of the dead person. Afterward, it travels to Yin. In Vietnam, it is believed that ancestors can protect their descendants, as well as the possibility of bringing evil and suffering to them.[521]

In Japan today, one company, Nihon Jujutsu Kenkyu Jukikai, which began over thirty years ago, offers a service to remove the curses of the ancestors, ranging in prices—depending on the nature of the curse, from ten thousand yen to three hundred thousand yen. The price also depends on the skill set of the practitioner and the level of the curse being administered.[522] This brings us to an analysis of our second cause in Buddhism of some examples of and causes of evil—the demonic.

The Demonic as a Source of Evil in Buddhism

Earlier in this chapter, we pointed out that one of the theological ideas that Buddhism inherited from Hinduism is the notion of the demonic. We also indicated that Gautama Buddha was believed to have been tempted while under the Bodhi Tree by three lovely daughters of the demon named *Kara* in the Buddhist Pali scriptures.

Scholar Gail Hinich Sutherland in her essay "Demons and the Demonic in Buddhism," begins her article this way:

> In contrast to Western representations of the demonic, the "demons" of Asia are primarily the powerful, ancient spirits of nature who require recognition and appeasement. Buddhism was more successful than any other missionary religion in making peace with the indigenous spirits.[523]

At first blush, it would appear that Ms. Sutherland was speaking of the practice of ancestor worship. But a little later in the same essay, she speaks of the "ultimate demon, Marra, who is a symbol of the inner demons of greed, aversion, and ignorance."[524] A few lines later, Sutherland remarks, "Those who are found lacking in these attributes have far more to fear from demons than those, like the Buddha, who has gained control over the ultimate demon, Mara."[525]

There are also a number of other demonic figures in Buddhism who are also symbols of greed, aversion and ignorance. The Buddhist god, *Yama*, for example, is the god of the dead. He is a wrathful deity who has the power to determine whether one has been a good person in this life or whether he has not. In other words, if you want to achieve nirvana, it is important to be morally good in this life and in one's lives to come.[526]

Another demonic figure in Buddhism is known as *Mahakala*, who is the "Protector of Education." Mahakala is also known as the "Black Demon" and can be identified by how he holds his hands, in which may be found a skull and an ax.[527] Another Buddhist demon is known as *Kubera* or by the name *Vaisravana*. Legend has it that it took him a thousand years of good deeds to finally become a god. Vaisravana is known as the "God of Wealth" in Buddhism. In Buddhist art, he is often depicted with a round body and many pieces of precious jewelry that cover him.[528]

Hayagriva is another Buddhist demon. He represents the passions that lie at the heart of anger. He is the embodiment of what the Buddhists call "Fierce Energy." Among the Tibetans, this demon may aid believers in controlling their fiercest emotions. Hayagriva is sometimes referred to as the "Horse-Necked One," In art he usually has two heads, one human and the other equine.[529]

Another Buddhist demon goes by the name *Palden Lhamo*. She has the job of taking care of the king's shrine, protecting it from danger. There is also a lake in Tibet known as the Palden Lhamo. She is the protector of this lake, as well.[530] Another Buddhist demon is known as *Ekajati*. She is the most potent of female spirits. In art, she is recognized for having only one eye, one tooth and one breast. She spends most of her time "stomping on the inner egos of humans."[531]

Another female demon is the goddess of war. Her name is *Beg-tse*. She is mostly venerated in Tibet, where they pray to her through tantric meditative practices. She is usually associated with combat.[532] There is a host of other demons in Buddhism that include *Jikininki*, *Oni* and *Rakshasha*. The first of these was borrowed from Hinduism. The name means "flesh-eaters." The second, *Oni*, is an ogre-like demon in Japanese Buddhism, usually shown as a giant beast with brightly colored skin. Oni is an extremely nasty spirit. Oni is often said to be the cause of societal breakdowns, like the Japanese defeat in World War II, for example.[533]

Finally, the Rakshasas, like their Indian counterpart, are man-eating spirits from Hindu cosmology and mythology. The class of spirits is known to possess black magic. They have long, toxic fingernails. Most of this class are very clever spirits. Some Buddhist traditions suggest that the Rakshasas are responsible for earthquakes.[534]

The relationship between these demons and spirits listed here and human beings is not always very clear. Often, however, they are identified in two ways. The first is that these demons are often the causes of Natural Evils and of mental diseases and disorders. The other way these demons come into play in Buddhism is that they are often seen as reifications of the worst personality traits found in human beings.[535]

The brings us to the cycle of karma as a source in Buddhism for evil and suffering, the topic of our next section of this fifth chapter on the phenomena of evil and suffering in the Buddhist faith.

The Karmic Cycle as a Source for Evil in Buddhism

The idea of the karmic cycle being a cause of evil and suffering in the world for the Buddhists may be seen with an illustration from writer Dale DeBakcsy in an article entitled, "The Dark Side of Buddhism," published on January 23, 2013, in the journal the *New Humanist*. In the article, he tells us a tale after having worked for nine years in a Buddhist school.[536] Mr. DeBakcsy relates:

> At first glance, Karma is a lovely idea, which encourages people to be good even when nobody is watching, for the sake of happiness in a future life. It is a bit of a carrot-and-stickish thing, but so are a lot of ways in which we get people routinely not to beat us up and take our stuff.[537]

Then DeBakcsy gets to the narrative he wishes to tell us:

> I remember one student who was having trouble memorizing material for tests. Distraught, she went to the monks, who explained to her that she was having such trouble now because, in a past life, she had been a murderous dictator who burned books. And so now, in this life, she is doomed to forever be learning challenged.[538]

Mr. DeBakcsy adds, "Not, 'let's look at changing your study habits,' but rather, 'Oh, this is because you have the soul of book burning murderer.'"[539] In this tale, the explanation provided by the Buddhist monks at the school, the evil associated with the student's troubles is "caused" by the fact that she was a book-burning murderer in a previous life. When we speak of the karma cycle being a cause of evil and suffering in this life, we mean just such a scenario.

Mr. DeBakcsy describes other similar cause and effect scenarios in which one's actions in one life have repercussions for one's behavior and environment in this life. Another example he gives is a Buddhist nun who gave a speech about "coming back from a near-death experience" and then being relegated to live in a sewer subsisting on human excrement.[540]

Even as early as the Buddha himself, the founder remarked:

All living beings have actions [Karma], as their own, their inheritance, their congenital cause, their kinsman, their refuge. It is karma that differentiates beings into low and high states.[541]

Thus, the Buddha firmly believed that all of one's good and evil actions have good and moral effects in subsequent lives, or even in this life. This is true when someone embodies love and compassion, as well as when he or she acts from greed and ignorance. Either way, moral actions have their effects in moral ways.

In a 2007 article on karma and the problem of evil, scholars Monima Chadha and Nick Trakakis responded to an earlier essay in the same journal by Whitley R. Kauffman. In their essay, Chadha and Trakakis put forward the view that "Seemingly undeserved suffering may have been caused by past lives."[542] The pair also takes Kaufman to task mostly because they believe that he does not fully understand the relationship between karma and evil in the Buddhist tradition.[543]

Another way to see the connection between karma and evil and suffering in Buddhism is to look at another example. Imagine someone in an office setting who has been rude and domineering with other workers on the same rung of the corporate structure. He is unpleasant to all around him, including yourself. Do you take it personally and thereby only notice your own needs and dislikes? Or do you notice that the co-worker is expressing his own insecurities and his own discomfort, which may be the product of this life or some previous life?

The traditional Buddhist might say that in a former life, the man was a slave to a boss who always had his way, and now he is working out that karma. Or he might say that his behavior is a product of earlier behavior in this life where he treated someone else harshly. Either way, there is a cause-and-effect relationship between bad behavior now and previous bad behavior.[544] For generations in the Buddhist faith, believers have been of the opinion that evil and suffering in this life may well have been caused by evil and suffering in a previous life or lives.

The Buddhist faith is fond of calling karma a collection of acts, germinal seeds if you will, that later bear fruit. They often employ farming images to express the relationship of one life to the next, and perhaps, beyond. The *Samyutta Nikaya* states this relationship quite clearly. It tells us:

According to the seed that's sown
So is the fruit you reap there from.
The Doer of Good will gather Good.
Doer of Evil, Evil reaps.
Down is the seed that thou shall taste.
The fruit thereof.[545]

The Buddhist *Dhammapada* speaks specifically about the possibility of someone changing his karma. It relates, "Not in the sky, nor in mid-ocean, nor entering a mountain cave can there be found a place on Earth where one may escape from the consequences of evil deeds."[546] In Buddhism, evil deeds always bring evil consequences. If not in this life, then in a life to come. In traditional Buddhism, both evil and good consequences follow from good and evil actions in a past life or lives.

Thus, we have seen three separate sources in Buddhism for the existence of evil and suffering in this life—ancestor worship, the Influences of Demonic Forces, and the Law of Karma that one reaps what he or she sows. If we add the emphases we saw earlier in this chapter in "Intentions," and its relationship to the Free Will Defense, as well as the nod in the direction of the Contrast View, we now see that Buddhism appears to endorse:

1. The Free Will Defense
2. The Contrast View
3. Ancestor Worship
4. Demonic Influences Theory
5. The Karma-Samsara View

One final way in which we see Buddhist responses to evil and suffering in the contemporary world are the many ways that the faith responds to issues of social justice. This is the subject matter of the final section of Chapter Five.

Buddhism, Evil and Social Justice

A final way that Buddhist tradition engages in the phenomena of evil and suffering is what the faith has had to say about the issue of social justice over the centuries. Since Buddhism originally began as a heresy of Hinduism, the Buddha clearly spoke out against race and class distinctions and discrimination, as well. In his *Sutta Nipata*, Gautama specifically spoke about the status of the Brahmin, as well as the untouchables—the bottom rung of the Indian caste system. In that text, he wrote:

No Brahmin is such by birth.
Nor outcaste is such by birth.
An outcaste is such by his deeds.
A Brahmin is such by his deeds.[547]

The Pali word "outcaste" in this section is *varna*. It originally meant the "Dark Ones," that is, the "Untouchables." The Sanskrit word *varna* is a cognate of the English "varnish," or to make a piece of furniture "dark." From the beginning, then, Buddhism was against the idea of separating people into races or social classes.

Another prime feature of social justice is the Buddha's treatment of slaves. Gautama condemned slavery in every form. In fact, the Buddha was a "Pioneer of Abolition." He sketched out five ways that a master should serve his slaves or boss his employees. These five prescriptions were:

1. Work should be proportional to the worker's health.
2. Proper food and wages should be given to them.
3. Proper care should be taken when the slave/worker is sick.
4. Treats and luxuries should be given periodically.
5. Holidays should be given at due intervals.[548]

Even early on, the Buddha reasoned that the worker-slave should be treated as one would treat a member of his own family. The Buddha also was conscious, even early on, of the status of women. In fact, he gave women a place of honor. He was against the prevailing Brahmanic view of his time that only a son is indispensable for salvation. It is true that in the beginning, women were denied the possibility of being a Buddhist monk. Later, however, he instituted an order of nuns into the *Sangha*, or "Buddhist Community."

The major way that Gautama preached about battling social caste, slavery and discrimination against women was to follow the Eight-Fold Path. Modern-day Tibetan monk Geshe Phelgye in a lecture on social justice, speaks of, "Planting seeds in the minds of children, so they may lead to a peaceful world."[549] Geshe also speaks of the need to adopt an attitude of responsibility and not simply to "walk away from political and social turmoil. We must avoid the expression, 'I don't want to get involved.'"[550]

In the same lecture, Master Geshe related:

If we walk away from being involved in social justice issues, that only allows the corruption and greed of the world to spread.[551]

Master Geshe believes it is in spiritual practice that can empower a person to take a stand. "We need to use our mindfulness and our awareness of spiritual ethics to monitor the events of the world, and to speak out to those in power, even when there is a personal discomfort involved."[552] Above all, for Master Geshe, as well as other Buddhist authorities, we must follow the five Moral Precepts mentioned earlier in this fifth chapter. These were:

1. Abstain from taking any life.
2. Do not take anything that is not your own.
3. Abstain from sexual impropriety.
4. Abstain from any false speech.
5. Abstain from drugs and alcohol.[553]

These five precepts are applicable to every Buddhist and every member of society, as well. To give in to the cravings associated with these moral rules is the core of Buddhist ethics. However, it is with these precepts in which Buddhism may play a role in social change, both in the *Sangha* and in the society as a whole.

This brings us to the major conclusions of this fifth chapter. The subject matter of Chapter Six of this study of evil and suffering in the world's religions is the Chinese faith of Confucianism and its perspectives on evil and suffering.

Conclusions to Chapter Five

The main focus of this fifth chapter has been how the Buddhist faith has dealt with the issue of evil and suffering over the course of is history. We began the chapter with a very short introductory section on the origins and foundations of Buddhism. After making some remarks about the life of Gautama Buddha, we went on to elaborate on the most important ideas in the Buddhist faith.

Among these ideas were the Three Universal Truths, the Four Noble Truths and the Eight-Fold Path. We also enumerated in the first section of Chapter Five the five most important moral precepts of the Buddhist faith. Additionally, we spoke in the same section of the Buddhist scriptures, including the Three Baskets, the Suttas and the *Tibetan Book of the Dead*.[554]

In the second section of Chapter Five, we introduced and discussed a variety of theological and philosophical ideas that the Buddhist tradition has adopted and adapted from classical Hinduism. Among those ideas were views on the nature of the Self, the understanding of karma, the idea of *Khansha*, or Skandas, the notions of moksha and nirvana, the idea of maya, views on the demonic in the two faiths, and perspectives on the demonic in Hinduism and Buddhism.[555]

These two sections were followed by the central section of the fifth chapter, in which we discussed the primary ways that the history of Buddhism has responded to the issues of evil and suffering. Among those answers or responses we introduced in this central section was a version of the Contrast View and the possibility that some evil is caused by the process of ancestor worship in Buddhism.[556]

In the next section of this chapter, we examined many of the demonic figures that have appeared in the history of Buddhism. In addition to Mara, we also have cataloged a list and description for several other demons in the Buddhist faith. This list included Yama, Mahakala, Kubera, Hayagriva, Palden lhamo, Beg Tse, Ekajati, the god Oni, and the demons called the Rakshasas.[557]

In the fifth section of Chapter Five, we introduced the view that one way Buddhism explains the existence of evil and suffering in the world is through the karmic cycle. By using some observations and examples from Dale DeBakcsy, we have shown that one way of explaining evil and suffering in Buddhism has been that it is sometimes caused by behavior in previous lives.[558]

In the sixth and final section of Chapter Five, we showed some of the ways that the Buddhist tradition have responded to issues related to social justice issues—both in terms of the Buddha's perspectives, as well as the observations of one contemporary Tibetan master Geshe Phelgye, who showed his reliance on traditional Buddhist responses related to the Eight-Fold Path. We also have shown Master Geshe's observation that the Five Moral Precepts of Buddhism may be an avenue or entry into discussions of issues related to social justice in the world.[559]

In summary, then, we have suggested that the Buddhist tradition has mentioned or has assented to the following views:

1. The Free Will Defense with its emphasis on Intentions
2. The Contrast View
3. Evil caused by Ancestral Spirits
4. Evil caused by the Influences of Demonic Forces
5. Evil caused the Karma-Samsara Cycle of Rebirth

This brings us to Chapter Six, an exploration of responses and answers to the phenomena of evil and suffering in the Chinese religion that has come to be known as Confucianism.

Chapter Six: Evil and Suffering in Confucian Thought

The Chinese title Lunyu means "collate conversations." Most modern scholars now believe that *The Analects* had been brought together over a period that lasted over the course of two or three centuries.

—*The Analects*, translation by Robert Eno

The Tao is not the name for a thing, but an underlying natural order of the universe whose ultimate essence is difficult to explain.

—Lao Tzu, *The Tao Te Ching*

Our greatest glory is not in never falling, but in the rising every time we fall.

—Kung Fu Tzu, *The Essential Writings of Confucianism*

Introduction

The purpose of this sixth chapter is to explore the movement and belief system known as Confucianism, a term developed in the eighteenth century by Jesuit missionaries in China.[560] By nearly all accounts, Confucianism is not a religion. Rather, it is a system of ethical living. For the Confucian, the collective—the family, the state, the nation—are far more important than the individual. In that sense, Confucianism is much more about ethics and ethical behavior than about metaphysics and theological speculation.

We will begin this sixth chapter with some general observations about the life of the movement's founder, Kung Fu Tzu, or Confucius, as well as his writings. We also will make some comments in the first two sections of the sacred places and personages in the Confucian faith. This will be followed by a description of a group of central beliefs of the believers in Confucianism, again, primarily about moral matters.

These two sections will be followed by the central section of Chapter Six, in which we will explore what Confucius, mostly in his *Analects*, has had to say about the phenomena of evil and suffering. In the final section of Chapter Six, we will make some observations about the Confucian system of beliefs. We move next, then, to the life and times of Confucius.

The Life and Times of Confucius

We must begin by pointing out that not a lot is known about the life of Confucius. His traditional dates are usually given as 551 BCE until around 479 BCE. His birth and his death both came in the Chinese state of Lu. His father was a soldier. His name was Kong He. He died when his son was three years old, at least according to tradition.[561] We do know that it is likely that Kung Fu Tzu spent his childhood living in poverty, since he was raised by his mother. It was rare at the time for Chinese women to work outside the home.[562]

Confucius' father was an important aid to a major aristocratic family, the ruling power holders in the Lu dynasty. Shortly before his birth, the family of Confucius relocated to the north of China. Because his wife had produced no progeny to continue his line, Kong He took on a concubine named Zou. It was she who gave birth to Kung Fu Tzu. Confucius' father died three years later, as indicated earlier.

Nevertheless, Confucius' family was part of a growing middle class called the *Shi*, who were not nobility but were above the lot of the common people, or peasant class. Confucius was of the belief, however, that people should be evaluated on what they say and do rather than their station in life. In early adulthood, Confucius worked a number of jobs, including being a shepherd and a clerk. Eventually, he came to work for the governor of his state of Lu, where he was among the leader's advisors.

The state of Lu prided itself with the fact that their lineage of its rightful Lords, the Dukes of Lu, had begun with the famous brother of the Zhou dynasty founder, the Duke of Zhou. The Zhou dynasty lasted for eight hundred years, from 1046 BCE until 256 BCE. It was in this dynasty that Confucius was born. Under the Zhou, culture flourished. The written Chinese language was codified, coinage came into use, and chopsticks became in use at meals.[563]

We know that Confucius was married at the age of nineteen and that he had one son whose name was Kong Li. We know little else about his married life beyond the fact that later on, he split with his wife—something highly unusual at the time— and that his son came to live with him after the break of the marriage.[564]

At the same time, Confucius began to develop his own philosophical system of living. This system did not become popular until long after his death when it became the basic philosophy of Chinese culture for over two thousand years.

Confucius' mastery of Zhou dynasty culture allowed him to become a teacher of young aristocrats of the day. Because of his associations with his students that allowed Confucius to secure his position in the state of Lu government.

In later life, Confucius quit his government job at the age of fifty-one. He was disappointed that the governor was no longer listening to his opinions. He then set out and traveled throughout China, teaching his philosophy to others. Eventually, some of his followers began to write down his ideas and principles. These were later to be called the *Analects*.[565] Confucius died around 479 BCE of natural causes. In his final years, he returned to his hometown of *Qufu* in Lu, spending most of his time still instructing his students.

Confucius' philosophy became the State philosophy during the Han dynasty. His teachings also became the basis of the Chinese Civil Service exam. The leaders of China adopted the system of Confucius because it put great emphasis on respect for authority and a centralized government. The Han dynasty was known as the "Golden Age" of China, with a prolonged period of stability and prosperity.[566] During the Han, China's territory was extended to what we now consider China proper. The Silk Road opened during the Han dynasty allowing China to connect to peoples to their west. This brought trade, foreign cultures, and Buddhism, among other things, to China.

The Han dynasty lasted from 206 BCE until 220 CE, making it one of the longest dynasties. Confucian thought was established as the official belief system in China during the time of Emperor Han Wudi, who ruled from 141 to 86 BCE.[567] *The Analects* also became the official state text during the time of the Han dynasty.

Scholar Robert Eno provides an introduction to *The Analects* of Confucius. He tells us:

> The Analects of Confucius is an anthology of brief passages that possess the words of Confucius and his disciples, describes Confucius as a man, and recount some of the events of his life. This book may have begun as a collection of Confucius' immediate disciples soon after their Master's death in 479 BCE. In traditional China, it was believed that its content was immediately assembled at that time, and that it was an accurate record.[568]

Professor Eno goes on to add:

> The Chinese title, *Lunyu*, means "collated conversations." Most modern scholars now believe that the Analects had been brought together over a period that lasted over the course of two or three centuries." Eno goes on to compare the development of the *Analects* to the "biblical Gospels, in which the text bears some resemblance," the Analects offers an "evolving record of the image of Confucius and his ideas through the changing standpoints of various branches of the school of thought he founded."

In the classical era of China, texts were recorded on thin strips of bamboo using brush and ink. One could fit about a dozen Chinese characters on each strip. Holes were drilled in the strips so they could be bound together by a string. Each large bundle became a "book." *The Analects*, composed of about five hundred independent passages, is divided into twenty of these books.[569]

The strips of Chinese texts were often arranged according to content or author. Other texts seem to have originated independently. The order of these strips and books seems to have been disrupted over time, either by disarrangement or the adding of strips later on to existing texts. Scholarly consensus now maintains that books sixteen to twenty of *The Analects* are very late additions.[570]

In terms of the subject matter of the books of *The Analects*, the following summary may be helpful:

Book I. An overall introduction
Book II. General issues of Governance
Book III. General issues of Ritual
Book IV. Discussion of Character
Book V. Discussion of Disciples and Historical Figures
Book VI. More on Disciples and Historical Figures
Book VII. On Confucius
Book VIII. Miscellaneous
Book IX. A version of Book VII
Book X. A portrait of ritualized perfection
Book XI. Comments on Disciples
Book XII. Issues of Governance
Book XIII. More issues on Governance
Book XIV. Theme of Reclusion
Book XV. A broad collection
Book XVI. Dominated by Lists of Numbers for Various Things
Book XVII. Re-imagining political Life in future
Book XVIII. Reclusion and Taoism
Book XIX. The Sayings of Disciples
Book XX. An Appendix[571]

The *Analects*, or *Lun Yu* in classical Chinese, is part of what is known as the "Four Books." These, along with the "Five Classics," are the principal texts in Confucian philosophy. The "Five Classics," or *Wu Jing*, are the following:

I. *Shu Ching*: The Classic of History. This is a collection of documents and speeches dating from the Late Han

Dynasty (23 to 220CE).

II. *Shih Ching*: The Classic of Odes. A collection of 300 poems
     and songs from the Early Chou Dynasty (1027–402
     BCE).

III. *I Ching*: The Book of Changes. Collection of texts on
     divination based on sixty-four hexagrams.

IV. *Ch'un Ching*: Spring and Autumn Annals. Extracts from the
     history of the state of Lu (722–484) said to be compiled
     by Confucius.

V.   *Li Ching*: Classic of Rites. Three books on *Li*, or Propriety.[572]

The "Four Books," on the other hand, of which *The Analects* is
one, are the following:

I.   The *Lin Yu*, or "Analects." These are the sayings of
     Confucius.

II. The *Chung Yung*, or "Doctrine of the Mean."

III. The *Ta Hsueh*, or "The Great Learning."

IV. The *Meng Tzu*, or "Book of Mencius."[573]

These are the holy books of Confucian philosophy. Of these,
the *Lun Yu*, or *Analects*, has been the most revered in the history of
Confucianism. It was not actually written by Confucius. Rather, it
was compiled by his students after his death, members of the second
generation of the movement. This brings us to the most important
sacred places and personages in Confucianism, our next topic.

Sacred Places and Persons in Confucianism

There are several sacred places in the Confucian faith. Among these
are the temple to Confucius, the cemetery where he and his family are
buried, the Kong family estate, and the house of Confucius in the state
of Lu. The Confucian Temple is in the city of Nanjing.[574] It became a
model for subsequent temples. Originally, they were used for worship.
Later, in places like Vietnam and China, they were used to administer
imperial examinations. Many of these early Confucian temples
also had schools. In this sense, they were often called "Temples of
Literature."[575]

These temples date back as far as the Tang dynasty. They usually had a front gate and either a pair or three courtyards. One temple in Qufu, China, had nine "halls" or great rooms. Each of these Confucian temples also had a shrine dedicated to the founder. Ritual dancing was performed in many of these temples, as well as offering sacrifices to the spirit of the dead Confucius.[576]

The cemetery of Confucius is also in the town of Qufu, in China's Shandong Province. The cemetery holds the remains of the founder, some of his disciples, and, of course, many of his family members. Since 1994, the cemetery has been a UNESCO World Heritage Site, alongside The Temple of Confucius and the Kong family mansion. The Kong family estate is also located in Shandong. Most of the surviving buildings of the estate are from the Qing and the Ming dynasties.

The Kong family took on a number of responsibilities like ceremonies honoring the ancestors, as well as the harvests. The Kong estate still has 152 buildings, with 1,480 rooms and a living area of 134,200 square feet.[577]

In addition to Kung Fu Tzu, the tradition recognizes two other holy leaders. These are Mencius (371–289 BCE) and Xun Zi (313–230 BCE). The former is considered the second most important Confucian thinker and philosopher. During his life, however, he was far more influential than Confucius himself, mostly because he taught generations of Confucian scholars.[578]

In contrast to Mencius, Xun Zi taught that human nature was basically evil, a Chinese version of Original Sin Theory. Xun Zi believed that humans were wayward from birth but that sophisticated teachers could cultivate the moral virtues through intense training. He argued for very swift laws governing human behavior.[579]

This brings us to a summary and discussion of the central ideas to be found in the thought of Kung Fu Tzu in general, and in *The Analects*, in particular—the subject matter of the next section of this sixth chapter.

Principal Ideas in Confucius and The Analects

This section will describe and discuss a dozen or so major ideas in the philosophy of Confucianism, mostly found in *The Analects*. We will list these ideas here and then speak of them one at a time. These ideas are:

1. Ren
2. Junzi
3. Dao/Tao
4. Li
5. Tian
6. De
7. Wen
8. Yi
9. Zhong
10. Xin
11. Jing
12. Xiao
13. Yong

The concept of *Ren* in classical Chinese thought is one of the most difficult to narrow down in terms of its meaning. In several places in *The Analects*, Confucius' disciples try to get the master to define what he means by *Ren*, with no success in doing so. The word *Ren*, pronounced "wren," is a kind of comprehensive word for ethical virtue, benevolence, or goodness, though a better translation might be "humanness" or "humanity."[580]

The Chinese character that makes up the word *Ren* has two parts. One part is the normal character for a human being, and the other part is two horizontal strokes that stand for the number "two." So, the idea of *Ren* has the feeling of being together with others—that is, a human being together with other human beings in a family or in society.[581]

The Chinese term *Junzi* is often used to denote an ideally ethical, as well as capable person. It sometimes refers to a person who holds power in a society. This is the original sense of *Junzi*. In many translations, the *Junzi* is translated as "Gentleman," or *Chun-Tzu*. He is the ideal person in Confucianism. In terms of education, the *Junzi* is a generalist who learns broad principles that govern the correct behavior in many circumstances.[582]

The *Dao*, or *Tao*, is a word related to having a certain teaching skill in some area of art or skill. The word *Dao* literally means a "way" or a "path," or even a "route." Sometimes it more loosely means a "doctrine" or a "principle." The *Dao* means the natural order of things. In Confucianism, it is not the name of a thing; it is the conceptual knowledge that cannot be grasped. It is the natural principle on which the universe continues to run.[583]

In the *Tao Te Ching*, Lao Tzu explains that "The Tao is not the name for a thing. But an underlying natural order of the universe whose ultimate essence is difficult to explain."[584] The word *Tao* lends itself to the naming of a religious movement called *Taoism*, which we shall discuss in Chapter Seven of this study.[585] The concept of *Li* is another Chinese idea difficult to define. It pertains to the ritual settings of the Zhou dynasty of which Kung Fu Tzu was a master. *Li*, pronounced "lee," is the name of a series of behaviors that requires certain behaviors in any social setting. It means something like "propriety."[586] In that sense, it also means what we call "etiquette."

The idea of *Tien* is perhaps the most difficult of these concepts to understand. It has the basic meaning of "Sky." It later designated a Supreme Being, often translated as "Heaven." Sometimes in *The Analects*, Tien is described as having anthropomorphic attributes. At other times, Tien seems to mean a "natural force."[587] Sometimes the expression *Tianming* is employed in Chinese thought. It means something like "The Mandate of Heaven," in which Heaven confers a mandate on a particular emperor, a *Tianzi*, or a "Son of Heaven."[588]

The idea of the "Mandate of Heaven" arose in Chinese society during the Zhou dynasty. The mandate's efficiency was believed to be based on the moral behavior of the emperor who possesses it. He was expected to lead a life filled with *Li* and *Yi*, a word that means "righteousness," as well as *Ren*, or benevolence. If the emperor had an immoral life or he acted as a dictator, Confucius suggested in Book XII of the *Analects* that he had lost his mandate and should no longer rule.[589]

The notion of *De* in *The Analects* is another idea hard to nail down. It was originally related to what we would call "Charisma," deriving from power and gift-giving. Later, it developed into a moral term that might be called "self-possession" or "self-realization," regarding the Moral Order. The word *De* is sometimes written as *Te*, such as in the *Tao Te Ching*. It was originally connected to the verbal form of *De*, which meant "to grab" or "to get." It is best to translate *De* as "contagious virtue," the kind of virtue that the *Junzi* can share with others.

Some time in the history of China, *De* came to mean the power by which men are ruled by the power of moral example. *De* was also used in discussions of ruling in Chinese government, where *De* refers to the fact that the best moral characteristic of a Chinese ruler, as Confucius says in the *Analects*, is his "Honesty." Truthfulness, for Confucius, was the most important of all virtues.[590]

Others translate *De* as an "inner power" or even "inner moral power," through which a person may positively influence others. Most modern interpreters simply translate *De* as "virtue," but that rendering would seem to fall short of the original intended meaning.[591] The classical Chinese word *Wen* is most often part of a conceptual pair along with *Wu*. These words come from the name of two emperors, King Wen and King Wu. The term *Wen* in modern times denotes features of a civilization or group that are peculiar to them. The term *Wen* was extensively used during the Zhou dynasty.[592]

In Confucian thought, the word *Yi* is often used as a companion to *Ren*. *Yi* is most often translated as "right" or "righteousness." *Yi* is almost always used in moral discourses where the topic of conversation is often how to behave. *Yi* is a moral disposition to do the Good. It is also a necessary condition for doing *Ren* in the Superior Man, or *Junzi*. Similarly, the word *Chih* is a kind of moral wisdom that is only known intuitively, at least according to Confucius. Some Chinese scholars compare the idea of *Chih* to what Freud called the "Super-Ego" or Plato's spirited element of his notion of the soul.[593]

Zhong is a classical Chinese word found many times in *The Analects*. The English word "loyalty" comes closest to the Chinese meaning. It is an attempt to align the self with the interests of others or with a social group. The word *Zhang* is also sometimes combined with *yong* to get the expression *Zhongyang*, or the "Doctrine of the Mean." It is a core idea among Confucians. It is quite like the same idea in Aristotle's *Ethics*. The Doctrine of the Mean in China meant that it is better to adhere to the idea of moderation in most activities, such as in eating, drinking or dancing, for example.[594]

The Confucian term *Xin* is found throughout *The Analects*. It means something like "faithfulness." It derives from a word that means "promise-keeping," meaning reliability in what one promises to others. Some also translate *Xin* as "trustworthiness." This is an unwavering dedication to what one has promised.[595]

The Confucian word *Jing* is derived from the idea of alertness. It is mostly used among Confucians when a boss or master wishes to make sure his followers are paying close attention. Some translators rendered *Jing* as "respectfulness."[596] One of the most important of these Confucian ideas is the notion of *Hsaio*, a word that is usually translated as "Filial Piety." The word is most often employed in *The Analects* to refer to the proper behavior toward one's parents.[597]

This idea of *hsaio*, or "Filial Piety," is related to all five of the primary relationship in Confucian thought. Those are:

1. Ruler and Ruled
2. Father and Son
3. Husband and Wife
4. Elder Brother and Younger Brother
5. Friend to Friend[598]

In each of these relationships, there is a hierarchy in which one submits to the other, the people to the ruler, the wife to her husband, the son to the father, the younger brother to the older brother, etcetera. Also, in each of these relationships is the keys to the proper moral behavior to whom he is submitting. In other words, the ruler demands from his people only what is good. Parents only demand of their children what is good for the children, as well as for the family as a whole.

So, when it comes to a properly designed society, at least according to Confucius, people find themselves in these fundamental relationships and their roles in those relationships are prescribed. Moreover, people at the top of the hierarchy care for those beneath them as a good parent takes care of his or her children. All the relations under Filial Piety should be understood in terms of *Hsaio*.

In *The Analects*, Confucius says each of these relationships should be characterized by respect and loyalty. He says, "even to the point of worship." Finally, the Confucian idea known as *Yong* was predominantly used in times of warfare. During what is called the "Warring States Period," for example, the concept of *Yong* was frequently used. The classical Chinese word is best translated as "Valor" or "Bravery."[599]

In *The Analects*, Kong Fu Tzu mostly employs the term *Yong* to refer to incessant warfare, bold warriors and adventures that required an inordinate amount of courage. On occasions in *The Analects*, Master Kong also points out that sometimes his followers may be required to display the attribute of *Yong*. In several places in *The Analects*, Confucius is asked if the *Junzi*, or Superior Man, should esteem *Jong*, or valor. In Book XVII, for example, a follower named Tsze-Lu asked Master Kong this question.[600] The answer that Confucius gives his student is this:

> The Superior Man should hold righteousness to be of the highest importance. A man in a superior situation, having valor without righteousness, will be guilty of insubordination. One of the lower people having valor without righteousness will commit robbery.[601]

This same exchange between Confucius and Tsze-Lu is repeated several times in *The Analects*, and in each time, the master points out that the attribute of *Yong* to be far less important than some of the other moral attributes.

In another place in *The Analects*, at Book XV, 23, Master Kong is asked by his student Zi Gong, "Is there one word that can serve as a principle for the conduct of life?" Confucius replied, "Perhaps the word reciprocity. Do not do to others what you would not want others to do to you."[602] The word for reciprocity in this passage is the classical Chinese term *Huhui*, another expression that means the same thing in the term *Dao Yi* that combines two of the ideas discussed earlier in this section of Chapter Six.

It is significant, however, to point out that the Chinese master, Kung Fu Tzu, had a version of the Golden Rule, even if it was a negative form of it, five hundred years before the version in the New Testament at the Gospel of Matthew 7:12.[603] This brings us to the third and central section of Chapter Six, in which we will explore the many places in his

Analects where Chinese philosopher Confucius mentions or discusses the ideas of good and evil.

Good and Evil in Confucius' Analects

In *The Analects*, Confucius makes three different kinds of comments about evil and suffering. First, there are those remarks when he speaks about human nature and how the individual is to deal with evil. The second variety of comments on evil in *The Analects* are very general remarks when he refers to the phenomena of evil and suffering. Finally, there are the places in *The Analects* where the Chinese philosopher gives answers or responses to evil and suffering that look like some of the views outlined in the opening chapter of this study.

In fact, as we shall see later in this section of Chapter Six, Confucius comes close to what we have labeled the Contrast View, the Retributive Justice Theory, the Test Theory, and the Influences of Demonic Forces Perspective. Before we go there, however, let us first turn to the other two varieties of comments on evil and suffering in *The Analects*. In terms of the very general comments, Confucius says things like, "Attack the Evil that is within yourself, rather than attacking the Evil in others." Master Kung remarks in another section of *The Analects,* "If a man sets his heart on benevolence, then he will be free of all evil."[604]

In another general comment on evil in *The Analects*, Confucius remarks, "Heaven [*Tien*] sends down its good and evil symbols, and wise men act accordingly." In another general remark about good and evil, Master Kung advises one to "Return Good for Good, and return Evil with Justice."[605]

Finally, in another general comment about good and evil, Confucius tells us this:

> The small man thinks that small acts of goodness are of no benefit, and does not do them; and that small deeds of evil do no harm, and he does not refrain from them. Hence, his wickedness becomes so great that it cannot be concealed.
> And his guilt is so great that it cannot be pardoned.[606]

In many other passages in *The Analects*, Master Kung either speaks about evil and human nature, or he provides some moral advice on how to deal with evil and suffering. We see one example of the latter, when Confucius says, "The man who searches for Evil must first look at his own reflection."[607] In another piece of advice, Master Kung advises, "Rate the task above the prize, and will not the mind be raised? Fight your own faults, not the faults of others. Then Evil will be mended."[608] In a similar remark from *The Analect,* the master advises:

> The mind of the Noble Man seeks to achieve the Good in others and not their own Evil. The little-minded man is the reverse of this.

Confucius also comments about evil when he relates:

> If out of all the three hundred songs I know and I had to take one line to personify my teachings, I would say instead, 'Let there be no Evil in your thoughts.

In another passage from *The Analects,* Master Kung tells us this about good and evil, "When you find Good in yourself, approve of it with determination. When you find Good within yourself, despise it in the most detestable way." Confucius was of the opinion that, "To see and listen to the wicked is already the beginning of wickedness.[609]

In several other aphorisms in *The Analects,* Master Kung makes comments that seem to be connected to the many theories sketched out in Chapter One of this study. Consider this comment that looks very much like the Contrast Theory:

> Yin and Yang, male and female, strong and weak, rigid and tender, Heaven and Earth, light and darkness, thunder and lightning, cold and warmth, Good and Evil... The interplay of opposite principles constitutes the universe.[610]

At times in *The Analects,* Confucius makes some remarks that remind us of Retributive Justice Theory, such as this observation, "There are those who say repay evil with kindness. But I ask, 'How then are we to repay kindness?' And I say, 'Repay kindness with more kindness, but repay Evil with Justice.'" The Master again comes close to Test Theory when he relates, "The gem cannot be polished without friction, nor man perfected without trials."[611]

In another book of *The Analects*, Master Kung again turns his attention to thoughts about evil and some advice. He observes:

> Riches and honors are what everyone desires, but if they only can be gained by doing Evil, they must not be held. Don't worry about not being in office. Worry about qualifying yourself for office. Don't worry that no one knows you, but seek to worry about being known.[612]

As in the Buddhist faith, believers in Confucian philosophy, at least early on, also practiced ancestor worship or veneration, as well as a belief in spirits and demons. In fact, there is one tradition among the Confucians that there was one area of life that "The Master Would Not Discuss."[613] This was the realm of spirits and demons. Indeed, there is a text that goes by that name. It first appeared in the eighteenth century CE. It was in sharp contrast to the prevailing Confucian orthodoxy, both at the time and in the ancient world.[614]

The text in question contains 746 tales of themes related to ghosts, sex, demons, revenge, homosexuality, betrayal, transvestism and spirits. These stories were collected over a lengthy period. The sources included oral accounts, official gazettes and other accounts and collections. In this collection, the supernatural creatures, spirits and demons, are known by the name *Hua Po*, which literally means "Flower Spirit."[615]

We bring up the Hua Po because some Confucian traditions believed that these spirits and demons had the ability to influence the lives of people on Earth—both for good and for evil. Thus, the Hua Po tradition may be a brand of the Influences of Demonic Forces View.[616]

There is also a long tradition, both in the ancient world and afterward, of the practice of ancestor worship among the Confucians. In fact, Confucius himself believed strongly that the category of *Hsaio*, or Filial Piety, extended to the dead. In fact, Confucius considered ancestor veneration to be one of the Five Fundamental Relationships discussed earlier in this chapter.

In *The Analects*, Confucius is clear about ancestor veneration being part of Filial Piety. He relates:

Hold, o hold, to strict decorum
This is virtue's vantage.
Proverb has it that even sages
Now and then the fools will join.
But the folly of the many must pay respect
To both the living and to the dead.

In the mind of Confucius, support and veneration of dead family members were interwoven into the fabric of Chinese society. Confucius did not prohibit the possibility that the spirits of the dead ancestors take part in the activities of the living. Scholar William Jennings, an early sinologist, tells us this about filial piety and the veneration of the dead:

> Filial piety is not limited to the living, to father and grandfather, but extends to the dead and finds expression in rituals, which are commonly called Ancestor Worship. It was practiced throughout China with great fidelity.[617]

In his essay "Spirits and the Soul in Confucian Ritual Discourse," Thomas A. Wilson points out that in *The Analects*, Confucius himself remarks, "I am as yet unable to understand the living, how then can I understand the ghosts and the demons?"[618] Nevertheless, Wilson goes on in his essay to describe rituals in which sacrifices were made to the dead in Ancient China.[619] Another student in *The Analects* confirms that "The Master did not speak of strange powers and Chaotic Spirits."[620]

However, in Book III of *The Analects*, we find the necessity of sacrificing to the spirits and that it be done properly. Confucius wonders in the same book, "if a mountain Spirit will decline to partake in a family's sacrifices that appear to be in violation of traditional rituals."[621]

The major conclusion we should make about this material should be clear. We should add ancestor worship and the Influences of Demonic Forces View to our Confucian answers and responses to the causes and meanings of evil and suffering in the philosophy of Kung Fu Tzu and his followers.[622]

Thus, we have shown in this section of Chapter Six that Confucius mentions or endorses the following views at one time or another in his classic work, *The Analects*:

Retributive Justice Theory
The Contrast View
The Test Theory
The Influences of Demonic Forces View
Ancestor Worship or Ancestor Veneration

Throughout *The Analects*, the philosopher Confucius also makes many comments and observations about the nature and extent of the Moral Good. This is the subject matter of the next section of this chapter.

The Analects and the Moral Good

The Analects of Confucius are filled with observations about moral goodness. Many of these are related to moral character that should be exemplified in Confucius' philosophy. Consider this comment, "People with virtue should speak out. People who speak out are not all virtuous." In another place, Master Kung remarks, "The demands that good people make are usually upon themselves."[623]

Other comments about the Moral Good from the *Yun Lu* also reveal a great deal of what Confucius believed about the make-up of Moral Goodness. One on occasion, he told his students, "Your life is what your thoughts have made it." In another time, he revealed, "You should act with kindness, but do not expect gratitude in return." Confucius often speaks of human nature in *The Analects*, such as this comment when he said, "All people are the same, only their habits differ."[624]

In several places of the *Yun Lu*, Master Kung relates that the most important moral traits for a leader are faithfulness and sincerity. Sometimes when Confucius speaks of Moral Goodness, it is to discuss goodness in the state, such as this comment when he says, "The strength of a nation begins with the integrity of the family."[625] Most often, however, when Confucius speaks of Moral Goodness in *The Analects*, it is about the individual and the Moral Good to be found there, such as this example:

> Fix your mind on Truth, and hold firm to Virtue. Rely on loving kindness and find your recreation in the arts.[626]

Some scholars of the Confucian philosophy have suggested that its views on ethics are comparable to what has come to be called in the modern world a version of "Virtue Ethics."[627] This is a philosophical view based on the philosophy of ancient Greek philosopher Aristotle, who maintained that the most important element in leading a moral life is to personify certain Moral Virtues like prudence, temperance, courage and justice.[628]

For Aristotle, in order to acquire a life of happiness, or what he calls *Eudemonia*, one must embody these Cardinal Virtues.[629] Similarly, Confucius believed that the moral life was only achieved by those who exemplify virtues like *Ren, Dao, Li, Wen, Yi, Zhong, Xin, Xiao,* and *Yong.* For Confucius, however, it is important to embody these virtues in the Five Basic Relationships; and that is the most important thing to understand about the nature and extent of Moral Goodness in Confucian Philosophy.

This brings us to one final section of Chapter Six, an examination of views on evil and suffering in the modern Confucian period.

Views on Evil and Suffering in Modern Confucian Period

Beginning in the High Middle Ages in the West, a movement in the East developed called neo-Confucianism. The movement first gained popularity during the Song dynasty in the eleventh century. More than anything, neo-Confucianism was a response to the incursions of Buddhism and Taoism into the Confucian philosophy. Among the most important ideas of the neo-Confucians was the emphasis away from the collective and a move instead toward the perfection of the individual.

Two other central ideas in the neo-Confucian movement was the belief that pragmatism should be applied to the rules of the state and that reason was far more important than intuition when it came to living a good life. Among the most important philosophical thinkers in neo-Confucian Movement was Ti Hwang (1501–1570), a prominent Korean, Confucian philosopher.[630]

Ti Hwang is important for our purposes because he firmly criticizes views about the origins of Moral Evil that suggested in his day that it was free will that was the source of Moral Evil. In its stead, Hwang emphasized a self-transcending way to remove evil and to do the good in human life.[631]

More specifically, Ti Hwang also suggested that the Confucian philosophy should return to its roots. He suggested the best way to eradicate Moral Evil was to embody the original virtues of the teachings of Confucius, such as *Ren* and *Li.* In this sense, Hwang was another proponent in the Confucian tradition of what we have called "Virtue Theory." Like the other neo-Confucians, Hwang was also critical of Buddhist and Taoist ideas entering the Confucian philosophy. He also was a believer that reason was the best way for evaluating any aspect of Confucian society.[632]

In contemporary neo-Confucian philosophy, some scholars, mostly Koreans, have revived the views of Master Ti Hwang on the phenomena of evil and suffering. One of the most important of these thinkers is Korean philosopher Yong Huang and his 2018 essay "Evil in neo-Confucian Thought."[633] In his analysis, Huang mostly relies on the earlier work of Master Ti Hwang and his works like *Songhak sipto* and the *Chasongnok.*[634]

In his article entitled "The Passions of the Soul in the Ministrations of Becoming," scholar Sachiko Murata also treats the question of how Islam interacted in China in the neo-Confucian movement.[635]

Before we move to the major conclusions of this chapter, we wish to return to our notion of what the religions of the world have tended to have in common. In Chapter One of this study, we suggested a group of ten family resemblance characteristics for calling something a religion. These were:

1. Conception of Ultimate Reality
2. Myths, Symbols and Rituals
3. Distinction Between Sacred and Profane
4. Religious Heroes, Places, and Things
5. A System of Ethics Sanctioned by Ultimate Reality
6. Explanations for Evil
7. View of the Self
8. Survival After Death
9. Holy Scriptures
10. Eschatology

Now when it comes to the philosophy of Confucius, it should be clear that his system does not have a view of ultimate reality unless we think of the notion of Tien as a god. It does have a system of myths, symbols and rituals, as well as religious heroes, sacred places and things, as we have indicated earlier in this chapter. It is certainly based on a system of ethics, but not one sanctioned by ultimate reality.

Confucianism also seems to fall short on having the nature of the self, as well as a view on survival after death. As we have shown, the Confucians do have a collection of holy writings, but it says very little about issues related to eschatology. In summary, then, Confucianism is lacking in items 1, 5, 6, 7 and 10, and only tangentially meet numbers 2, 3, 4, 6 and 9. The bottom line on Confucianism should clearly be it does not have enough family resemblance characteristics for calling something a "religion."

This brings us to a summary of the major conclusions in Chapter Six of this study of evil and suffering in comparative religions. Chapter Seven of this study is dedicated to the perspectives on evil and suffering that may be found in Taoism and in the faith called Shinto.

Conclusions to Chapter Six

We began Chapter Six with some very general comments on the life and times of the founder of Confucianism, including the written woks that have been attributed to him, particularly the *Lun Yu* or "Analects" of Confucius. Indeed, after a description of the "Four Books" and the "Five Classics" of the Confucians, we went on in Chapter Six to the second section, in which we explored the most important sacred places and sacred people in Confucianism.

In the former category, we mentioned the Confucius temple, the Confucius cemetery and the Kong family estate in Shandong.[636] Under the category of sacred people, in addition to the founder, we also mentioned Mencius and philosopher and reformer Xun Zi.[637]

In the third section of Chapter Six, we described and discussed at some length a group of thirteen ideas and virtues that frequently appear in the philosophy of Confucius. Among these ideas were:

1. Ren
2. Junzi
3. Dao/Tao
4. Li
5. Tian
6. De
7. Wen
8. Yi
9. Zhong
10. Xin
11. Jing
12. Xiao
13. Yong

We have shown that these thirteen ideas and virtues have made important contributions to understanding the philosophy of Confucius. In the central section of this chapter on "Good and Evil in Confucius' Analects," we described and discussed three separate ways in which discussions of evil and suffering can be found in *The* Analects. The first of these types is when the master speaks of evil in a very general way. In the second group of comments, we spoke of when Confucius mentions evil in the context of human nature or when giving moral advice to his students.

In a third variety in which Master Kong discusses evil and suffering, we mentioned several places in *The Analects* where the master seems to be mentioning, or even assenting to, many of the theories and responses outlined in the first chapter of this study. In that regard, we have seen what may be examples of the Contrast View, the Test Perspective, Retributive Justice Theory, the Influences of Demonic Forces Approach, and the Veneration of Ancestors Theory.[638]

In the fourth section of Chapter Six, we examined a number of passages in *The Analects*, where Moral Goodness was the subject matter of a discussion of Confucius with his students. Altogether, we looked at a half dozen of these examples. We commented that many Confucian scholars are of the view that the Chinese philosopher had a version of "Virtue Theory."[639]

In the fifth and final section of Chapter Six, we had two separate goals. The first of these was to examine how the neo-Confucian movement has responded to the issues of evil and suffering in that period. The second goal was to answer the philosophical question, "Is Confucianism a Religion?" The answer we gave to that query was no.

In Chapter Seven, we will turn our attention to two other East-Asian religions or philosophical movements. Namely, Taoism and Shinto.

Chapter Seven:
Evil and Suffering in Taoism and Shintoism

Taoism (also spelled Daoism) is a life philosophy and practice of living in harmony with the *Tao*. The word Tao means "way" or "path"—a sort of double meaning as both the "way of nature" and the "way to happiness."

—D. T. Strain, "Taoism: An Introduction"

If there was one, single, broad definition of Shinto that could be put forward, it would be that "Shinto is a belief in Kami, the supernatural entities at the center of the religion."

—Joseph Cali, "Shintoism"

The perennial human quest for an answer to the existence of evil and its results is of interest to every human being as everyone seems to be affected by pain and suffering. Every culture poses this question in one way or another.

—Delia Ursulescu, "A Christian Response to the Problem of Evil in the Shinto Religion"

Introduction

The purpose of this seventh chapter is to introduce and discuss what two other Asian religions have had to say about the issues of evil and suffering in their respective traditions. These religions are Taoism and the Japanese faith called Shintoism. We will begin Chapter Seven with an introduction to Taoism. This opening section will be followed by some observations about how the tradition of Taoism has responded to, or have answered, questions related to the phenomena of evil and suffering.

These two sections of Chapter Seven on Taoism will be followed by two more on Shintoism. The first of these will give a brief introduction to the Shinto faith, who, what, where and when. In the fourth section of this chapter, we shall explore how the Shinto faith has responded to the issues of evil and suffering. We move now, then, to some introductory comments on Taoism and its History.

An Introduction to Taoism

The faith known as Taoism is an organized religion that has been around for thousands of years. Its roots in China are believed to go all the way back to shamanistic beliefs that even predate the Hsia dynasty that began around 2200 BCE. Today, Taoism can rightly be called a world religion with followers from many cultural and ethnic backgrounds. Some of these followers choose to identify themselves to Taoist temples and monasteries—the formal, organized faith—and others do not.

Indeed, some Taoists choose to walk the path of a hermit of solitary cultivation of the self, and still, others adopt aspects of the institutional faith, while not adhering to all of its precepts. For all Taoists, however, their world view is rooted in a close examination of the natural world—the patterns of constant change that exist within that world.

There is no identifiable time when Taoism began. The ideas that came to be known as Taoism developed through ancient Chinese oral tradition. In the sixth century BCE, the philosopher Lao Tzu began to assemble those ideas or his interpretation of them in his work the *Tao Te Ching*.

Indeed, the primary source for understanding the teachings of Taoism is the *Tao Te Ching*, usually translated as "The Book of the Way of Nature, Virtue, and Empowerment." This book is believed to have been written by Lao Tzu, the founder of Taoism, in the sixth century BCE. The next most prominent thinker in Taoism is Chuang Tzu, a philosopher in the fourth century BCE. His writings are also considered as authoritative and foundational in the Taoist faith. The canon of scriptures in Taoism is called the *Daozang*, or the "treasury of the Tao." [640]

Throughout the vast history of East Asia, there has been much meshing and cross-influencing between Taoism, Buddhism and Confucianism, with many elements of each faith to be found in the other two, particularly as they are practiced today.

Taoism is a complex system of thought. Its customs and beliefs are related to a subtle form of wisdom that is fully compatible with the systems of the natural order. The most important principle or idea in Taoism is the Tao itself. The Tao is the ineffable flow of the universe— the true nature of things that lies beyond description in any language. In some ways, the Tao may be compared to the Western philosophical school called Stoicism, which speaks of the *Logos* as the rational order by which the cosmos operates.[641]

The goal in the Taoist faith is to be "One with the Tao." This essentially means that the individual has freed himself or herself from selfishness and desire, to having been released from one's narrow ego, and to live in harmony with the nature of things. Many of the central beliefs of Taoism are aimed at helping the follower to achieve the state of being one with the Tao.

Taoist ethics includes a principle known as *Wu Wei*, or "effortless action." This is the art of moving in unison with the natural flow of events to achieve one's goals, rather than crudely going against the flow. Some of the hallmark characteristics of the Taoist are compassion, frugality and humility.[642] These three attributes are sometimes called the "Three Treasures."[643] One of the elements of Taoism that people find most attractive is how its prescriptions are intimately connected to the "way the universe works."

The Taoist faith grew out of the observations of the natural world and the notion that there is a cosmic balance maintained and regulated by the Tao. It is unlikely that the earliest forms of Taoism said anything about belief in spirits or ancestor worship, but these practices gradually found a role in the Taoist faith.[644]

Taoism began to exert a great influence in Chinese culture during the Tang dynasty (618–907 CE). Emperor Xuanzong, who reigned from 712 to 756 CE, declared Taoism to be the official state religion. He also mandated that all his subjects keep Taoist writings in their homes.[645] Taoism fell out of favor in the Tang dynasty (seventh to the tenth centuries), but it revived after that time.[646]

The Taoist historian Sima Qian (145 to 86 BCE) tells the tale of Lao Tzu, who at the time was a curator of the Royal Library in the State of Chu. Qian says of Lao Tzu, "He believed in the harmony of all things and that people could live easily together and if they considered each other's feelings, and that self-interest is not always in the interests of the State."[647] Qian also tells us that:

> Lao Tzu grew impatient with people, as well as with the corruption he saw in Government that caused people much pain and suffering. He was so frustrated about the possibility of changing people's behavior that he went into Exile.

As he was leaving China through the Western Pass, the gatekeeper, a man named Yin Hsi, stopped him because he knew Lo Tzu was a noted philosopher. The gatekeeper asked the philosopher if he would write him a book. So, as the story goes, Lao Tzu sat down next to a rock and wrote out the *Tao Te Ching*. When he had finished writing, he handed the book to Yin Hsi and walked through the Western Pass.[648]

The name *Tao Te Ching* was first used during the Han dynasty (206 BCE to 220 CE).[649] The book presents a way of life intended to restore harmony and tranquility to a kingdom that was racked by widespread disorder. The book advocates beliefs in spontaneity, non-interference and letting things take their natural course. As Lao Tzu puts it, "Do nothing and everything will take its course."[650]

In the nineteenth century, doubts began to be raised about whether Lao Tzu was the true author of the *Tao Te Ching*. Some scholars even doubted the existence of the historical Lao Tzu.[651] The work consists of eighty-one chapters in two major parts, the first of which has thirty-seven chapters and the second, forty-three chapters.[652] Some scholars believe an earlier work known as the "Songs of Chu" that focused on diet and meditation, may have been one of the sources of the *Tao Te Ching*.[653]

In addition to the idea of the Tao and *Wu Wei*, the faith has also had a number of other key ideas. Among these are *Yin* and *Yang*, as well as many of the Chinese ideas and virtues we saw back in Chapter Six, such as *Ren, De, Tian,* etc. Other important concepts in Taoism include the *sheng ren,* or "ideal person," the *shen yi,* or "spirits," and the *zhenren,* or "a feeling of invincibility," and finally, *ziran,* or "naturalness."[654]

The ideas of *Yin* and *Yang* in Taoism, next to the *Tao* and the idea of *Wu Wei,* are the most important ideas in the faith. These two ideas are opposites, and when they are depicted, it is usually when the opposite idea is shown to be embedded. The thought behind this is that opposites are necessary in order to have harmony. In fact, Taoism seems to imply that you cannot have one without the other idea.

In Taoism, *Yin* is the female. It is passive, dry, soft and unassertive. *Yang,* on the other hand, is male—hard, aggressive, wet and assertive. *Yin* is the night to the *Yang's* day. Lao Tzu relates, "All things carry Yin and yet embrace Yang."[655] He adds, "They blend their life and breaths in order to produce a harmony."[656] It is important to remember, however, that Lao Tzu says, "The Tao that can be spoken of is not the real Tao."[657] This may be interpreted as Divine Plan Theory.

The second most important thinker in Taoism is the figure of Chuang Tzu, who lived in one of China's northern states, south of the Yellow River, in the fourth century BCE. Chuang Tzu was intelligent, clever, witty, and at times, very cutting and abrasive toward his enemies. Although he revered Lao Tzu, he had no interest in reforming human society, governance or even politics. Instead, he preferred a quiet life "off the beaten path."

Chuang Tzu's traditional dates are given as 399 to 295 BCE. His style of writing was full of parables and tales, such as the famous Chuang who dreamed he was a butterfly who dreamed he was Chuang.[658] At times Chuang Tzu's thoughts seem well beyond the views of Lao Tzu, like his comment:

> The mind of the perfect man is like a mirror. It does not lean forward, nor back in response to things, but conceals nothing on its own. Therefore, it is able to deal with things without injury to his reality.[659]

Chuang Tzu does, however, at times reflects on issues that may seem questions in Western philosophy, like the nature of the self, for example. He thought that identifying the origins of things like pleasure, anger and sorrow is far more important to understanding the nature of the self than a soul or spirit.[660] Chuang Tzu also wrote a great deal about the nature and use of language. He calls language "not blowing breathe" and suggests that language can "never be fixed."[661] This comment may be similar to theories in twentieth-century linguistics or even to the philosophy of Ludwig Wittgenstein in regard to the nature of language.

The closest thing to the work of Chuang Tzu in Western philosophy is probably skepticism. He was quite skeptical, for example, about the idea of the sages in Chinese history. He also came very close to the dictum of Socrates that "The wise man is the one who knows nothing."[662] Because his ideas are often related in parables, his ideas are not always very clear, but nearly all interpreters see him as a skeptic and as a relativist.

Between the figures of Lao Tzu and Chuang Tzu, some add the figure of Hui Shih, who was born in Song (Henan in Modern China) around 380 BCE. He represented a school of thought known as the "Dialecticians." Much of what survives of his work are series of paradoxes, quite like Zeno of Elea in the West around the same time.[663]

This brings us to the places in the Taoist faith where the issues of evil and suffering have come to the fore in the history of that faith, the subject matter of section two of this seventh chapter.

Evil and Suffering in Taoism

In terms of the phenomena of evil and suffering in Taoism, we should begin with some obvious conclusions. First, Goodness is anything that "flows with the Tao." Second, Evil is the opposite. It is anything that puts resistance to, stops, interferes with, or damages the flow of the Tao. For Taoism, good things help you grow and to follow the Tao. Each person in Taoism has what is called their own *Yuen Sun*, the Tao of an individual life. Anything that aids in achieving one's Yuen Sun is Good. Anything that goes against one's Yuen Sun is Evil. Anything that does harm to, or gives resistance to your Yuen Sun, is by its very nature an Evil.[664]

Lao Tzu points out that one cannot judge a person's actions unless he knows the entire situation. He gives the example of a man who killed someone, and everyone will think he is a bad person, only to find out the slain man was on a rampage killing many other people in the process.[665]

In an essay called "Evil in Taoism," scholar Mojtaba Zarvani sums up Lao Tzu's views on evil in four premises. These are the following:

1. The Tao is the *Summum Bonum*, or Highest Good.
2. The Tao is the ultimate source of all things and events.
3. All things and events are good if they are not the results of some interference with the spontaneous evolution of the Tao.
4. The assertive use of the human will is an interference with the spontaneous evolution of the Tao.[666]

From these four premises, Zarvani arrives at the conclusion:

Therefore, every thing or event that is caused by the assertive use of the human will is Evil.[667]

Zervani goes on to tells us about premise number four that "It may be revised to say that only the assertive use of the will is an interference with the spontaneous evolution of the Tao." And then he adds:

In that case, all evils are either some assertive uses of the will or their Consequences.

Zervani then points out that premises one, two and three are the basic beliefs or assumptions of the philosophy of Lao Tzu. The problem is whether premise four is consistent with them.

One response to evil and suffering in the *Tao Te Ching* that is clear is the view that to understand what is evil in Taoism, you might first understand what is good. As Lao Tzu tells us, "Without Light, it is impossible to know what the Dark is. In order for something to exist, there must be two extremes of things."[668] In this passage, it should be clear that the Chinese philosopher is endorsing a version of what we have called the Contrast View.

Another way to see this view in the *Tao Te Ching* is to examine what Lao Tzu has to say about *Yin* and *Yang*. In his book, the central relationship between yin and yang is called *Hsisang*, a pattern of mutual development that cannot be separated from each other. The philosopher in chapter two tells us:

...which exists and which does not create each other.
It's hard and easy to support each other...
Before and after following each other.

Lao Tzu illustrates the nature of the yin-yang binary in a story that illustrates the relationship:

There was once a farmer who lost his horse. At dusk, the farmer was met by a neighbor after he had lost the horse. The neighbor told the farmer that he had lousy luck. The next day, the horse returned and six wild horses came along with his horse. The neighbor saw what had happened, and he told the farmer he had good luck.

The next day the farmer's son attempted to mount one of the wild horses and the boy fell and broke his leg. The neighbor again saw what transpired and told the farmer he had bad luck.

The next day a military officer came around to find all the boys to become soldiers, but the farmer's son was not taken because of the broken leg. The neighbor saw what had happened and he told the farmer, "You are a lucky man."[669]

The tale is like the yin-yang binary because inside every good act in the tale, there is a hidden evil. And each evil in the tale leads to another good. So too is the relationship of yin to yang, and like the diagram of the yin-yang binary, there is a spot of yin in the yang and a corresponding spot of yang in the yin.[670] The yin-yang relationship represents a symbol of harmony. One must have both elements to protect the balance of things. Thus, again, Lao Tzu seems to be assenting to the Contrast View as introduced in the first chapter of this study.

In the article by Mojtaba Zarvani mentioned above, the Iranian scholar suggests that "In the Taoist tradition, especially in the *Tao Te Ching*, evil is divided into two categories, Causal Evil and Consequential Evil.[671] Zervani adds:

Causal evils are those evils that are said to be the causes of
other evils. Causal evils originate from human will and cause
suffering. This means that evil is not equivalent to suffering.

In Zarvani's analysis of Lao Tzu, Consequential Evils are said to
be the byproducts or consequences of the Causal Evils. It appears that
what Lao Tzu and Zarvani mean by this analysis is this: Causal Evils is
another name for Moral Evils, and Consequential Evils is another name
for Natural Evils. If one thinks about humans making bad decisions
that later affect the environment, we see an example of Causal Evils
bringing about Consequential Evils, like unclean water or soil that has
been tainted by toxic compounds.[672]

In this analysis we have sketched out so far, in the view of Lao
Tzu there are only man-made evils. But it raises an interesting question,
Are all of the Consequential Evils always a by-product of the uses of
the human will? Now we do not know how Lao Tzu would answer
our question, but it seems like his answer can only be that there are no
Natural Evils.[673] In other words, in his view, there can be no physical
or mental suffering that was not caused by the human will. Thus, Lao
Tzu was against the idea of cancer being a Natural Evil, and the worry
about the disease, a metaphysical evil, as defined in the opening chapter
of this study.

In chapter thirty-two of his book, Lao Tzu observes, "If one
follows the Tao, all things will take their proper places spontaneously."
In a very real way, this pronouncement deems to come close to the
adage that "Everything works out in the end." If that is the proper
understanding of the passage from chapter thirty-two, we can add the
Divine Plan Theory to our list of responses from Lao Tzu.

In another section of his book, the Chinese philosopher observes:

The Tao that can be told is not the Eternal Tao. The name that
can be named is not the Eternal Name. The unnamable is the
only Eternally Real. Naming is the origin of all particular things.

Although this passage is a cryptic one, to say the least, it
nevertheless speaks of the gulf that the Taoist believes exists between
the knowledge of human beings and the phenomenon of the Tao itself.
Again, this may be seen as an indication of Divine Plan Theory.

If we follow our analysis of evil in Taoism so far, it appears that Lao Tzu assented to, or endorsed, the following views:

1. The Free Will Defense (Causal Evil)
2. The Contrast View (Yin-Yang binary)
3. Natural Evil (Consequent Evils)
4. Divine Plan Theory

We might add, however, that not all Taoists held these same positions in regard to the phenomena of evil and suffering. Chuang Tzu, for example, differs from Lao Tzu on the relation of Causal and Consequential Evil. Chuang Tzu definitely recognizes the existence of Natural Evils, which he explains as "The wonderful transformation of all things in the Tao," in chapter six of his work.[674]

Chuang Tzu also advises his followers that "pains should be accepted as they are and should not be regarded as evils."[675] But it is not clear what the philosopher means by "as they are."

In several other places in the *Tao Te Ching*, Lao Tzu makes random comments about evil, such as when he remarked, "Weapons are the instruments of Evil, not the instruments of Good Rulers."[676] This comment is consistent with the Chinese philosopher's overall view that one should be distrustful of kings and the elite.[677] In another section of the *Tao Te Ching*, Lao Tzu relates, "Give Evil nothing to oppose it and it will disappear by itself."[678] This may be another application of the Contrast View of evil and suffering.

In chapter sixty of the *Tao Te Ching*, Lao Tzu cryptically remarks that "When all the world recognizes the Good as Good, it becomes Evil."[679] Throughout his work, the words for "good" and "evil" have no absolute or defined meanings glued to them. Rather those meanings are fluid and ever-changing, much like the sense of the Tao itself.

In Taoism, the word "evil" does not have an absolute, definitive meaning. Rather, it is anything that keeps the believer from achieving one's personal Yuen Sun. Anything that promotes that achievement is good; anything that does not is often labeled evil in the Taoist faith.[680] In Taoist belief, what is good for one person may not be good for another. Something evil to one person may not be evil to another.

The Taoist sages all agree that human beings are born to make choices and to make decisions. In this sense, Lao Tzu and Chuang Tzu are both strong advocates of what we have called the Free Will Defense in Chapter One of this study. In an article called "Free Will: The Cornerstone of Taoism," Master Mikel Steenrod tells us simply, "We live in a choice-driven universe."[681] The Tao has constructed a universe of choice in which all things, including ourselves, must move through the flow of choices according to our own selections. In other words, our choices are the manifestations of Divine Law.

It is important to point out, however, that the Tao is not a tyrant. It creates without possessing. It acts without expecting. It guides without interfering. What the Tao is, instead, is love. Not a subjective love that makes distinctions, but an objective love, the love of the Tao that is at the heart of the very nature of things. In Taoism, you are free to choose. You can choose not to love, but that would go against your very nature. In Taoism, you are free to choose, so choose wisely.[682]

Finally, it is common in Taoist literature to read about demons, exorcism, ancestor worship, spirits, and other metaphysical realities. There are also many references to spirit mediums that serve as conduits to the spirit world. In this section, we will remark about some of these phenomena.

In the history of Taoism, we find many comments about a class of beings known as the *Yaogua*, or *Yaojing*. These are mostly malevolent animal spirits or fallen celestial beings who have acquired magical powers through the practice of Taoism. The goal of these creatures is to achieve immortality and deification. The Chinese text where we learn the most about the nature and functions of the Yaojing is the 1592 novel *Hsu Chi-yu*, or the *Journey to the West*.[683] What may strike the reader most about this text is the pervasiveness of the demons and monsters throughout. One way the Yaoguai seek to achieve their goals is by the abduction and the consumption of holy men, particularly noted Taoist sages. The purpose of these activities is to dissuade these holy men from their dedication to the Tao.[684]

In *Journey to the West*, many of the Yaojing appear as fox spirits, or as demonic pets of other spirits. In Chinese folklore, the classical Chinese word for "Hell" is *Diyu*. It is a place that is populated by various kinds of demons similar to the Sanskrit notion of the *Rakshasa*. In Japanese culture, the Yaojung are called *Yokai*, or *Mononoke*.[685]

In the Taoist tradition, there are several Yaojing that appear in Chinese mythology. A figure known as *Baigujing* is perhaps the best known. Her name literally means "Skeleton Spirit." In *Journey to the West*, she is one of the chief antagonists. She desires to possess human beings and to eat their flesh. Baigujing is considered one of the most cunning of the demons. She is also a trickster who enjoys tricking humans, so she can eventually eat their flesh.[686]

Another prominent Taoist demon is known as *Niumowang*, or the "Bull Demon King." He is also known as the "Great Sage who pacifies Heaven" and appears in *Journeys to the West*, as does a figure known in Taoism as the *Pipa Jing*. Pipa Jing is also a fictional character in the Ming dynasty novel *Fengshen Yanyi*, where she is put in charge of jade pipe.[687] Over and against all of these descriptions of demons and demonic possession in Taoism, there is also the line from the *Tao Te Ching*, where Lao Tzu reminds us, "The enemies of people are not demons, but people like themselves."[688]

There is also a long tradition in Taoism going all the way back to ancient times of exorcism. For the most part, there are three different varieties in Taoism. The first is related to Taoist priests, who are generally a more refined group of Taoists. They have had the power of exorcising demons from the bodies of humans and of animals.[689]

Another class of exorcists, particularly during the Song dynasty (960 to 1279 CE), is called the *Fashi*. The classical Chinese *fa* means "method" or "technique." It refers to a method of exorcising that is often used in conjunction with Taoist priests and spirit mediums.[690] Spirit medium is the lowest class of exorcists in Taoism. These exorcists were responsible for the removal of demons from the common people.[691] This class of exorcists mostly function as the voices of spirits and demons that connects the phenomenal world with the spiritual world.

The upshot of this discussion now should be clear. We should add the Influences of Demonic Forces Theory to our list of Taoist responses to the phenomena of evil and suffering in this Chinese faith. That list now includes:

The Free Will Defense (Moral Evil)

The Contrast View

Natural Evil (Consequential Evil)

Divine Plan Theory

The Influences of Demonic Forces View

This brings us to an introduction to the religion known as Shintoism, the subject matter of the next section of this seventh chapter of this study of evil and suffering in the religions of the world. We move next, then, to Shintoism.

Introduction to Shintoism

The word "Shinto" is a general term for the religious faith popular in Japan that reveres all the *Kami* of heaven and earth. The origins of the Shinto faith are as old as the history of Japan itself. It was only at the end of the sixth century CE when the movement began to be called "Shinto."

It is peculiar among some scholars to call it a religion, for it has no particular founder, and there is very little of what might be called dogma. The Shinto faith has no sectarian groups. It has no codified sacred scripture, and, unlike other Asian faiths, there is no belief in Shintoism of reincarnation, nor even a notion of what would be called the "Soul" in the Western tradition.

The Shinto faith does have a land of the dead. It is called *Yomi*. Everyone who dies eventually goes there, but it is a very cumbersome process that includes twenty steps outlined in the faith. The practice of purification is a very central idea in Shintoism. Among the twenty steps are instructions for how to wash the body, as well as how to purify the earth before burial.

The land of Yomi is comparable to the Greek idea of Hades, or the ancient Hebrew notion of *Sheol*. It is a murky, dusty place from which one may not return to the land of the living on earth. Yomi is often identified with the tale of Izanami, who follows his lover, Izanagi, to the land of Yomi. When he discovered that he could not bring her back, he returned himself, still pining for her all the more.

In Japanese, the land of the dead is known as *ne-no-Katasukuni*, an expression that means something like "firm-hard-packed place" because of the number of people who have already traveled there.

Most Shinto believers are now cremated, and the ashes are usually brought back to home shrines for subsequent rituals. When a Shinto child is born, its name is added to a list at the temple. When that person dies, the name is removed from the birth list and added to the death list, which contains all the names of the dead ancestors.

The Japanese religion known as Shinto is also called *Kami no michi*.[692] It is classified among the East Asian religions by scholars of the history of religions, and it is sometimes referred to as a Japanese "indigenous faith" and as a "nature religion." The Shinto faith is polytheistic and revolves around the idea of the *Kami*, which means "gods" or "spirits." These Kami are worshipped in household shrines, family shrines, as well as in public shrines. These public shrines are usually staffed by Shinto priests who oversee gifts and offerings to the Kami and the religious paraphernalia associated with the faith, such as amulets.[693]

The notion of the *Kami* in Shinto thought is an all-embracing term that signifies gods, spirits, ancestors, natural phenomena and supernatural powers. All of the Kami can influence the everyday lives of believers. The Kami are worshipped, venerated and given offerings. They are solicited for aid and sometimes even appealed to for skills in divination. The Kami are attracted to examples of purity—both physical and spiritual. The Kami are also repelled by impurity and the lack of harmony.

The Kami are never entirely good. There are several Kami that are recognized in the Shinto faith as evil Kami. The Shinto believes that all Kami have the ability to become angry even though they more often protect people. The Kami, like humans, can also make mistakes. One Kami known as the *Magatsuhi kami* a force who brings ill-will and negative aspects of life to humans.[694]

The Kami are particularly associated with nature and are often present in places like mountains, waterfalls, trees and unusually shaped rocks. For these reasons, there is an enormous number of Kami, certainly in the millions.

The Kami are appealed to, nourished and appeased so that their influence on those on earth is positive. Offerings of rice wine, food, flowers, prayers and tea, are regularly offered in Kami shrines. Every year an object called a *Goshintai*, a physical representation of the Kami, is carried around a local community to purify it and to ensure its future well-being. The Kami are thought to be related to great natural features and great storms. One prime example is Mount Fuji, which is visited by many worshippers in pilgrimages to the site.[695]

There are many common rituals associated with the Kami, including the *Kangura*, a ritual dance. The Japanese noun *Matsuri* is employed to refer to celebrations and seasonal festivals. Ritual purity is a very important idea in the Shinto faith, so there are a variety of rituals, including ritual washing and bathing, related to the faith.[696]

Unlike other faiths, Shintoism has no specified founder, nor do they have a designated moral code. It also has no specified written texts, mostly because the faith exists in localized and regional places. The belief in the idea of the Kami can be traced back to the *Yayoi* period of Japan from 300 BCE to 300 CE.[697] Buddhism entered Japan during the Kofun period, 300 to 538 CE. This began the practice of understanding the Kami in anthropomorphic ways. The Shinto faith may be characterized by syncretism, where one Asian religion borrows from and transfers ideas.

The earliest written sources in the Shinto faith were developed in the eighteenth century. They are called the *Kojiki* and the *Nihon Shoki*. The Kojiki, or the "Records of Ancient Matters," is an early Japanese collection of myths, legends, songs, genealogies and oral traditions from Japanese antiquity until the year 641 CE. It contains myths about the beginning of the world, the Japanese peninsula, the origins of the Kami and the sanctioning of the Japanese Imperial line.[698]

The *Nihon Shoki* is sometimes translated as the "Chronicles of Japan." It was produced and published in 720 under the editorial supervision of Prince Toneri. The *Nihon* also contains a version of the Japanese creation myth, as well as the formation of the first seven generations of divine beings. It also contains several Japanese tales and narratives about virtuous rulers and those who were not so virtuous.[699]

William George Aston did the first English translations of these works in 1869. In the Aston edition, the *Nihon Shoki* contains thirty chapters, mostly about the Japanese Imperial line.[700] During the Meiji Era, 1868 to 1912, Shinto was adopted as the Imperial religion. It was also at this time that the emperor began to be identified as the son of the Sun Kami.[701]

Around the same time, the emperors began an effort to purge the state religion from Buddhist influences, and this fomented a period of Japanese nationalism and imperial worship. After their defeat in World War II, Shinto was formally separated from the state.[702]

Today, there are about 80,000 public shrines in Japan, as well as many more home and family shrines. Some of the Kami are only venerated in a single shrine, while others have shrines dedicated to them all over Japan. The process of establishing a shrine is called *Bunrei*, or "dividing the spirit," meaning that the spirit of an ancestor has been separated from the living.[703]

In the Shinto faith, the creative spirit that permeates all living things is known as *Mutsubi*.[704] Within traditional Shinto thought, there is no concept of an over-arching duality between good and evil. The Japanese word *Aki* refers to misfortune, unhappiness or disaster, like a monsoon or hurricane.[705]

Shinto priests are recognizable because they wear distinctive black caps and long white dresses. These indicate that a person knows the rituals that are tied to rituals related to the Kami and to other spirits. The offerings to the Kami and the ancestors in Shinto are similar to those in Buddhism and Confucians discussed in earlier chapters. They are offered flowers, fruit, rice and tea. On the front of every Shinto shrine is a "Sacred Rope" called a *Shimenawa*, a symbol of the purity that should be embodied in all followers of the Shinto faith.[706]

Other values respected by the Shinto faith in addition to purity are inclusiveness, particularly in regard to other faiths; intuition is far more valued than reason; veneration and respect, particularly in regard to the Kami; as well as a devotion to the idea of the family, both past and present.

Scholar of the Shinto faith, Brian Bocking, points out that there are several versions or kinds of Shinto. He relates:

> Some scholars suggest we talk about types of Shinto such
> as Folk Shinto, Domestic Shinto, Sectarian Shinto, Imperial
> Shinto, Shrine Shinto, State Shinto, New Shinto. This approach
> can be helpful, but it begs the question of what is meant by
> "Shinto." In each case, particularly since each category incor-
> porates or has incorporated Buddhist, Confucian. Taoist, Folk
> Religion as well as other elements.[707]

Bocking is correct that it is not so easy to narrow down just what is meant by the "Shinto faith." But we believe that we have in this section of Chapter Seven given at least a short introduction to that faith. This brings us to an analysis of what the Shinto faith has had to say about the phenomena of evil and suffering.

Perspectives on Evil and Suffering in the Shinto Faith

The first thing that the Shinto faith has to say about evil and suffering should be clear. In the idea of purity is the highest value among the Shinto followers, the notion of impurity becomes the chief anti-value. Many Shinto scholars like Norinaga equate the ancient Japanese as a pure natural state. Along with this belief is Norinaga's belief that people are born basically good.[708]

Motoori Norinaga (1730–1801) was a Japanese philosopher in the Edo period of Japanese history. He trained as a physician as well as a philosopher. He is important for our purposes because he wrote and lectured a great deal about the phenomena of evil and suffering, human nature, and many other philosophical topics.

For Norinaga, impurity creates a condition in which one is incapable of sensing his interconnectedness to the world of the Kami, which causes the person to act in ways that go against his nature. On the other hand, Norinaga seems to be endorsing the Free Will Defense because the philosopher believes that the doing of evil by human beings is inevitable. Norinaga clearly believes that when one departs from the realm of purity, those decisions are intentional and are free. Thus, he appears to assent to the Free Will Defense when humans do impure things.[709]

Another aspect of Norinaga is that moral eminence, as he called it, applies to the Kami, as well as to human beings. He tells us this about the Kami:

> Generally speaking, "Kami" denotes, in the first place, the deities of Heaven and Earth that appear in the ancient texts, and also the spirits enshrined in the shrines; furthermore, among all kinds of beings—including not only human beings but also such objects as birds, beast, trees, grass, mountains and so forth—any being whatsoever, which possesses some eminent quality out of the ordinary and is all-inspiring, is called Kami... Evil or queer things, if they are extraordinarily awe-inspiring, are also called Kami.[710]

For Norinaga, moral eminence could apply to Kami, human beings, and even non-human objects. In another place in the same work, he suggests that each of the Kami has two different spirits. He calls the first *ara-mitama*, or the rough or aggressive spirit, and the *nigi-mitama*, or "gentle spirit." In fact, Norinaga tells us that a "Kami may erupt into rage, while evil spirits may soften their hearts when happy. This is possible because each Kami possesses these two spirits."[711] It appears that Norinaga is endorsing here a Free Will Defense Theory for Kami, as well as for humans.

The solution that the Shinto faith endorses for the removal of evil is essentially the implementation of purification rituals. This ritual usually takes place twice a year. The goal, they say, "is to remove dust" that causes one's heart to become opaque and to be disrupted from the generative power called *Musubi*.[712] This is the interconnected energy that flows through all things that are living.

Impurities that are removed during this rite have become accumulated either because of ignorance or out of negligence. When Norinaga was asked what the reason or cause is for the removal of these impurities, the eighteenth-century Shinto philosopher said, "It cannot be known because there is no tradition transmitted about it."[713] This notion of "not being known," of course, seems to imply the Divine Plan Point of View.

Norinaga offers the same response when discussing the value of intuition over reason. Norinaga observes:

> Reason cannot help one in the process of rediscovering the
> truth because human intelligence is incapable of compre-
> hending the profound principles of the Ways of the Gods."[714]

Again, this language about "human incapability" pushes Motoori Norinaga in the direction of Divine Plan Theory.

An important Shinto scholar, Urabe no Kanetomo, tells us that the "Man derives his essential nature from the same source as the Kami and all living things.[715] He puts the matter this way:

> That which is in the universe is called Kami. That which is in all
> things is called Spirit [toma], and that which is in man is called
> heart [kokoro.]

Some Shinto thinkers believe there is no objective concept of good and evil. Shinto monk Taishi Kato, for example, in a 2016 interview tells us:

> There is no concept of Good and Evil in Shinto. Everything in
> the universe is changing based on the principles of nature. Ev-
> ery human being is changing by interacting with the universe.
> Therefore, one cannot judge what is absolute Good or Evil.[716]

We have suggested so far in our analysis that Shinto thinkers have assented to, or endorsed:

Retributive Justice Theory (for Kami)
Retributive Justice Theory (for humans)
Divine Plan Theory

The demonic in the Shinto faith has a very deep and long history. In Japanese mythology, the demons are called *Tengu*. These are supernatural demons and spirits who often have the ability to fly, have great physical strength, magical powers and secret martial arts skills. There are several types of Tengu. One is called *Daitengu*. His most prominent feature is his long nose and large wings. He is usually red in color.[717] Another type of Tengu is called the *Kotengu, or the*

Karasutengo. The word *Karasu* means "crow," but this type may take the form of any bird of prey.[718]

By the eleventh century, many Tengu legends had developed in Shinto literature. These have been collected in a thirty-one-volume work called the *Konjaku Monogatari*, but only twenty-eight volumes are still extant.[719] One tradition that has survived about the Tengu is that they often attack Shinto priests, chiefly because they know about Shinto enlightenment. The Tengu possess the bodies of these priests and try to lead them in the path of impurity.[720]

By the thirteenth century, the Tengu appear in the guise of *Yamabushi*, ascetic Shinto mountain priests. Rather than leading these monks astray, the major goal of the Tengu was to get humans to worship them.[721] By the nineteenth century, a figure known as the *Tengu Kanji* began to appear. This figure is depicted as a celestial dog. The Tengu Kanji has the ability to change shapes whenever he likes.[722]

The first extant record of the use of the word Tengu comes from 637 CE. One story from 1672 tells the tale of a villager who saw a creature on the roof of his neighbor's house, which looked like a dog but stood upright like a man. It had a sharp beak, and the upper body was red, and the lower half was blue indigo. Its tail was a broom.[723]

During the Edo period, the Tengu abducted Shinto priests and would also kidnap children. Some of these people were permanently damaged, or so says the legends. Japanese author, Hirata Asuntane, wrote a book about these abducted children published in Japan in 1822.[724]

Another bad spirit in the Shinto faith is named *Kitsune*. He is an evil fox. The Kitsune attempts to deceive humans, often by spirit possession. They also want to possess human beings for a variety of reasons, like revenge, killing one of its cubs or destroying the Kitsune's afternoon nap.[725] Another fox demon is known as *Inari*. He is responsible for mysterious, flickering lights seen in the sky at night—often in bogs, marshes, sand and other wet places.[726]

Another nineteenth-century Japanese tradition related to the demonic is the making and wearing of what were called *Noh-Masks*. These were masks with frightening faces worn by Shinto priests to ward off other evil spirits. Many of these masks still survive, one from the 1840s.[727]

From all these examples, it should be clear that we may add the Influences of Demonic Forces Theory in our list of Shinto responses to the phenomena of evil and suffering in the Japanese religion.

Finally, another way that Shinto thought and art in which the subject matter is sometimes Natural Evils can be seen in paintings like *The Great Wave of Kanagawa*, a painting by Hokusai completed sometime between 1829 and 1833. The painting is now owned by the Metropolitan Museum of Art in New York City.[728] The image depicts an enormous wave threatening three boats off the coast of the town of Kanagawa. Mount Fuji rises in the background.

It is sometimes assumed that the wave is a tsunami, but it is more likely to be a very large rogue wave. The painting is part of a series that depicts the area and activities around Mount Fuji under various conditions. These paintings come from woodblock prints. Katsushika Hokusai (1760–1849) was a Japanese painter and printmaker during the Edo period of Japanese history.[729]

In the Shinto faith, of course, the natural world is infinitely more powerful than human beings, as is the wave compared to the people on the boats. Shinto rituals show enormous respect for the Kami of nature. The block carver who makes such prints is called the *Horishi*.[730]

Many other Japanese painters and poets created works based on the March 11, 2011, tsunami and earthquake. The event is also called the "Great Sendai Earthquake." It was the most powerful earthquake ever recorded in Japanese history since record-keeping began in 1900. The tsunami swept the mainland and killed 16,000 people, with many more injured.

We mentioned these examples of Natural Evil because another way that Shinto thinkers have expressed their views on evil and suffering many times come in the context of great natural disasters. This brings us to the major conclusions we have made in this seventh chapter. The subject matter of Chapter Eight is the phenomena of evil and suffering in the Christian tradition.

Conclusions to Chapter Seven

The main purpose of this chapter was to explore two other East Asian religions—Taoism and Shintoism—and show how these two faiths responded to the phenomena of evil and suffering in them. We began Chapter Seven with some very general comments on the nature of Taoism and its history.

In the first section of Chapter Seven, we introduced the figures of Lao Tzu and Chuang Tzu and the former's work, the *Tao Te Ching*. We have shown that, since the nineteenth century, much criticism has arisen in Taoist scholarship about the reality of the historical Lao Tzu and the time in which his work was written.[731]

In the opening section of Chapter Seven, we also introduced the most central philosophical categories in the Taoist faith. In addition to the Tao itself, these included wu wei, the yin and yang, and the Taoist incorporation of Buddhist and Confucian ideas of *Ren, De, Tien*, and many others.

This first section of Chapter Seven was followed by the second section in which we identified and discussed many ways that the Taoist faith has responded to the issues of evil and suffering. Many of these were identified and discussed because they are mentioned in the *Tao Te Ching*.

Among the theological answers and responses that the Taoist faith has assented to, or clearly has endorsed, were: The Free Will Defense, The Contrast View, the idea of Consequent Evil as Natural Evil, the Influences of Demonic Influences View, and the Divine Plan Theory. As we have shown, we have found some of these responses in Lao Tzu and others in the work of Chuang Tzu.

In the third section of Chapter Seven, we provided a short introduction to the study of the Japanese faith known as Shintoism. As we have shown, the origins of the faith are not entirely clear. We do know, however, that the principal idea among the Shinto is the idea of the *Kami*, gods and spirits in Heaven and on the Earth.

In this third section of Chapter Seven, we introduced and discussed a number of the main values that can be found among the Shinto. Among these were the idea of ritual purity, inclusiveness in regard to other faiths, the reverence of intuition over reason, as well as the idea of devotion to ancestors, family and the government.

At the end of the third section of Chapter Seven, we also quoted scholar Brian Bocking about the "varieties of Shinto" and how difficult it is to narrow down just what the word "Shinto" means in the modern world.[732]

In the fourth and final section of Chapter Seven, we indicated the many ways in the Shinto faith where believers and experts alike have answered or responded to the phenomena of evil and suffering. As we have shown, one of the ways to establish these views was to refer to the work of Shinto philosopher Motoori Norinaga (1730–1801), who is one of the major thinkers in modern Shinto thought. We have also garnered Shinto perspectives on evil and suffering from Shito monk Taishi Kato, as well as many other Japanese Shinto thinkers.

From our analysis in the final section of Chapter Seven, we concluded that several of the responses to evil and suffering that we introduced in Chapter One of this study on evil and suffering in the religions of the world, may be found in the Shinto faith. Among those answers and responses in Shinto that we have seen were:

Retributive Justice (for Kami)

Retributive Justice (for humans)

Divine Plan Theory

And the Influences of Demonic Forces View

This brings us to Chapter Eight, in which our major goal shall be the exploration of how the Christian tradition has responded to the phenomena of evil and suffering in its history.

Chapter Eight:
Evil and Suffering in Christianity

To those who love God, all things work together for the
Good.

—Romans 8:28

Evil is not a positive substance, the loss of the Good has
been given the name Evil.

—Augustine, *The City of God*

The Book of Job offers us a series of intellectual gems or
beauties that cannot be found in other books of the Old
Testament.

—G. K. Chesterton, "Essay on the Book of Job"

Introduction

The purpose of this eighth chapter is to explore and discuss how the
phenomena of evil and suffering have been treated in the Christian
tradition from the time of the New Testament up to and including to
present times in the late twentieth and early twenty-first centuries in
the Christian Church.

We will open Chapter Eight with some general remarks about how
the issues of evil and suffering are treated or responded to in the New
Testament. This will be followed by the second section of Chapter Eight
on what the Christian Church has had to say about evil and suffering in
the medieval period, from the fifth to the fifteenth centuries.

Stephen J. Vicchio, Ph.D.

These two sections will be followed by a description of early modern Christian views on evil and suffering, from the sixteenth to the eighteenth centuries, and those three sections of Chapter Eight will be followed by a similar section on Christian views from the nineteenth to the twenty-first centuries. Rather than examining a wide range of Christian thinkers in each of these periods, we will only treat representative examples of each of those periods.

We move, then, to evil and suffering in the New Testament.

Evil and Suffering in the New Testament

In the twenty-seven books of the New Testament, there are fourteen different answers and responses to the phenomena of evil and suffering in the early Christian Church. We will list these views here and then discuss them one at a time. These theological views are the following:

1. The Influences of Demonic Forces Theory
2. The Original Sin Theory
3. The Retributive Justice Theory
4. The Free Will Defense
5. The Two Yetzerim Theory
6. The Test View
7. The Moral Qualities Perspective
8. The Contrast View
9. Divine Plan Theory
10. The Practical Approach
11. The Deprivation of the Good View
12. Determinism
13. Eschatological Verification
14. Other Miscellaneous Theories

We now will move to an explication and representative examples of each of these positions on early Christian attitudes toward evil and suffering. The first position—the Influences of Demonic Forces Theory—can be seen in dozens of places in the New Testament. We will look at six representative examples. These come from the Gospels of Matthew, Mark, Luke and John, as well as Acts of the Apostles and the letters of Paul. More specifically, these come at Matthew 12:43–45, Mark 1:23–27, Luke 4:5–7, the Gospel of John 10:20, the Acts of the Apostles 19:15, and Second Corinthians 4:4.

The Gospel of Matthew 12:43–45 speaks of "unclean spirits that have gone out of a person and then wander aimlessly looking for a place to rest." Similarly, in the Gospel of Mark 1:23–27, we are told:

> Just then, there was in the Synagogue a man with an unclean spirit and he cried out, "What have you to do with us, Jesus of Nazareth?"

Later, in the same passage, Jesus commands the unclean spirit to leave the man, and it obeyed. In the Gospel of Luke 4:5–7, the Evangelist informs us about Jesus and the Devil in the desert. The text relates:

> Then the Devil led him up and showed him in an instant all the kingdoms of the world. And the Devil said to him, "To you I will give all their glory and authority if you will bow down and worship me."

In the Gospel of John 10:20, the disciples of Jesus inform him about a man of whom they tell Jesus, "He has a demon and is out of his mind. Why listen to him?" From these four New Testament passages alone, we may assume that the people living in and around Palestine in the first century CE were of the belief that humans could be influenced by demonic entities.

In the Acts of the Apostles 19:15, we may make the same conclusion. This text speaks of an evil spirit speaking to Jesus, and the text then says, "Then the man with the evil spirit leaped on him…" an obvious reference to the Demonic Forces Theory. At Second Corinthians 4:4, Paul relates that "In this case, the god of this world has blinded the minds of unbelievers." The "god of this world" in the New Testament is a reference to the fact that first-century Christians were of the belief that the Devil controlled the world in that period. See, for examples, Ephesians 1:1 to3 and the Gospel of John 12:31, for representative examples of this view.

We move now to several places in the New Testament where Original Sin Theory is at play. Consider, for example, Romans 5:12,

"Therefore, just as sin came into the world through one man, and death came through sin, and death spread to all because all have sinned." Paul repeats this conclusion a few verses later at 5:18, where he relates:

Therefore, just as one man's trespass led to condemnation
for all, so one man's act of righteousness leads to justification
and life for all.

Saint Paul again declares his belief in Original Sin Theory in First Corinthians 15:22, when he observes, "For as all die in Adam, so all will be made alive in Christ." Another passage in the New Testament that may indicate a belief in original sin comes in the Gospel of John 3:3. In that narrative, a man named Nicodemus comes to Jesus and asks how he may enter the Kingdom of God. Jesus responds by saying, "Unless you are born again from above," you will not enter it. Later in verse five, Jesus adds, "You cannot enter the kingdom without being reborn of water and spirit."

Among New Testament scholars, rarely is this tale interpreted as concerning original sin; but the being reborn of the spirit "with water" may be precisely what this text means. From these passages, we have established that Original Sin Theory is one way that may explain evil and suffering in the New Testament. This brings us to Retributive Justice Theory.

In the Gospel of Mark 2:9, Jesus meets a paralyzed man. After seeing faith in the man, Jesus said to him, "Arise, your sins have been forgiven." And the man did just that. This text, of course, would seem to imply the belief that the man was paralyzed because of his sins.

In the Gospel of Luke 6:37, Jesus gives some advice about judging others. He relates:

Do not judge and you will not be judged. Do not condemn
and you will not be condemned. Forgive and you will be
forgiven. Give and it will be given to you. A good measure,
pressed down and shaken together, and running over, will be
put into your lap, for the measure that you give will be the
measure that you will get back.

From this passage, we see a clear pronouncement of what Jesus believed about his followers who did the moral good—that they will get good things back. Another passage where Jesus speaks of Retributive Justice Theory comes in a narrative at the beginning of chapter thirteen of the Gospel of Luke. It involves a passage related to something called the Tower of Siloam. The tower was a structure that fell upon eighteen people, killing them instantly.

Referring to the fall of the tower, Jesus asks if the dead were more sinful than other people? Clearly, this is an argument against Retributive Justice Theory. It is of some interest that some twentieth-century archeology may have uncovered the remains of the tower.[733] Perhaps the best example of Jesus' negative response to both Individual and Collective Retributive Justice Theories comes in the ninth chapter of the Gospel of John.

The scene in question involves a man who was born blind. Now the disciple asks Jesus, "Rabbi, who sinned, this man or his parents so that he was born blind?" Jesus responds by saying, "Neither, this man was born blind for the greater glory of God."[734] It should be clear that behind the question of the disciples was the specter of Retributive Justice Theory, but Jesus rejects that theory and replaces it with one that may be a version of the Divine Plan Theory. Again, it is clear that Retributive justice Theory was alive and well in first-century Christianity. This brings us to the Free Will Defense.

In the Gospel of John 8:31, Jesus speaks to some Jews who believed in him, and he says to them, "If you continue in my word you are truly my disciples, and you will know the truth and the truth shall make you free." In this passage, it is not clear whether Jesus is speaking of his followers being released from original sin and thereby possess free will, or some other interpretation of the passage. A similar passage may be seen in Paul's letter to the Romans at 6:18 and 22, where Paul relates:

> And you have been set free from sin, and you have become
> slaves of righteousness.

Again, we have the same question here about the idea of freedom that we saw in the Gospel of John in the above passage. Free will is much clearer, however, at the Book of Revelation 22:17, where the text advises us to, "…Come, and let everyone who hears, Come! And let everyone who is thirsty come. Let everyone who wishes to take the water of life as a gift." Now this text seems to imply that human beings have free will, for if they did not, they could not use it to decide if they will come or not. Thus, we have established that the Free Will Defense is employed in the New Testament, as well.

This brings us to some places in the New Testament where we may find the Two Yetzerim Theory. In the tenth chapter of the letter to the Romans, at verses six to eight, Paul tells us:

> Do not say in your heart, "Who will ascend into Heaven, that
> is to bring Christ down, or who will descend into the abyss,
> that is to bring Christ up from the dead. But what does it say?
> The word is near you, on your lips and in your heart."

It is not initially clear how this is connected to the Two Yetzer Theory. But if we remember that for the ancient Jews, the organ of the mind is the heat and not the brain, and it is the part of a person that makes moral decisions, then it is clear that the Two Yetzerim Theory is probably at work here. Similarly, in the Gospel of Matthew 5:27 and 28, when Jesus is speaking of adultery, he tells us:

> You have heard it said, "You shall not commit adultery, but I
> see to you for everyone who looks at a woman with lust has
> already committed adultery in his heart."

Again, this is an example of when someone makes a moral decision in first-century Palestine. It is the heart that makes that decision, that is, the *yetzer hara*, or the "evil imagination," or "evil inclination," that all people are born with. Thus, so far in this eighth chapter, we have seen assent to the Influences of Demonic Forces Theory, Original Sin Perspective, Retributive Justice Theory, the Free Will Defense, as well as assent to the Two Yetzerim Theory. We move now to the Test View.

We may establish that the writers of the New Testament endorsed what we have called the Test Theory. At the Gospel of Matthew 6:13, the Evangelist combines the Test View with the Demonic Influences Theory when he writes:

> And do not bring us to the time of trial,
> but rescue us from the Evil One.

At Hebrews 2:18 and 4:15, Paul also endorses the Test Perspective. In the first of these, he relates:

> Because he himself suffered when he was tested, he
> is able to help those who have been tested.

In the latter passage, the one from chapter four of Hebrews, Paul tells us:

> Because he himself suffered when he was tested, he is able to
> help those who are now being tested.

In the Epistle of James, in the opening of the book at Chapter 1:2–4, James also refers to testing. He relates:

> Consider it pure joy, my brothers and sisters that whenev-
> er you face trials of many kinds because you know that the
> testing of your faith produces perseverance, let perseverance
> finish its work so that it may be mature and complete, and
> not lacking in anything.

What we see in these short verses is really a combination of two theories on evil and suffering—the Test View and the Moral Qualities Perspective. In this case, the moral quality to be developed is perseverance, or *Hupomeno*, in New Testament Greek. The same word is employed at Luke 8:15 and 21:19, Romans 2:7 and 5:3–4, James 5:11, Second Peter 1:6, First Timothy 6:11, and many other New Testament passages. From these passages, it is clear that we can add the Test Perspective and the Moral Qualities Theory to our New Testament responses on evil and suffering.

We also can see the Contrast View in several places in the New Testament. Consider, for example, the Gospel of John 3:19. This verse relates:

> This is the verdict, Light has come into the world, but
> people loved the darkness instead of the Light
> because their deeds were evil.

In the Gospel of John at 1:5 and 8:12, we also see examples of the Contrast Perspective. In the first of these, John relates, "The Light shines in the Darkness, and the Darkness has not overcome it." At 8:12,

John has Jesus say, "I am the Light of the world. Whoever follows me shall not walk in darkness but will have the Light of Life." At Acts of the Apostles 26:18, we find another example of the Contrast Perspective. This verse relates:

> To open their eyes so that they may turn from darkness to light and from the power of Satan to God, that they may receive forgiveness of sins and a place among those who are sanctified by faith in me.

From these passages, we may add the Contrast View to our theological responses to evil and suffering in the New Testament. This brings us to an analysis of Divine Plan Theory to be found in the New Testament. We have already indicated that the apostle John combines Retributive Justice Theory with the Divine Plan View in the Nicodemus tale of chapter nine. We also see this view at the Gospel of Luke's 22:22, where Luke relates, "For the Son of Man is going as it had been determined, but woe to the one by whom he is betrayed."

In this verse, Luke seems to be suggesting that human actions were determined long before they occur. At Acts of the Apostles 2:23 and 4:24–28, we may find a similar conclusion. In the former passage, we find, "This man handed over to you according to the definite plan and foreknowledge of God…" At Acts 4:28, the text speaks of, "To do whatever your hand and your plan had predestined to take place." Again, it is clear from these passages that the Divine Plan Theory was also alive and well in first-century Palestine.

One final way that the Divine Plan Theory can be seen in the New Testament at the letter to the Romans, chapter eight, verse 38. Here Paul tells us, "To those who love God, all things work together for the Good."

By the Practical Approach, we mean a theory about evil and suffering in the New Testament that may be garnered from the behaviors and thoughts of the historical Jesus in the Gospels. In short, he appears to respond to evil and suffering in the best practical way he can, so that he helps the sufferer. This practical approach may be seen in a variety of passages, but we will look at three places where Jesus suggests metaphors about God's relationship to believers. These come at Mark 6:34, Matthew 9:36 and Luke 13:34.

In the first of these, the one from the Gospel of Mark, the text relates, "And so he went ashore and saw a great crowd, and he had compassion for them because they were like sheep without a shepherd. We find a similar incident at Matthew 9:36, but at Luke 13:34, the metaphor changes. There the Evangelist says, "Jerusalem, Jerusalem, the city that kills the prophets and stones those who are sent to it. How often have I desired to gather your children together as a hen who gathers her chicks under her wings."

What we mean by the "Practical Approach," then, is that when it comes to Jesus and his views on evil and suffering, often the simplest way he responds is to say he helps in whatever is the most practical way possible. This brings us to the "Deprivation of the Good Theory," another approach we find in the New Testament. Although the theory does not explicitly appear, it may appear implicitly in passages like Romans 5:13 and First John 3:4. The latter of these passages tells us, "Everyone who sins breaks the law. In fact, sin is lawlessness." At Romans 5:13, Paul relates, "People sinned even before the law was given, but sin was not charged against anyone's account, because there was not yet any law to break."

Already we have indicated a couple of New Testament passages related to Determinism and the Divine Plan Perspective. At First Peter 2:7 and 8, we find another example in which, "Those who do not believe... stumble because they disobeyed the word, as they were destined to do." The Greek word *athod*, or "destines," appears in many places in the New Testament, including Luke 2:34; John 17:12; Acts 13:48, 17:31, and 22:10, 11 and 14, in addition to Romans 8:29.

There are even a variety of places that looks very much like what we have called "Eschatological Verification" back in Chapter One. Among these are Matthew 12:36, Acts 17:30–31, Romans 2:16, Second Corinthians 5:9–11, and Revelation 20:11–15. In addition to all of these New Testament responses to the phenomena of evil and suffering, there also can be found a number of other miscellaneous views that cannot be cataloged in the other theories. We turn to these next.

At Romans 1:30, we learn that humans are the "inventors" of evil. First Peter 2:16 tells us not to use free will in the presence of evil. Romans 5:13 and First John 3:4 speak of lawlessness and its relationship to evil. And the letter to the Philippians at 2:5–8 seems to imply a doctrine like *Kenosis* regarding evil and suffering.

From our analysis in this first section of Chapter Eight, we have established that the writers of the New Testament have assented to, or endorsed, the following theories with respect to the phenomena of evil and suffering:

1. The Influences of Demonic Forces Theory
2. The Original Sin View
3. Retributive Justice Theory (Individual and Collective)
4. The Two Yetzerim Theory
5. The Free Will Defense
6. The Test View
7. The Moral Qualities Perspective
8. The Contrast View
9. Divine Plan Theory
10. The Practical Approach
11. The Deprivation of the Good Theory
12. Determinism
13. Eschatological Verification
14. Other miscellaneous theories

This brings us to an analysis of attitudes toward evil and suffering in the early Church. We have chosen the work of Augustine of Hippo as a representative example from this period. This will be followed by an examination of the perspectives of Thomas Aquinas in the second section of Chapter Eight, as well.

Evil and Suffering in the Early and the Medieval Church

Of the important thinkers in the first five centuries of the Christian Church, the two most important figures for the study of evil and suffering were Irenaeus and Augustine of Hippo. Augustine of Hippo (354–430) wrote a great deal on the problem of evil. The primary sources for his views include *The Confessions, On Free Will*, in *The City of God, The Enchiridion*, and his comments on the Book of Job entitled the *Adnationes*.[735]

In *The City of God*, book XI, chapter 22, Augustine tells us about his definition of evil:

> Evil is not a positive substance, the loss of the
> Good has been given the name Evil.

Augustine makes the same conclusion in chapter 28:3 of *The Enchiridion*, when he says, "Evil contributes to the perfection of the universe as do shadows in the perfection of a picture." In book XI, chapter 22, of *The City of God*, Augustine says more about the nature of evil:

> As darkness is nothing more than the absence of light,
> so Evil is merely a defect in the Good.

This looks very much like a combination of the Contrast View and the Deprivation of the Good Theory.

In his commentary *On Genesis*, chapter 22, Augustine tells us that "Evil is to be permitted for the punishment of the wicked, as well as the trial of the Good. Again, in Book XI of *The City of God*, Chapter 11, he observes,

> The nature of the good is pleasing to God, not because
> of what it is, but because of where it is, as penalty and
> just consequences of sin.

Thus, the Bishop of Hippo endorses the Retributive Justice Theory, as well.

In terms of Augustine's views on evil and suffering, the two most important biblical texts for him were Genesis 3 and Romans 5:12–20. Of course, the former is important because it depicts the fall of Adam and Eve and their expulsion from the Garden of Eden. The verses from Romans are crucial because "Death spread to all men because all men have sinned."

There are six different propositions that are the foundations of Augustine's views of evil and suffering. These are the following:

1. God is perfect, and the world he created reflects that perfection.
2. Humans were created with free will.

3. Sin and death entered the world through Adam and Eve and
   their disobedience.
4. Adam and Eve's disobedience brought about disharmony
   because all other human beings were seminally present in
   the loins of Adam.
5. Natural Evil is the consequence of the disharmony.
6. God is justified in not intervening because the suffering is a
   consequence and a punishment for human actions.

From these six propositions, it should be clear that Augustine
endorsed the Free Will Defense, Original Sin Theory and Retributive
Justice. We can add these to the Privation of the Good Theory, the Test
View and the Contrast Perspective indicated earlier. In his commentary
on Job 1:20–22, Augustine says this about Eliphaz, Bildad and Zophar,
Job's friends:

> The friends of Job do nothing more than say the
> patriarch is suffering for no other than he must
> have done something wrong.[736]

In the same work, still in his comments about the biblical Job,
Augustine refers to those, "Evil Spirits who though they cannot be said
to prefer earthly possessions to Christ, still hang on to them with a
somewhat moderate attachment to them."[737] Here, of course, Augustine
refers to the angels who have gone bad and followed Satan. He speaks
of them again in the same work when he says:

> What are ordained are beyond us, yet always what is
> arranged for us by Him who is wise and who loves us so
> is to be accepted, be it ever so grievous to endure.[738]

The phrase, "What is ordained by God is beyond us," of course,
refers to Divine Providence that goes well beyond the understandings of
all human beings. Augustine makes a similar point in his *Commentary
on Genesis* when the bishop remarks:

> Nothing is without a cause. Nothing is by chance.
> Everything happens for a purpose. Everything
> possesses some ineffable Wisdom.[739]

In another section of *The City of God*, the Bishop speaks of "bringing good out of evil," another reference to the Greater Good or Divine Plan point of view.[740] In another place in *The City of God*, Augustine again endorses the Contrast Theory, followed by these words:

> Nevertheless, Satan here, it is merely stated that he
> "came" before God, but not that he would have seen Him,
> for the vision of God is a specific grace of heavenly happiness
> according to the words of Jesus, who explained, "I tell
> you that in heaven their angels always behold the face of
> my Father, Who is in the heaven."

Chapter 16 of Book XI of *The City of God* entitled "Of the Ranks and Differences of the Creatures Estimated by Their Utility, or According to the Natural Gradations of Being," appears to consent to what we have called the Principle of Plenitude Theory. There are also places in Augustine's corpus, in his *Commentary on Genesis*, chapter 22, for example, where the bishop implies that the world he made was, in fact, the "Best of All possible Worlds."

From our analyses of Augustine of Hippo, then, we have suggested that he assents to, or believed in:

1. The Free Will Defense
2. The Contrast View
3. Original Sin Theory
4. The Demonic Forces View
5. Retributive Justice Theory
6. The Deprivation of the Good Perspective
7. The Best of All Possible Worlds Theory
8. The Divine Plan Perspective
9. The Test View
10. The Principle of Plenitude Perspective

Our other representative thinker in this period is Italian philosopher Thomas Aquinas (1225–1274), who speaks of the issues of evil and suffering in at least nine of his major works. These are: *On Potential, On Evil, On the Merits of Grace, On Original Justice*, his *Treatise on*

Angels, his lengthy *Commentary on the Book of Job*, his *Commentary on Lombard's Sentences*, and his two most important works, the *Summa Theologica* and the *Summa Contra Gentiles*.[741]

From these nine works, we can make several conclusions about what the Italian saint believed about the issues of evil and suffering. In addition to the Bible, the sources for Thomas' views include Augustine of Hippo and Thomas' German mentor Albertus Magnus.

From his *Commentary on the Book of Job*, as well as volume II, chapter 71, of the *Summa Contra Gentiles*, Thomas shows his dedication to the Divine Plan Theory. In his views on Job, he remarks:

> Now God indeed does what He wants, one thing for the sake of another, but without any stirring of His mind, because from eternity, He had in mind what He wanted to do and for what purposes. The Lord has disposed from eternity, then, to afflict Job temporarily to demonstrate the truth of virtue, so that every calumny od malicious men would be excluded.

The passage in the *Summa Contra Gentiles* is even clearer about Divine Plan Theory. It tells us:

> In God's plan, this process of becoming involves the appearance of certain beings and the disappearance of others, the existence of the more perfect, alongside the less perfect.

In volume III, chapters six to fifteen of the *Summa Contra Gentiles*, Thomas Aquinas displays his dedication to the Deprivation of the Good Perspective. He also advocates the same view in part one, question 25 of his *Summa Theologica*, as well as question 48 of the same work, where he remarks:

> In so far as anything has being, it is intelligible and suitable for a rational desire, and so rationally Good, as both Plato and Aristotle held. Therefore, evil is a "missing" Good, a privation, an absence of the Good that, either naturally or morally, ought to be there. It is privation like blindness in a person, not mere absence like blindness in a stone.

Later on, in the same chapter, Thomas adds:

Nothing in so far as it has been, is or can be Evil. It is not possible for God to make something that is less than it ought to
be... Nothing can be essentially bad. Further, there is nothing that absolutely ought not to be, not even the worst free,
rational creatures. God can be the cause of what ought not to
be by causing a penalty fit to justice.

In this passage, it should be clear that Thomas Aquinas begins
with the Privation of the Good Theory and ends with references to the
Free Will Defense, as well as Retributive Justice Theory. In part II of
the *Summa Theologica*, Thomas again refers to the Free Will Defense
as a cause of human evil at questions 2, 24 and 55. In the latter of these,
Thomas relates:

But man, judging from his course of action by the power of his
reason, can also judge about his own decision in as much as
he knows the meaning of the end and the means to that end,
and the relationship of one to the other... He is, therefore,
endowed with free choice—that is to say, with free judgment
about acting or not acting.

In part one, question 83, of the *Summa Theologica*, Thomas again
turns to the topic of free will. He observes, "Free will is the cause of its
own movement because by his own man moves himself to act." That
Thomas was a firm believer that some evil in the world was caused
by original sin is established in several of his major works mentioned
earlier. Two good examples are in questions four and five in *De Malo*,
or "On Evil," as well as in questions 81 and 82 in part one of the *Summa
Theologica*.

Similarly, in question 97 of part one of the *Summa Theologica*, in
commenting upon Romans 5:12, the Italian comments:

By sin, death came into the world, wherefore original justice
was forfeited through the sin of our first parents, as human
nature was stricken in the soul... also, it became subject to
corruption.

In question 83, article 1 of the *Summa Theologica*, Thomas
maintains that original sin was most certainly a sin against God, and he

quotes Romans 7:23 as a proof text for that view, for "Original sin is in the flesh, since unnatural concupiscence, the other law of my members, is in the flesh." A little later on, in the same text, Thomas adds:

> Whoever maintains that human nature at any point required not the Second Adam for its physician, because it was not corrupted in the First Adam, is considered as an enemy to the grace of God.

Thomas Aquinas comes close to concluding that the world that God made was the best of possible worlds, in part one, question 25 of the *Summa Theologica*, when he says, "The Universe is the best one possible." He combines this view with the "Principle of Plenitude," just a few paragraphs later in the same work: "Metaphysical Evil, or imperfection, is necessarily involved in its constitution, since it must be finite, and could not have been involved with infinite perfection that belongs to God alone."

Thomas Aquinas also endorses the Influences of Demonic Forces Approach in a variety of his other major works, as well. In part II of the *Summa Theologica*, for examples, in questions 24, 49 and 55, as well as part I, question 114, Thomas deals explicitly with the notion of the demonic as one of the causes of human evil and suffering. Another place where we can see this view is in his comments on Satan in the Book of Job. In that regard, Thomas asks in his *Commentary of the Book of Job,* "Whether there can be one supreme evil that is the cause of all evil?" After raising six objections to answer this question in the negative, Thomas goes on to say:

> Because the First Principle of the Good is the highest and more perfect Good, there can be no Supreme Evil because Evil is a deprivation of the Good. If there could be a wholly Evil being, it would destroy itself, because the subject of Evil is always the Good.[742]

In other words, If Satan is purely evil, and evil is nothing more than a Deprivation of the Good, then it follows that there can be no totally evil creature. Also in question 49 in the same book, Thomas Aquinas again speaks of the demonic when he relates:

> Now certain spirits are evil—not by nature or by creation—
> since the Author of both natures is God and the Supreme
> Good and God only causes good things, so they become evil
> by their own fault.

This passage begins as an endorsement of Deprivation of the Good Theory, and then it morphs into an assent to the Free Will Defense when it says, "by their own fault." In part I of the *Summa Theologica*, in question 61, Thomas suggests that the sins of the bad angels are "Envy and Pride." Thomas relates, "Under envy and pride, as found in the demons, are comprised all other sins derived from them." In Question 64 of the same book, Thomas turns to the punishment of the bad angels. Hs suggests that that the "punishment of them may be deferred until the Final Judgment."

In question 48 of the first part of the *Summa Theologica*, as well as articles one and three of *De Malo*, Thomas appears to lean in the direction of the idea that one cannot have evil unless we have good. Thomas believes that evil and good are bound up with each other, in the sense that the former is dependent on the latter because it is a privation of it. So, perhaps we may add the Contrast View to the positions of evil and suffering held by Thomas Aquinas.

Finally, in his 1936 book *The Great Chain of Being*, Arthur Lovejoy held the opinion that Thomas Aquinas had a "modified version of the principle of plenitude."[743] If Lovejoy is correct about that, we may add that view to our list of responses to the issues of evil and suffering in the works of Thomas Aquinas. Indeed, from our analyses, we may conclude that Italian philosopher Thomas Aquinas assented to, or endorsed, the following points of view:

1. Retributive Justice Theory
2. The Demonic Forces View
3. Original Sin Theory
4. The Free Will Defense
5. The Divine Plan Theory
6. The Contrast View
7. The Test Theory
8. The Moral Qualities Perspective

9. The Best of All Possible Worlds Theory
10. The Deprivation of the Good View
11. The Principle of Plenitude Position
12. Eschatological Verification Theory

This brings us to the next section of Chapter Eight—views on evil and suffering in the Reformation period, in which we will examine the contributions of Martin Luther and John Calvin.

Evil and Suffering in the Christian Reformation

Both Martin Luther (1483–1546) and John Calvin (1509–1564) had much to say about evil and suffering in the Christian Reformation of the sixteenth century. Luther's sources for his views on the matter were the following: Augustine, Luther's method of exegesis, his translation of the Book of Job, his *Table Talk*, *On the Bondage of the Will*, his great exchange with Erasmus, the German's *Commentary on Romans*, as well as many of his other written works.

From these sources, Luther's most significant contributions to the issues of evil and suffering were versions of the Divine Plan View, Retributive Justice Theory, the Original Sin Perspective, and an indication of the use of the Hidden God Perspective. We will examine these one at a time here.

For the most part, Luther agreed that God created the world *Ex Nihilo*, or "out of nothing." This belief for him emphasizes God's complete omnipotence. It also carries the added consequence that anything that is wrong with the universe cannot be attributed to God since He is also All-Good and All-Knowing. For Luther, the entrance point of evil and suffering in the world is the work of Satan and the actions of Adam and Eve in the Garden of Eden.[744]

One response that Luther does not take, however, is the Free Will Defense. Indeed, in his response to Erasmus, Luther was decidedly against the idea of human freedom as a source for human evil and suffering. For Luther, power is a zero-sum game. All of it resides in the Divine and none in human beings. For Luther, salvation is not won or lost by human moral choices. It is decided simply by the Grave of God.[745]

In the fifth section of *On the Bondage of the Will*, Luther explicitly takes up the issue of theodicy. He reasons that "If there is no human free will and all that occurs happens by necessity," then in his view, God is the author of sin. Erasmus counters this argument by indicating that the blame for the presence of evil and suffering in the world, at least in part, is owed to the exercise of free choice. Erasmus's response is in his 1526 work *Hyperaspistes*.[746]

The debate between the two centered on two biblical passages, Exodus 9:12 and Romans 9:14ff. In both of these places, God is said to have "hardened the heart" of Pharaoh. Erasmus began the debate in September of 1524 when he wrote his essay "On Free Will."[747] Luther responded with *On the Bondage of the Will*, published in December of 1525.[748] Erasmus answered Luther again in February of 1526. And Luther responded again in 1527.[749]

Ten years later, on July 9, 1537, Luther wrote about the issue of free will:

> Regarding the plan to collect my writings in volumes, I am not eager about it, for I acknowledge none of my books with the exceptions of the *Bondage of the Will* and the *Catechism*.[750]

The theological position of Erasmus was quite simple. Many things in scripture are obscure and complicated, such as the dual natures of Jesus and the nature of the Trinity. The issue of free will is another of these obscurities. In Erasmus, humans are rewarded or punished according to the moral decisions they have made.[751] For Erasmus, the church fathers and the allegorical method of scripture are the most fundamental tools for interpreting the Bible.[752]

Luther's position in the debate is also quite clear. He eschews allegory in favor of the letter and the spirit. Salvation occurs through the Grace of God. "Free will," Luther says, "is a fiction among real things, a name with no reality."[753] Luther concludes on the matter:

> Therefore, we must go to extremes, deny free will altogether and ascribe everything to God.[754]

For Luther, salvation occurs through predestination. "God has put my salvation out of my control and will and under the control of His

Will and Grace."[755] In Luther's view, then, evil and suffering occur in the world, most fundamentally, because of the Divine Plan that God has set out long before the existence of human beings in the universe. As part of that plan, it was mandated that Adam and Eve would fall through the dispensation of God's Grace.[756]

With that mandate and with that plan—at least according to Martin Luther—God's actions are often incomprehensible to human beings. In this sense, Luther tells us, the deity is often a "Hidden God." In his *On the Bondage of the Will*, Luther tells us:

> It is not for us to inquire into these mysteries, but to adore them...God is He Whose Will no cause or ground may be laid down as its rule or standard, for nothing is on the level of it, but it is itself the rule of all things. What God wills is not right because He ought, or was bound, so to will; on the contrary, what takes place must be right because He so wills it.[757]

Here Luther alludes to the Divine Plan Theory, as well as the hiddenness of God. The German theologian also says a great deal about the role of Satan in His Divine Plan. Indeed, Luther believes that Satan primarily acts in his own self-interest. He relates:

> ...Like Satan, His Prince, is wholly turned to self and to his own. He does not seek God... He seeks his own riches, and glory, and works, and wisdom, and power, and sovereignty in everything, and wants to enjoy it in peace... He can no more restrain His fury than he can stop his self-seeking; and he can no more stop his self-seeking than he can stop his existing.[758]

In speaking of those who are outside the community of God, Luther relates, "The evil that we experience is not comparable to theirs, for they are caught in their sins of disbelief, in a trap of the devil and those who follow him."[759] For Luther, the entrance point for evil and suffering in the universe is the works of Satan that result in human sin. The work of Satan is the cause of evil, and human evil is the most significant manifestation of this evil. But sin and evil, in the final analysis for Luther, were a mystery.[760] As he concludes in *On the Bondage of the Will*, "Don't try to explain it. We simply don't know."[761]

Finally, many interpreters of Luther have suggested that another fundamental position of Luther's about evil and suffering is the view called "kenosis." This word refers to the doctrine that Christ "self-empties" in his incarnation. The word comes from the Greek of Philippians 2:7 that relates that Jesus "emptied himself by taking the form of a servant." In other words, Jesus laid aside his divine nature so that he could display his human nature.

In terms of Jesus' relationship to humans, Luther thought that the best moral behavior of believers is to imitate, in the best way possible, the moral life of Jesus Christ, what we have called the *Jobus Christi* Model, as a basic response to evil and suffering.

In summary, then, when it came to the issues of evil and suffering, reformer Martin Luther assented to the following views: Divine Plan; the Influences of Demonic Forces Theory; the Hidden God Perspective; and the Kenosis Response, or Jobus Christi View. This brings us to what John Calvin has had to say about the issues of evil and suffering.

The sources for ascertaining the views of reformer John Calvin on the phenomena of evil and suffering include Augustine of Hippo; Calvin's *The Institutes of the Christian Religion*, particularly chapter fourteen, sections 17 and 18; and Calvin's 159 sermons on the biblical Book of Job. Like his fellow reformer, Luther, Calvin rejected the Free Will Defense as a response to the issues of evil and suffering. At the same time, Calvin can be seen to endorse the following responses and answers on:

Theodicy and the Problem of Evil
Retributive Justice Theory
The Moral Qualities View
The Test Perspective
Eschatological Verification Theory
The Divine Plan Perspective
The Influences of Demonic Forces View

In volume III of *The Institutes*, Calvin tells us this about the Will of God:

> For God's will is so much the highest rule of righteousness
> that whatever He wills by the very fact that He willed it, it

must be considered righteous. When, therefore, one asks why
God so willed, you are seeking something greater and higher
than God's Will, which cannot be found.[762]

From this passage, it should be clear that Calvin assents to the
Divine Plan Theory. In his *Commentary on Genesis*, in commenting
on Genesis 3:7, "and their eyes were opened," Calvin suggests that
in the eating of the fruit, Adam and Eve were "confused," and they
"felt shame" because of the "stirring of sexual concupiscence." Thus,
it should be clear that Calvin assented to Original Sin Theory, as well.

It is just as clear that Calvin identified the serpent in Genesis 3
with the figure of Satan. He makes this point continually throughout
The Institutes of the Christian Religion, particularly in book IV of that
work. In fact, in that book, the reformer relates:

As angelic hosts, they help in God's Plan, the Demons are
in opposition to His work, though always under His control.
Scriptures warn us against the adversary and equips us for
combat against the adversary.

Here Calvin combines Divine Plan Theory with the view that
demons, at times, try to influence the behaviors of human beings. In
discussing the fallen angels narrative, Calvin remarks in *The Institutes*:

Wherever they may travel, they draw their chains after them,
and they remained involved in their own shades. And mean-
while, their final torment is put off until the final day.

Calvin employs Retributive Justice Theory here and, by extension,
also asserts the Eschatological Verification Point of View. In the first
book of his *Institutes*, at 14.18, Calvin speaks of "unclean spirits"
and that God "occasionally wounds" these spirits. This language of
wounding may be assenting either to the Moral Qualities View or to the
Test Perspective.

In sum, if you have followed our analysis here, John Calvin appears
to have endorsed: Retributive Justice Theory, The Moral Qualities
Perspective, the Test Theory, the Eschatological Verification View, the
Influences of Demonic Forces Perspective, Original Sin Theory, and,
of course, Divine Plan Theory. This brings us to Christian responses to

the phenomena of evil and suffering in the eighteenth century, or early modern period, the subject matter of the next section of this Chapter Eight.

Early Modern Christian Responses to Evil and Suffering: Eighteenth and Nineteenth Centuries

We have chosen as representative Christian thinkers from this period the works of German philosopher Immanuel Kant (1724–1804) and British artist William Blake (1757–1827). The former thinker, in his "On the Failure of All Attempted Philosophical Theodicies," critically discusses many of the theological responses cataloged in Chapter One of this study on evil and suffering in the world's religions.[763] In that work, Kant correctly identifies the view of Job's first three friends as Retributive Justice Theory. Kant also maintains that the Book of Job goes from that theory to a position much like G. W. Leibniz's Best of All Possible World Theory, as well as the Divine Plan View that Kant found in the Elihu and in the God speeches of the Book of Job.[764]

Another important view that can be found in Kant's "Failure" is that the German suggests that Job's morality is not the result of his faith. Rather his faith is the result of his morality.[765] Kant says nothing, however, about the angry speeches of Job, mostly found in places like chapter three, where Job curses the day of his birth. For Kant, there is only the Patient Job, as exemplified in the prose prologue and epilogue.[766]

Another element of Kant's "Failure" is that he completely dismisses the Free Will Defense, Original Sin Theory and the Retributive Justice View and favors instead what he calls "Optimism," a modified version of G. W. Leibniz's theory.[767]

Immanuel Kant also wrote a great deal about natural disasters and earthquakes, particularly in his essay, "The Only Possible Argument in Support of a Demonstration of the Existence of God," published in December of 1762.[768] In that article, Kant raises the possibility of natural disasters being "predestined by God as acts of Divine Punishment for the sins of human beings."[769]

Kant also completed two separate essays on the phenomenon of earthquakes, particularly after the Lisbon earthquake in November of

1755. The first of these was written in early 1756. The second was written and published a few months later in what Kant considered a "second installment."[770] In this second essay on earthquakes, Kant gives a much more scientific and rational explanation of the phenomena, not unlike what has come to be called the "Science of Tectonics" in the twentieth century.[771]

In this second essay, Kant also takes a different theological position on earthquakes. In fact, in the second missive, Kant suggests that God uses earthquakes and other natural disasters to "teach people something." And what Kant had in mind was something close to the Test Theory, as well as the Moral Qualities Point of View.[772]

Later in 1756, Immanuel Kant wrote a fascinating article about the nature of the wind and another on the comet that appeared on July 23, 1762, across the skies of Europe.[773] Kant wrote another essay entitled, "On the Volcanoes on the Moon."[774] He also wrote extensively on the phenomenon of the weather in an essay completed in 1794.[775]

Another question that Kant raises in many of these works described here is whether "There is more good in the world or more evil?" The philosopher of Konigsberg comes down on the side of the good. This is another factor that contributed to his view of optimism when it came to responding to the phenomena of evil and suffering.[776]

Finally, Kant believed in a philosophical category he calls "Radical Evil." He says we become radically evil when we subordinate the moral law to our own self-interest. Kant claims that we never do wrong for the sake of doing wrong, but only for the sake of prudence or from the inclinations to more limited goods. Kant introduced the category of Radical Evil to explain events like the Holocaust or a serial murderer or rapist. It is a category of evil reserved for the most evil among us.[777]

Our other representative figure from this period of Christian history is the artist and poet William Blake (1757 to 1827), who is considered the first of the great British Romantics. Blake began writing poetry at age twelve and began an apprenticeship to a London engraver at fourteen. Blake is important for our purposes because he completed a set of twenty-four illustrations of the Book of Job in 1825, just eighteen months before his death.[778]

In examining these illustrations, it soon becomes clear that Blake had his own peculiar system of metaphysical thought, often far from what we would consider reality. For example, in the Job illustrations, the right is the good or the spiritual foot. The left is the evil or material foot. All the calamities that come to visit Job always come with the left foot first. The face of God in the Job illustrations and the face of Job are identical.[779]

Blake takes a page out of the work of Sigmund Freud when he indicates that the characters of the Book of Job are reifications of different aspects of Job's personality. Stan is shown as the demonic, destructive aspect in Job. In the illustrations, Job's wife is the feminine side of the patriarch. Job's children are not lost to him in a physical sense but in a spiritual sense. Each character goes into the fuller understanding of the patriarch from the land of Uz.[780]

William Blake produced illustrations of the Book of Job throughout his adult life. Even as early as 1785, he completed an illustration of Job "Protesting His Innocence."[781] The same piece was completely redone seven years later as a powerful, septile painting. Then came the construction of the Job series in the early years of the 1820s and their publication in 1825.[782] This brings us to the final section of this chapter on evil and suffering in the Christian tradition, in which we will explore representative Christian attitudes toward evil and suffering in the twentieth and twenty-first centuries.

Contemporary Christian Views of Evil and Suffering: Twentieth and Twenty-first Centuries

We have chosen in this section to speak of the Christian attitudes toward evil and suffering in the works of William James, John Henry Newman and Gilbert Chesterton as key representative examples of this contemporary period. William James (1842–1910) makes several observations about evil and suffering throughout his major works, including his *Principles of Psychology* (1890), *The Varieties of Religious Experiences* (1902) and his *Pragmatism* (1907).

In each of these works, James mentions the biblical Book of Job and how the patriarch deals with evil and suffering. His overall view of the book is that it is about the impotence of man and the omnipotence of God. In general, in his views on the phenomena of evil and suffering, James takes a view quite like the Divine Plan Point of View in relationship to the man from Uz.

John Henry Newman (1801–1890) wrote a great deal about evil and suffering in his scholarly works, as well as in his literary output. In his *Parochial and Plain Sermons*, Newman included many sermons on the Book of Job, including one on Job 8:15. Newman chose this passage because it is one of the few in the poetry portions of Job that is consistent with the Patient Job Point of View of the prose of the book.[783]

Apparently, this was because Newman's overall theory about the phenomena of evil and suffering is a very optimistic view, perfectly consistent with the Divine Plan Point of View. Newman was well aware of the new movement in Christian exegesis on the Bible that concentrated on form-critical and literary aspects of the text. But, for the most part, Newman eschews those, and he concentrates instead on the poetic and theological value of the book.

Finally, Gilbert Chesterton (1874–1936) brought out an edition of the Book of Job in which he accompanied the text with a lengthy essay about the meaning of the book.[784] In that essay, Chesterton suggests that the main idea of the book of Job is what he calls "The loneliness of God," or what we have called the "Hiddenness of God" in this study.[785]

Chesterton goes on to suggest that the Book of Job offers a "series of intellectual gems," or "beauties," that cannot be found in most other books of the Old Testament. He also raises the question if Job is an optimistic or a pessimistic book, and the British critic is deeply affected by God's two speeches from the whirlwind. Indeed, he describes them as possessing "grandeur."[786]

Chesterton also wrote about evil and suffering in many of his other works, including his novel *The Man Who Was Thursday*.[787] Chesterton also explicitly employed what we have referred to as the Free Will Defense throughout his work *The Surprise*.[788] In fact, when it comes to Chesterton's novels, the approaches he seems to take toward evil and suffering are among the most classical responses to be found in the contemporary Christian period. He is, at once, an advocate of the Hidden God Theory, while at the same time, he uses many of the traditional theological categories of the Christian Church.

When it comes to evil and suffering in the contemporary Christian period, Chesterton's work has the flavor of modern existentialism, while at the same time, his characters often express what we only can call the deepest expressions of faith. This brings us to the major conclusions of Chapter Eight. The subject matter of the ninth chapter to follow is responses to evil and suffering in the Islamic faith.

Conclusions to Chapter Eight

We began this eighth chapter with the goal of discussing attitudes toward the phenomena of evil and suffering in the Christian Church from the writings of the New Testament in the first century up to and including contemporary times in the late twentieth and early twenty-first centuries. We have also shown examples in the New Testament where these many theories have been employed.

In the remainder of Chapter Eight, we provided a series of historical periods in the history of Christianity, where the subjects of evil and suffering had come to the fore. Rather than giving many details and figures in these periods, we instead described and discussed representative thinkers in those periods. In the early and medieval period of the Church, we concentrated on the views of Augustine of Hippo and Italian philosopher Thomas Aquinas.

In the Reformation period of Christian history, we chose the works of Martin Luther and John Calvin and their views on evil and suffering in the Reformation Church. These sections of Chapter Eight were followed by a discussion of two more representative Christian thinkers in the eighteenth and nineteenth centuries, Immanuel Kant and Romantic poet and illustrator William Blake, who completed a series of illustrations on the Book of Job published in 1825.

In the final section of Chapter Eight, we examined three twentieth-century Christian thinkers and their views on the phenomena of evil and suffering. These were philosopher William James, theologian and exegete John Henry Newman, and British author and literary critic Gilbert Chesterton. These three thinkers, as we have shown, have made important contributions to the history of Christian answers and responses to the issues of evil and suffering.

The next chapter—Chapter Nine—is dedicated to a discussion of many of the ways that the Muslim faith has responded to the issues of evil and suffering, beginning with the inception of the faith in the seventh century CE and continuing up to Muslim responses to the phenomena of evil and suffering in the contemporary Muslim world.

Chapter Nine will be followed by a conclusive chapter in which we will catalog the major conclusions we have made in this study about the responses to evil and suffering that may be found in the religions of the world. The tenth chapter will be followed by a group of appendices in which we list the many foreign words and phrases that we have mentioned in this study.

Chapter Nine: Evil and Suffering in the Islamic Faith

> Those who believe and perform good deeds will not be held guilty for what they have done in the past if they fear Allah.
>
> —The Holy Qur'an (Author's translation)

> Repel Evil with that which is best. We know best what they describe, and we seek refuge from the suggestions of the Devils.
>
> —The Holy Qur'an 6:96 (Author's translation)

> No fatigue, nor disease, nor sorrow, nor sadness, nor hurt, nor distress, will befall a Muslim, even if it was the prick he received from a thorn, but that Allah expiates some of his sins for that.
>
> —Sahih Al-Bukhari, *Hadith* (Author's translation)

Introduction

The purpose of this ninth chapter is to describe and discuss the many ways the religion of Islam has responded to the issues of evil and suffering in its history. To that end, we will begin Chapter Nine with a short introduction to the religion of Islam. This will be followed by the second section of Chapter Nine by an analysis of the many places in the Muslim Holy Book, *Al-Qur'an*, where the phenomenon of *Sharr*, or "Evil" in Arabic, is discussed.

These two sections of this chapter will be followed by an analysis of several places in Hadith literature where the origins and the meanings of *Sharr* are a central topic of conversation. In the fourth section of this chapter, we shall indicate many places in medieval Islamic philosophy where evil and suffering are discussed. Finally, we will end Chapter Nine with some comments on how modern Islamic philosophy has dealt with the phenomena of evil and suffering.

However, before moving to these other tasks, we will first make some comments on the classical Arabic vocabulary about words related to "Good" and "Evil." The normal Arabic word for "good" is *tayyib*, whose plural form is *tayyabin*. The moral sense of the word good in classical Arabic is *khayir*, such as in expressions like *khayir wa sharr*, or "good and evil." When evil is used as an adjective, it is generally the word *sharir*, whose plural is *ashrar*. As indicated earlier, when "evil" is used as a noun, the word is usually *Sharr*.

Another classical Arabic word used to designate "bad" is *kharab* and is often employed in modern Arabic. Another word used as both a verb and a noun is the Arabic word *kidder* and the noun form *keddir*. Other classical words related to evil are the word *ghish* meaning "deceit," and its derivatives like *ghashash*, "deceitful," and *ghashsh*, which is the verb, "to deceive." The Arabic equivalent of "sly" is the term *hayyal*, and its plural form, *hayyalin*.

The Arabic words for "tempt" and "temptation" are *jedheb* and *tajriba*, while "tempting" is the word *mushawwiq*. The Arabic *baliya* is rendered "trial" or "test" in English. *Darif* is the normal word used when something is "vulgar." And the word for "fraud" is usually *tadlis*.

The Arabic nouns for the demonic are *Shaytan* and *Iblis*. The plurals of these words are *Shayatin* and *Abalis*. The Arabic *'aqsi* means "perverse," and *qabih* is usually rendered "repulsive." Other classical Arabic terms related to the good and the right are *addal* (right); *salah*, or "righteousness," and *bil haqq*, or "rightfully." Both *zeniyah* and *salah* are often translated as "virtue," and *fadhl* is "virtuous."

In short, classical Arabic has a rich vocabulary when it comes to words related to good and evil, as well as terms connected to bad, right, perversity, deception, temptation and righteousness. This brings us to a section of Chapter Nine, where we will give a short introduction to the religion of Islam.

A Short Introduction to Islam

The religion known as Islam began in the seventh century CE with its prophet, or *Nabi*, a man named Muhammad. The words *Islam, Muslim, Moslem* and *Salam*, all come from the Semitic root SLM, which are connected to words associated with "Peace," such as *Shalom*, in classical Hebrew, or *Salaam*, in classical Arabic. Like Judaism and Christianity, Islam arose in the Middle East, but it soon became a world religion.

In the world today, there are more than a billion Muslims across the globe—from Bosnia to Zanzibar, as well as in the United States and even in the People's Republic of China. At its most fundamental base, Islam is a form of monotheism, or belief in one God. The days of its founder are usually given as 570 to 632 CE. He was originally a merchant in the city of Mecca in the Arabian Peninsula. From the year 620 until his death in 632, the Prophet Muhammad received a series of visions for his God, Allah. In these visions, the Angel *Jibril* instructed Muhammad to "Recite" what he had learned in these visitations. These recitations became the Muslim holy book *Al-Qur'an*. The Prophet Muhammad died in 632 CE. His followers believed that he was the final of a long line of prophets stretching back to Abraham, Moses and Jesus.

There are six major beliefs of the Islamic faith. These may be summarized this way:

1. Tawhid
2. Mala'ika
3. Al-Qur'an
4. Nabiim
5. Yawm Qayamah
6. Al-Qadar[789]

The first of these beliefs is that any Muslim must believe that there is only one God, Allah, and that He was the Creator of all things. Allah is All-Good, All-Knowing and All-Powerful. He has no offspring, no race, no gender and no physical body. Allah is a Pure Spirit, and He is not affected by any characteristics of life on Earth.

The second of the "Six Pillars of Islam" is that the Muslim must believe in the existence of the *Mala'ika*, the classical Arabic plural of the word for "angels." These are unseen beings who worship Allah and carry out His orders throughout the universe. Among the *Mala'ika* are several notable members of the race, including the Angel *Jibril*, or Gabriel, who brought the revelations of Al-Qur'an to the Prophet Muhammad.[790] Other notable angels in Islam include *Mika'il*, or "Michael," and the *Churribim*, or "Cherubim," as well as many other noted angels.

The third of the Six Pillars is that the believing Muslim must assent to the Book of Allah, the Holy Qur'an, as well as other holy books including the Torah, given to Moses, the Psalms revealed to King David (*Daud* in Arabic), as well as the *Scrolls* given to Ibrahim, or Abraham, and the *Injil*, or "Gospels," given to *Isa*, or "Jesus." All Muslims are required to believe that these earlier scriptures in their original forms also were divinely revealed to these other prophets.[791]

The fourth of the Six Pillars of Islam is belief in the *Nabiim*, or the "Prophets." All Muslims must believe that Allah brought revelations to a long series of prophets going all the way back to Adam himself. Twenty-five of these prophets are mentioned in Al-Qur'an. Among these include Adam; Nuh, or Noah; *Ibrahim*, or Abraham; *Musa*, or Moses; and *Isa*, or Jesus, among many others.[792]

The idea of the *Yawm Qiyamah*, or the "Day of Judgment," is the fifth of the Six Pillars. This is a belief that all humans will be judged for their actions in this life at the End of Time. Those who followed the prescriptions of Allah will be rewarded with Paradise or, *Jannah*. Those who had strayed from those prescriptions will take up residence in *Jahahnam*, or Hell in Arabic.[793]

Finally, the believing Muslim is required to assent to what is called *Al-Qadar*, in classical Arabic. This term might be translated as "Allah's Decrees." That is, that all that happens, in the Heavens as well as on the Earth are governed by Divine Decree.[794]

The religion of Islam also has five basic requirements that all believers are bound to follow. These are:

1. The *Shahadah*
2. The *Salaat*
3. The *Sawm*

4. The *Zakat*
5. The *Hajj*[795]

The first of these is a "Declaration of Faith." It simply says, "There is no God but Allah and Muhammad is His Prophet."[796] The word *Salaat* means "prayer." All believing Muslims are required to pray five times a day, and that this reminds the believer to remember that Allah is indeed the greatest virtue, and He helps people adhere to the path of Righteousness.[797] The classical Arabic word, *Sawm.* means "fasting." It requires that all believing Muslims must fast during the daylight hours of the month of Ramadan of the Muslim calendar, which includes abstinence from eating, drinking, smoking and sexual relations in those hours. This reminds the believer of his or her dependence on Allah, as well as their kinship with, and responsibility for, the millions of human beings in the world who experience involuntary fasting because they have no food.[798]

The Arabic word *Zakat* is associated with the "Purification of Wealth," in that all Muslims are required annually to give a certain portion of their wealth to the poor, the disabled and the deprived. It is supposed to remind all believing Muslims that all bounties, ultimately, come from Allah.[799]

Finally, the fifth requirement is that of the *Hajj*, or "Pilgrimage" to the holy city of Mecca, that all Muslims are required to make at least once in their life if personal circumstances permit one to do so. Muslim believers perform prescribed acts of worship at the Ka'baa in Mecca, which, according to Al-Qur'an, was built by Ibrahim and his son Ishmael. Each of these five prescribed acts of worship brings daily and repeated sustenance to all believers of the Muslim faith.[800]

In Islam, there are several holidays. *Al-Hijra* is the Islamic New Year. It marks the end of Muhammad's journey from Mecca to Medina. The *Eid Al-Adha* is the "Festival of Sacrifice." This is a four-day holiday celebrating Ibrahim's sacrifice of his son, which in Islam is Ishmael. The Prophet Muhammad's birthday is also considered a holiday. The Feast of *Eid Al-Fitr* is a celebration that marks the end of Ramadan, the month of fasting.[801]

Followers of the Islamic faith believe in both the immortality of the soul as well as in the resurrection of the body at the end of time.[802]

Muslim history also posits the belief in a place known as *Barzakh,* where the *nafs* or soul of a believer exists between life on Earth and the Great Beyond. It is an intermediary state, almost like the Roman Church's purgatory.[803]

Muslims also believe that God, or Allah, has ninety-nine different names and a hundredth name that is only known by Allah.[804] They believe that *Al-Dajjal,* or the Antichrist, will appear at the End of Time after a series of signs that will harken his arrival.[805]

The Antichrist will do battle with the *Mahdi,* or the "Messiah." At that time, one of Allah's angels, *Israfil,* will blow his special *Sur,* or horn, to begin the End Times in Islam. Indeed, he is scheduled to blow the horn three times, with each time ushering in a different sign.[806]

There are seven levels of Heaven, or Paradise, in Islam. They are in ascending and in descending orders, and the expression "being in Seventh Heaven" was originally an expression in the early Arabic of the Islamic faith.[807]

In the Islamic faith, the one unforgivable sin is called *Shirk,* the classical Arabic word for "idolatry." This is a prohibition against worshipping anyone or anything other than the god Allah. Those who practiced *Shirk* are sometimes called *muskrikun,* the plural form of the word *muskrat.* Those who practiced *Shirk* may be forgiven by Allah if he or she asks for forgiveness before his last breath on Earth. It is likely that one of the reasons for the need to instigate the prohibition of *Shirk* was the Christian Trinity that early Islam saw as a belief in three gods.[808]

In terms of sacred places in Islam, the most sacred place in the faith is the *Ka'ba,* the supposed shrine built by Ibrahim according to Muslim tradition around a sacred black stone. The Prophet Muhammad specifically designated Mecca as the holy city of Islam and the direction of the *Qibla,* or direction to which Muslims should orient their prayers.[809]

The second most important place in Islam is Medina, the "City of the Prophet." It is in the Hejaz region of the western portion of Saudi Arabia. It was to Medina that Muhammad fled when he was initially driven out of Mecca, and the place where he attracted his first followers.

The third most sacred city in the Islamic faith is Jerusalem, which was the original *Qibla* before it was changed to Mecca. Jerusalem is revered in Islam because, in Muslim tradition, the Prophet Muhammad miraculously traveled to Jerusalem in what is called the "Night Journey," in which Muhammad was guided to the city by the Angel Jibril, and when they arrived there, Muhammad ascended into Heaven, or *Jannah*.[810]

In Shiite Islam, two other cities are revered. The first is Karbala, about one hundred kilometers southwest of the city of Baghdad. Shiites consider Karbala to be the second holiest place in the world, second only to Mecca.[811] The other sacred city for the Shia tradition is Najaf. It is the center of political power in Iraq.

In terms of sacred persons in Islam, there are many traditional religious leaders like the *Caliph*, the *Imam*, the *Grand Imam*, the *Grand Mufti,* the office of the *Ayatollah*, and the *Grand Ayatollah*. The *Caliph* was the name of the head of the Muslim community after the death of the Prophet Muhammad. The word *Imam* means "Leader" in Arabic and is used to designate members of the clergy in Islam. The "Grand Imam" is a title only used in Egypt to refer to the most renowned of Sheikhs. The title "Grand Mufti" refers to the highest official of religious law, or *Shariah*, in Sunni Islam.[812]

The Farsi title *Ayatollah* is a prestigious station given to major clergymen in Shia Islam. The "Grand Ayatollah" is the highest rank member of the clergy in the Shiite tradition. He is considered to be the most theologically authoritative clergyman in the Shia, as well as the most authentic source of Shiite Shariah.[813]

This brings us to the second section of Chapter Nine, in which we examine how the phenomena of evil and suffering are mentioned in the Muslim holy book Al-Qur'an.

Evil and Suffering in Al-Qur'an

Many of the comments made about evil and suffering in the Al-Qur'an are very general remarks about good and evil. Take, for example, Surah 5:100, where the text relates, "Tell them that the Evil and the Good are not equal, even though the examples of the Evil may be pleasing to you. So fear God, O men of wisdom, and you may happily find success."[814] Just a few verses earlier in the same Surah, we learn:

> Those who believe and perform good deeds will not be held
> guilty for what they have done in the past, if they fear Allah
> and believe and do good things and are conscious of Allah
> and believe and will fear Him and do the good, for Allah loves
> those who do the Good.[815]

At Surah 29:4–5 of the Holy Book, the text asks, "Do those who do evil think that they will get the better of us? How bad in the judgment that they make. He who hopes to meet Allah should know that Allah's appointed time will surely arrive. He is all-Hearing as well as All-Knowing." Surah 39:51 also speaks of those who do evil. It relates:

> Then the worst of what they had done overtook them. So
> will the evil deeds of those who are sinners among them will
> recoil back on them.

At Surah 41:34 of the Qur'an, we see the relative values of good and evil. The text relates, "Good and Evil are not alike. Repel Evil with what is Good. That you will find your enemy like a close, affectionate friend."

In many places in the Muslim Holy Book, the idea of evil is mentioned simply to remind the reader about the demonic. Consider, for example, Surah 17:27 that tells us, "Those who dissipate their wealth are the brothers of the *Shayatin* [devils], and *Shaytan* was ungrateful to his Lord." At 58:19, we see a similar example:

> *Shaytan* has gotten the better of them, and he made them
> forget the name of Allah. Indeed, they belong to the factions
> of *Shaytan*. Will not *Shaytan's* faction not perish in the end?

At Surah 2:168–169, we see another example of the ways in which the demonic attempts to influence believing Muslims. We also can see the Test Theory at *ayat* 155 of the same Surah; The Free Will Defense at Surah 4:79. And Retributive Justice Theory is embodied at 17:16.

In Muhammad's Farewell Sermon, the prophet gives us advice about the demonic when he said: "Beware of *Shaytan*. He is desperate to divert you from the worship of Allah, so be wary of him in matters about religion." At Surah 6:96 to 98, we also find some advice regarding the demonic. These verses related:

Repel Evil with that which is best. We know best what they describe. And say, 'My Lord, I seek refuge in you from the suggestions of the *Shayatin*. And I seek refuge in you, my Lord, lest they attend me.

Many passages in Al-Qur'an suggest that much evil in the world is caused by Iblis' refusal to prostrate himself to Adam. Surah 15:28 is typical of these. This *ayat*, or verse, tells us:

O Iblis, what is your reason for not being among those who prostrated themselves? Iblis said, "I am not one to prostrate myself to a man, whom Thou did create from sounding clay, from mud molded into shape." Then Allah said, 'Then get yourself out of here, for you are rejected, accursed, and the curse shall be on you until the Judgment Day.

In several places of Al-Qur'an when evil is mentioned, it comes in the context of other things that are thought to be evil, like ignorance. Consider Surah 7:199, which gives us the advice to "Hold to forgiveness, command what is right, but turn away from the ignorant."

Many other verses about *Sharr*, or evil in Al-Qur'an, are simply a reiteration of what happens to evil-doers on Judgment Day. Consider, for example, Surah 30: 10, "Therefore, Evil is the end for those who do Evil, for they denied the signs of Allah and made fun of them." To cite another example, Surah 22:23 tells us that "Whoever puts obstruction in the plans of Allah will receive violent punishment." This appears to be a combination of the Divine Plan Theory with the Retributive Justice view, as outlined in Chapter One.

In surah 2:210, the Holy Book of Islam provides an example of Retributive Justice Theory, when the text asks:

Do you reckon that you will enter the Garden without there coming upon you the like of those who have passed away before you?

Evils and griefs afflicted them, and they trembled so much that the Apostle and those who were with him said, 'When will the help of Allah come? O truly, the help of Allah is near.

At the Battle of Uhud, it was reported that Muhammad said, "When a blow strikes you and you already have struck back, will you say, 'What just happened?' And you say, 'It was from themselves. Truly, Allah has power over every little thing.'"[816] Obviously, this is another example of Retributive Justice Theory, perhaps combined with Divine Plan Theory in its language of "power over every little thing."

At Surah 2:109, we find Divine Plan Theory in these words:

> To Allah belongs East and West.
> No matter where you turn,
> There is the face of Allah.
> Truly, Allah is All-Embracing and All-Knowing.

Allah's plan even extends as far as the splits that open grain and the date-stone. "He brings forth the living and the dead, and he brings forth the dead from the living. That, precisely, is Allah." At Surah 9:92–94, we find an example of the Moral Qualities Theory, when the Holy Book relates:

> We never sent any Prophets into a town without catching
> hold of its people with misery and affliction, that they might
> perhaps be humbled.

At Surah 5:95, we learn that "Suffering not only forms character, it also exposes it," another example of the Moral Qualities Perspective. At Surah 31:36, Al-Qur'an relates:

> Every soul tastes death, and We test you with Evil and with
> Good, as a trial, and to us you will return.

This is a clear example of the Test Theory, as are these words from 5:95, "You who believe, Allah tests you in the manner of a game." We find another example of the Moral Qualities Perspective, where the virtue to be developed is *Sabir*, or "patience," at Surah 2:150. One final way that the subjects of evil and suffering arise in the context of the Muslim Holy Book is what has come to be known as the "Evil Eye" in the Muslim faith. References to this phenomenon can be found in several places in Al-Qur'an, such as at 68:51 and 113:1 to 5. The expression refers to harm that comes to a person because of someone else's jealousy towards them.

Many Muslims believe the Evil Eye to be real, and some incorporate specific practices in order to protect themselves or their loved ones from the effects of the Evil Eye. Others in modern Islam reject the idea as nothing more than superstition or an "old wives' tale." Several passages in Al-Qur'an suggest that the two principal causes of the Evil Eye are envy and ignorance. Among these passages are 2:109, 68:51 and 113:5.

From this discussion, we have shown that Al-Qur'an assents to, or outright endorses, Retributive Justice Theory, the Free Will Defense, the Moral Qualities Perspective, the Test Theory, the Influences of Demonic Forces View, as well as Eschatological Verification Theory, and, of course, the Divine Plan Perspective.

These theological views and these employments of Arabic vocabulary about evil and suffering employed in Al-Qur'an can also be seen in many of the comments in traditional Hadith literature, where the topics of evil and suffering appear. This is the topic of the next section of Chapter Nine.

Evil and Suffering in Hadith Literature

For the most part, the same themes about evil and suffering in Hadith literature may be found as those we have seen in Al-Qur'an, as well. Sa'id Al-Khudri, for example, reports that Muhammad said, "Whoever among you sees an evil, he must change it with his hand. If he is not able to do so, then with his lips, and if he cannot do that, then he should change it with his heart, and that is the weakest level of faith."[817]

The Hadith is consistent with several passages in Surah three, such as *ayat* 104 and 110. The first of these tells us, "Let there arise among you a band of people inviting to all that is good, enjoining what is right and forbidding what is wrong. They are the ones to achieve felicity." At Surah 3:110, we find a similar piece of advice. It tells us:

You are the best of peoples, evolved from mankind, enjoining
what is right and forbidding what is wrong. And believing in
Allah. If the people of the Scripture deny it, it had been better
for some of the believers, but most of them are Evil-Doers.

Sahih Al-Bukhari relates that the Prophet Muhammad said:

No fatigue, nor disease, nor sorrow, nor sadness, nor hurt,
nor distress befalls a Muslim, even if it was the prick he
received from a thorn, but that Allah expiates some of
his sins for that.[818]

This book also relates that "Illness has a religious purpose and that through the experience of suffering a patient might earn merit and attain a status of a true believer." Bukhari adds, "When Allah intends to do good to somebody, He afflicts him with trials." This is clearly a version of the Test View.[819]

Hadith collector Sahih Muslim relates that the Prophet Muhammad said:

When a person fell ill, the Prophet used to rub him with his
right hand and then pray to Allah saying, "O Lord of the people, grant him health, heal him, for Thou art the Greatest of
Healers."[820]

In another tradition from Abu Bukhari, he tells us that when someone is born, an angel is sent to that person with four commands, for his sustenance, the length of his days, whether he is to be wretched or happy, and his work."[821] From the Sunnah of Abu Daud, he relates that the Prophet Muhammad said:

Allah first created the Pen, and he said, "Write." And it asked,
"What shall I write?" And He said, "Write the destinies of all
things until the coming of the Hour."[822]

Another Hadith from Sahih Hurayra, the prophet asked among his companions, "Whom do you reckon to be a martyr among yourselves?" And they said, "Oh messenger, whoever is killed in the cause of Allah is a martyr." And Muhammad said, "In that case, the martyrs of my community would be few. He who is killed in the cause of Allah is a martyr. He who dies in the cause of Allah is a martyr. He who dies of the plague is a martyr. And he who dies of Cholera is a martyr."[823]

Another way we see references to evil and suffering in Hadith literature is what the traditional collectors say about *Shaytan* or *Iblis*. Abu Hurayra, for example, says this about Ayyub's, or Job's suffering:

> While Ayyub was naked and taking a bath, a swarm of locusts fell upon him. He began collecting them in his garment, and his Lord cried out to him, "Oh Ayyub, have I not made you rich to need what you see?" He said, "Yes, oh Lord, but I cannot shun Your blessings."[824]

Abu Hurayra suggests that it is Iblis who was responsible for removing the Prophet Ayyub's clothing in this tale. Ninth-century Qur'anic interpreter Jafar Al-Tabari gives this account of Ayyub's troubles:

> Shaytan rushes back and forth from Heaven to Earth. He resorts to various ruses and disguises. He causes female breasts to grow on Ayyub's chest and warts the size of sheep's buttocks.[825]

This pair of *Ahadith*, the plural form of Hadith, are versions of the Influences of Demonic Forces Theory. Similar sentiments may be found in Abu Hurayra's number 53 of the same book relates, "Tell my servants what is best. Indeed, *Shaytan* induces dissension among them. Indeed, he is forever an enemy to mankind."[826] At Hadith 134 of the same book, Sahih Hurayra relates:

> No one disputes concerning the signs of Allah except those who disbelieve. So be not deceived by their uninhibited movement throughout the land.

Again, it seems clear here that Sahih Hurayra is referring to the movements of the *Shayatin* throughout the earth, tempting those who are true believers. From all this, we may conclude that the Influences of Demonic Forces Theory, with respect to the phenomena of evil and suffering, can also be found in classical Hadith literature.

This brings us to a discussion of Muslim views of evil and suffering in the medieval philosophical period, which is the subject matter of the fourth section of this ninth chapter of this study of evil and suffering in the world's religious traditions.

Evil and Suffering in Medieval Islamic Philosophy

We have suggested earlier in this chapter that as early as the seventh century CE, we begin to see medieval Islamic perspectives on the issues of evil and suffering. In fact, from the seventh century to the fourteenth century, we see a plethora of points of view about evil and suffering in the Islamic faith.

One way we see some of these theological perspectives is in the debate between what was known as the *Mu'tazila* school of philosophy and the *Asharite* school. The former approached the problem of evil within a framework of what was called "Moral Realism."[827] This view maintains that moral values are accessible to unaided reason so that human beings may make their own moral judgments about Divine intervention in the world with *Sharr*, or Evil. Those in the Mu'tazila camp argued that the Divine act of Creation is Good, or *Khyar*, despite the existence of evil and suffering. They posited that human beings have the capacity to commit evil acts using their own free will. Thus, the Mu'tazalites endorsed the Free Will Defense with respect to the issues of evil and suffering in Islam.[828]

The Asharites, on the other hand, reject the position of the Mu'tazila. The Asharite school was founded by Abu al-Hasan Al-Ash'ari in the early tenth century. When it comes to free will, the Asharites argued:

> Humans have some freedom of action and total freedom of thought, but only Allah has the power to create actions—humans do not create this power. Humans cannot truly understand ideas about freedom and justice that are the domains of Allah alone.[829]

In the Asharite view:

> Allah may send a person to Hell; or to Heaven, even though it seems unfair sometimes to human beings. Ultimately, everything that Allah does is fair and just, but much of it is beyond human understanding.[830]

Here we see a combination of the Eschatological Verification Theory with a Divine Plan Perspective that is "beyond human understanding." Many other medieval Islamic perspectives on the issues of evil and suffering can also be seen among some of the great philosophers of the period. These include figures such as:

1. Al-Ghazali
2. Ibn Sina, or Avicenna
3. Ibn Arabi
4. Fakhir al-Din al-Razi
5. Ibn Taymiyyah
6. Ibn al-Qayyim
7. The mystic Rumi

We will look at each of these seven Islamic theological thinkers, in turn, to ascertain their contributions to the discussion of the phenomena of evil and suffering in medieval Islam, beginning with Al-Ghazali and continuing through the other Muslim philosophers listed here.

Abu Hamid Ghazali (1058–1111) is important for our purposes because he endorsed the view that this is the "Best of All Possible Worlds."[831] The Persian polymath Ibn Sina (980–1037) dealt with evil from a purely Neo-Platonic point of view. Thus, he assented to the Evil as Privation Theory.[832] Fakhr al-Din al-Razi (1150–1210), who is sometimes referred to as the "Sultan of the Theologians," in his early Sunni views, challenged Ibn Sina's Privation Theory and argued that "There is more pain in the world than there is pleasure."[833]

Hanbali scholar Ibn Al-Taymiyyah (1263–1328) noted Muslim judge, theologian and logician, argued that human, free acts are responsible for their good and bad deeds, for they are agents of their own acts.[834] Taymiyyah also suggests that "Evil is actually Good when considering its purposes." Thus, Ibn Al-Taymiyyah combines the Free Will Defense with Divine Plan Theory. Al-Taymiyyah also suggests that pure evil cannot exist.[835]

This latter view was developed further by Ibn Al-Qayyim (1292–1350), another great Hanbali scholar, who maintains that Allah created the figure of Iblis because he is to serve a purpose in "Allah's Grand Scheme" of things. This is obviously a nod in the direction of Divine Plan Theory.[836]

Finally, this brings us to the writings of Jalal Al-Din Rumi (1207 until 1273), who is mostly known in the West for his mystical poetry. For Rumi, the purpose of the study of philosophy is to get to know one's "True Self," or what he calls *ma'rifat al-nafs*, in his Arabic and Persian.

Ultimately, Rumi believed that one should come to the realization that the True Self has become separated from its True Source, or *Asl*.[837]

For Rumi, one must exercise his *Ikhtiar*, or freedom of choice, and to find ways to return to its True Source. He states, "Human beings have a tendency to forget Allah, particularly in two kinds of situations. The first of these is when a person acquires wealth, and the second is when the believer has good health." As Rumi puts the matter:

> Between Allah and His servant, there are two veils between them, and all other veils are manifestations of either wealth or health.[838]

Rumi points out that the man who is healthy says, "Where is Allah, I do not know." But as soon as he gets sick, he starts saying, "Oh Allah, oh Allah, where are You?"[839] Rumi believes in the final analysis—one should seek union with one's "True Self" with its "True Source," no other than Allah Himself. This notion of "Union" may, indeed, push Rumi in the direction of assenting to a Religion of Dissolution, as developed back in the opening chapter of this study on evil and suffering in the world's religions.

From this material from the medieval period of Islamic philosophy, we have seen assent to the following points of view:

1. The Free Will Defense (the Mu'tazila and Ibn Taymiyyah)
2. Retributive Justice Theory (the Asharites)
3. The Eschatological Verification View (the Asharites)
4. The Deprivation of the Good Theory (Ibn Sina and Al-Razi)
5. The Best of All Possible Worlds Perspective (Al-Ghazali)
6. The Divine Plan Theory (Al-Qayyim)
7. Islam as a Religion of Dissolution (Rumi)

This brings us to the fifth section of this ninth chapter, in which we will explore many of the modern Islamic views of evil and suffering from the sixteenth century until the twentieth century.

Evil and Suffering in Modern Islamic Philosophy

In the modern period of Islamic philosophy, several Muslim thinkers have made some substantial comments on the phenomena of evil

and suffering. Among the most important of these modern thinkers
are:

1. Mulla Sadra (1571–1640.]
2. Muhammad Abduh (1849–1905)
3. Jamal al-Din Afghani (1838–1897)
4. Sayyid Nursi (1877–1960)
5. Sayyid Qutb (1906–1966)
6. Tubanur Yesilhark Ozkan
7. Muhammad Iqbal

Of these philosophical treatments in the modern Islamic period,
the fullest treatments on evil and suffering in the Muslim faith are those
of Mulla Sadra and Said Nursi. Tubanur Yesilhark Ozkan's work, *A
Muslim's Response to Evil: Said Nursi on Theodicy*, is a treatment and
critique of the Turkish philosopher's treatment of the phenomena of evil
and suffering.[840] Ozkan also puts Nursi's views on evil and suffering in
the context of Western secular treatments of those same issues.[841] She
also demonstrates a range of Western thinkers such as Isaac Newton,
Rene Descartes, G. W. Leibniz, Baruch Spinoza, David Hume and
Immanuel Kant and their views on evil and suffering.[842]

Jamal al-Din Afghani (1838–1897) was a political activist and
writer, perhaps best known in his role in the Pan-Islamic movement.
As a boy, Afghani traveled to India and saw the effect of colonization
on that country and occasioned his life-long hatred of the British,
particularly British rule in Muslim lands. Afghani was a great influence
on subsequent Muslim thinkers.[843]

Muhammad Abduh (1849–1905) was an Egyptian writer, religious
scholar, jurist and liberal reformer. Some regard him to be the founder
of what is known as Islamic Modernism. Among other works, Abduh
wrote a treatise on *Tawhid*, or "The Oneness of Allah."[844] He also
completed a voluminous work that is a commentary on Al-Qur'an that
consists of thirty volumes.[845]

Sayyid Ibrahim Qutb (1906–1966) was an Egyptian author,
educator and Islamic theorist. He was also one of the leading figures
in the Egyptian Muslim Brotherhood in the 1950s and 1960s. He was

convicted of plotting an assassination of Egyptian President Gamel Abdel Nasser and was executed by hanging in 1966.[846]

Sayyid Qutb wrote extensively on social justice issues, particularly in his books *Social Justice* and *Milestones*.[847] Qutb also had an intense dislike for the United States, which he saw as far too materialistic, and was obsessed with violence and sexual pleasures. Qutb advocated the violent uses of Jihad. He was greatly influenced by Jamal Afghani in that regard and was one of the thinkers relied on by Osama bin Laden and the terrorist attacks of September 11, 2001, and a foundation of his movement Al-Qaeda.[848]

As we have indicated earlier in this section of Chapter Nine, the fullest treatments of the phenomena of evil and suffering in the modern Islamic world came from Mulla Sadra and Turkish philosopher Said Nursi. We will bring this chapter to a close with specific comments on these two figures, as well as Pakistani philosopher Muhammad Iqbal.

Evil and Suffering in Mulla Sadra and Said Nursi

Many of the perspectives of Mulla Sadra on the issues of evil and suffering come in the context of what he had to say about resurrection and eschatology. He suggests that only those who have "actualized themselves" will benefit from the full resurrection of the body. He calls these people the *al-uqul al-khalisa*, or "Those who have been actualized."[849] Sadra makes it clear, however, that the resurrection "is not primarily about rewards and punishments."[850]

Instead, Sadra ties the resurrection to his view of what he calls "teleology." In this regard, Sadra tells us:

> Allah, Most High, does not create anything without a
> Telos [*ghaya*]. Therefore, all present things must have an
> activity and a Telos...It has been confirmed that through proof
> that the Final Telos of His most High activity is His essence.
> His essence of all Teloi, as it is the base of all bases. Doubtless,
> the Telos of a thing, then, is to arrive and to finish its essence.
> Indeed, it cannot be imagined any other way, even
> metaphorically, to have a Telos.[851]

Thus, Sadra tells us that all things in the universe have a telos and that all of reality taken together, in Sadra's view, becomes the telos of Allah, which is the very essence of Allah.[852] For Sadra, the *Eschaton* is nothing more than an act of Divine Mercy, in that Allah has allowed all of His creations to come forward. Sadra tells us:

> It is as if Allah reaches His hand down to the Earth, where most souls are confused and helpless, and He lifts these souls up to a higher level, where they might have a better view of reality.[853]

Again, in the words of Mulla Sadra himself:

> Certainly, He will destroy the world and will turn all that is on the Earth and in the Heavens into oblivion. Nature will return into the world of the soul. The soul will return into the world of intelligence. The intelligence will return into the One, the Almighty. As he, Most High says, 'He will blow the Horn and those in the Heavens and the Earth, will come to an End.[854]

The Mulla Sadra concludes:

> Thus, if things return to their original place, after leaving the world of motion, of transformation, evils, pains of the sadness of death, treachery, terror, and of being struck down, the Divine Mercy will show compassion on them another time with a life that has no death, a permanence that will not be broken.[855]

In this passage, Sadra is quoting Surah 39:48 of Al-Qur'an. It is traditionally thought to be about resurrection. Yet, Sadra applies the verse to all existing things. They will all be transformed into a new and an elevated state, into a Heavenly Jerusalem, to borrow a biblical phrase.[856]

Mulla Sadra seems to pull together here a combination of Retributive Justice Theory, along with the Free Will Defense, Eschatological Verification Theory, and, of course, Divine Plan Theory.

Said Nursi begins with Al-Qur'an when speaking of evil and suffering in his thought. He starts with verses like the Qur'an's 32:7 that maintains that "All that Allah has made is beautiful."[857] Nursi relates:

> Everything and every event in the universe is either directly beautiful, beautiful in essence, or consequentially beautiful.[858]

For Nursi, there are certain things that appear ugly or evil. However, at least according to Nursi, these things are "under a veil of ugliness or evil that hides the true beauty and harmony of the event or thing."[859] Nursi relates:

> Hidden in the torrent of the Spring rainstorm are the smiling faces of Summer Flowers Under the veils of events such as storms and earthquakes, and disease There are unseen blossoms.[860]

Nursi seems to be endorsing here what we have called the Hidden God Theory. In his analysis of evil and suffering, Nursi also says that people are too quick to cast judgments on the results of apparently evil events. He says that human weaknesses are many of the reasons that people do not always see the beauty in events. The judgments of human beings are often superficial and selfish; therefore, we often only judge on the uglier face of an event selfishly, and we only see the aspect of an event that affects us.[861]

Said Nursi also at times criticizes some of the traditional explanations of evil events. When two major earthquakes hit Turkey in the 1930s, for example, when many people interpreted them as Allah's wrath for human sin, Nursi simply asks, "Then why did some who were sinless suffer from the quakes?"[862] In regard to the earthquakes, Nursi refers the believer to the Qur'an's 8:25, "Take refuge in Allah from the trial. It will not touch only the wrong-doers among you."

For Nursi, this verse suggests that this world is a place of testing and character building, a place for examination, responsibility, and Jihad for doing good things.[863] Nursi says, "Innocents do suffer in calamitous situations, but their suffering will be compensated for greatly in the life to come."[864] As Nursi puts the matter:

> Their transient properties will become eternal, their ephemeral life will be forever. With a relatively small and temporary difficulty, they will have tremendous benefit in Eternity. Such an earthquake is a mercy for them.[865]

To bolster this point, Said Nursi quotes another Qur'anic verse at 2:216 that tells us, "You may hate something which, in fact, is better for you and you may love something that is, in fact, detrimental to you."[866]

This *ayat*, or verse, suggests that every event has two phases. The first phase is the "appearance" of the event that may appear evil, but in the other phase, the beauty of the event is revealed.

Nursi tells us that if "Evil deeds are not punished in this life, it does not mean that the Justice of Allah will not be served in the Afterlife." As the Qur'an's 35: 45 tells us, and a verse quoted by Said Nursi on evil:

> If Allah were to punish people for what they have done,
> then He would not leave a living creature on the surface
> of the Earth. But Allah reprieves them for an appointed time.
> When their time comes, they will see that Allah has
> observed closely all of Allah's people.[867]

Thus, Said Nursi appears to agree that Allah may not apply the rules about sin and their punishment consistently in this world, but there will be no escape from justice in the life to come. In fact, Nursi says it may be the smallest evils that are punished in this world, just as local crimes are settled in small claims court, while much bigger crimes are punished at a higher level, that is, after we are dead.[868] At any rate, Nursi seems to be endorsing here a combination of Eschatological Verification Theory, Retributive Justice and the Divine Plan Theory.

Said Nursi also believed that the absolute justice of Allah could be seen in the world through the practice of prayer. Disasters and evil events, though seemingly unjust, are, in fact, opportunities for believers to grow closer to Allah through prayer and patience, or *Sabir*. Nursi points out that "Allah really cares about your prayers. If you do not pray, then, he asks, 'What is important to you?'"[869] Nursi hints here at the Moral Qualities Perspective, as well as the Test View.

Nursi also indicates that many afflictions are some of the ways that Allah "tests" through which one may prove his or her closeness to Allah. This, of course, is another reference to the Test Perspective. For Nursi, this world is a "field" to gain eternal life when seeds have been planted to be harvested in the next life. In this sense, Nursi appears to endorse the Divine Plan View, along with Eschatological Verification Theory at the same time.[870]

Thus, in the works of Mulla Sadra and Said Nursi, we have seen assent to, or endorsement of, Retributive Justice Theory, the Eschatological Verification View, the Hidden God Perspective, the Test View, the Moral Qualities Theory, and Divine Plan Theory, in regard to the phenomena of evil and suffering in the Muslim faith.

This brings us to the figure who is perhaps the most influential modern Islamic thinker on the issues of evil and suffering, Pakistani philosopher and poet Muhammad Iqbal, the subject matter of the final section of Chapter Nine.

Muhammad Iqbal on Evil and Suffering

One final Muslim philosopher who has written a great deal about evil and suffering in the context of the faith of Islam is Muhammad Iqbal (1877–1938), a Pakistani poet, philosopher and barrister in British India. Iqbal commented on the phenomena of evil and suffering in a variety of his works and in a variety of ways. In his 1980 work, *The Development of Metaphysics*, for example, the Pakistani philosopher, gives a cogent summary of the history of metaphysics in Islam, beginning with Persian dualism, and then continuing on to Greek dualism and Plato and the Neo-Platonists, then what he calls "Islamic Rationalism," "Rational Idealism," popular in his own time, and then finally to Sufism.[871]

Another way that Iqbal made remarks about evil and suffering was in his poetry. In his collection called *Tulip in the Desert*, Iqbal imagines a dialogue between the Angel Jibril and Iblis, or *Shaytan*.[872] In another poem entitled "Give Me Another Adversary," Iblis is frustrated that his opponent is the Omnipotent Allah and thus imagines another foe.[873] From 1929 until 1931, Muhammad Iqbal gave a series of seven lectures on the topic of omniscience and human freedom, and in the process of these lectures, Iqbal made many comments about the idea of *Sharr*, or Evil.[874]

In many of his major philosophical works, the issues of evil and suffering are at the heart of these tomes. The most important of these works of Iqbal is *The Reconstruction of Religious Thought in Islam*.[875] This book is as much about what he rejects about evil and suffering as it is what he proposes about these matters. Among those views on evil that Iqbal outright rejects are the Deprivation of the Good Theory, the Buddhist version of a Religion of Dissolution, and the Christian doctrine of Original Sin.[876] For Iqbal, the image of Iblis is nothing more than a fiction, so he rejects the Influences of Demonic Forces Theory, as well.[877]

What he replaces these theories with is a version of the Limited God Theories that we have seen in figures like E. E. Brightman and William James. The Western source that Iqbal found for his version of dualism, or panentheism, is the philosophy of Charles Sanders Peirce (1839–1914). What Iqbal adopts from Peirce is a view of God that the American called "panentheism."[878]

While the metaphysical view known as "pantheism" asserts that "All is God," the panentheist claims that God is greater and distinct from the universe. In Peirce's view, God cooperates with his creatures of the world, human beings, to bring them and the universe to the fullest realization of itself.[879] The name panentheism was coined by German philosopher Karl Christian Krause (1781–1832), who had sought to reconcile monotheism with pantheism.

Peirce read Krause, and Iqbal then read Peirce, and subsequently arrived at a version of panentheism. The metaphysical point of view is also reflected in some of his poetry like the following:

What is the purpose of this whirling of time?
That thy ego may be revealed to thee;
Thou art the conqueror of the world of good and evil
I dare not reveal the great destiny ahead of me.[880]

In this poem, Muhammad Iqbal speaks of the cooperation of Allah with human beings so that we finally see that the world of good and evil will be reconciled in a "destiny that is to come." In this view, Iqbal believes God limits Himself so that He can cooperate more with humans. This idea of "limiting" on God's part is something that Charles Peirce found in Plato's *Timaeus*. And ultimately, it was adopted by Muhammad Iqbal, as well.[881]

Muhammad Iqbal also speaks in his *Reconstruction* of the human use of the Free Will Defense. Indeed, he makes two main points about it. First, Adam's first act of disobedience is also the first human use of free will.[882] And secondly, only acts that can be characterized as good are free acts. Since goodness is a condition of a free act, we may add the Free Will Defense to the points of view on evil and suffering of Pakistani philosopher and poet Muhammad Iqbal.[883]

This brings us to the major conclusions we have made in this ninth chapter. Chapter Ten to follow is an attempt to pull together the major conclusions we have made in this study of the phenomena of evil and suffering in the major religions of the world. But first, we move to the conclusions of Chapter Nine.

Conclusions to Chapter Nine

The chief function of this ninth chapter has been to describe and discuss many of the ways in the faith of Islam where evil and suffering have been topics of conversation in the history of that faith. To that end, we began the chapter with a short history of an introduction to Islam that included its founder, its Holy Book, Al-Qur'an, what is known as Islam's "Five Pillars," as well as five other basic requirements that all Muslims are bound to follow: profession of faith, prayer, fasting, alms, and a pilgrimage to Mecca.

We have also shown in this first section of Chapter Nine, the Muslim holidays, views on the survival of death, that Allah has ninety-nine names, the seven levels of Heaven and of Hell in Islam, the most Holy of places in the faith, and the most unforgivable sin, or *Shirk*. In this same section, we gave a description of sacred persons and titles in the Islamic faith that included the *Imam*, the *Grand Mufti*, and the *Grand Ayatollah*, among many other titles and descriptions of office in Islam.

In the second and central section of Chapter Nine, we have explored and discussed many of the places in the Muslim Holy Book, where the subject matter is *Sharr*, or Evil, in Islam. Altogether we have examined over two dozen places where the issues of evil and suffering arise in Al-Qur'an. This section of Chapter Nine was concluded with a summary of the many ways that the Muslim Holy Book has responded to the phenomena of evil and suffering.

In the material in the third section of Chapter Nine of this study, we have introduced and discussed a number of places in traditional

Hadith Literature where evil and suffering have been written about or discussed. In that section, we have seen Hadith from Sa'id Al-Khudri, Al-Bukhari, Sahih Muslim, Abu Hurayra, Jafar Al-Tabari, and many other prominent Islamic scholars.

These sections of Chapter Nine have been followed by a series of sections on historical periods within Islam where evil and suffering have been topics for discussion or for written works. The first of these periods was that of medieval Islamic philosophy. In that section, we examined the beliefs of the Mutazites, the Asharites, and philosophers Abu Hamid Al-Ghazali, Ibn Sina, Ibn Arabi, Al-Razi, Ibn Taymiyyah, al-Qayyim, and the mystical philosopher and poet Rumi.

The second historical Islamic period we examined where views on evil and suffering have been discussed is in modern Islamic philosophy from the sixteenth to the twenty-first centuries. In this section of Chapter Nine, we introduced and discussed the perspectives of Mulla Sadra, Muhammad Abduh, Jamal Afghani, Said Nursi, Egyptian Sayyid Qutb, as well as contemporary female philosopher Tubanur Ozkan who has written a recent critique on the views of Said Nursi on the issues of evil and suffering.

For the most part, what we have found in this modern material is that these modern Islamic thinkers have fallen back on employing the same responses and answers to evil and suffering that can be found in Al-Qur'an and in traditional Hadith literature.

Indeed, in the final sections of Chapter Nine, we examined and discussed the more detailed views of the two most prominent modern Islamic perspectives on our issues at hand. These were Mulla Sadra and Said Nursi, as well as a separate section on the philosophy of Muhammad Iqbal.

In these perspectives we have examined from Sadra and Nursi, we have found the employments of the Retributive Justice Theory, the Eschatological Verification View, the Free Will Defense, and the Divine Plan Theory. Among the perspectives we examined from Muhammad Iqbal, references were made on evil and suffering in his poetry, in his public lectures, as well as in his major philosophical works. The most important realizations we found in Muhammad Iqbal's observations about evil and suffering are, first, what needs to be rejected, Original Sin Theory, the Deprivation of the Good Perspective, and the Religions of Dissolution Approach in Hinayana Buddhism. And second, what needs to be adopted, and that is Charles Peirce's view of panentheism.

We turn now to Chapter Ten, a conclusive chapter on what conclusions we have made in this entire study. This will be followedby Chapter Eleven and then by a series of appendices in which we catalog the many foreign words and phrases we have employed in this study of evil and suffering in the religions of the world.

Chapter Ten: Evil and Suffering in African Religions

In regard to the Yoruba and evil, instead of running away,
they simply live with it, seeking whatever solutions are
possible and accepting with little or no complaints whatever cannot be overcome, as their lot in life.

—E. O. Oyelade, "Evil in Yoruba Religion and Culture"

The study of sacred texts of any religion, whether oral
or written, is the primary way to understand the theology of a religion rather than the modern preoccupation of
scholars of religion and anthropology with interviews of
believers.

—Wande Abimbola, "God Versus Anti-Gods"

Ori, we salute you
Who quickly remembers His own.
You who blesses a person more quickly than the Orisa.
There is no Orisa who by himself blesses a man
Without the consent of his Ori.

—Traditional Yoruba poem

Introduction

The purpose of this tenth chapter is to make some observations and
evaluation of how African religions have dealt with the phenomena of
evil and suffering. We will begin the chapter with some geographical
distinctions and traditional ideas regarding the relationships of evil and
suffering to African religions.

This material will be followed by an introduction and discussion of two test cases in examining the issues of evil and suffering in Africa's faiths. More specifically, we will examine the belief systems of the Yoruba and the Igbo peoples in terms of what they have to say about the phenomena of evil and suffering. In that regard, we will introduce and discuss the Yoruba and the Igbo people of evil and suffering in three separate sections.

These may be summarized this way:

1. The origin of evil.
2. Types of evil.
3. Methods and responses to evil.

Before we get to that material, however, we first will turn to African geography and indigenous beliefs. In that regard, East Africa was very different from West Africa, and sub-Saharan Africa has been very different from the North, as we shall see next. Before we get to that material, however, we first will outline a collection of beliefs and practices that most traditional African societies believe in and have ritually engaged in for many centuries.

Traditional African Beliefs

For the most part, traditional African societies have a collection of myths, symbols, and rituals that are related to their religious beliefs and practices. Among those beliefs and practices are the following:

Belief in a Supreme or High God.

Belief in many minor gods.

Belief in spirits and a spirit world

Belief in ancestral spirits.

Belief in the efficacy of sacrifice.

Rites of passage.

A creation myth.

The use of divination.

The use of magic.

A cosmology.

For the most part, traditional African societies believe that there are many gods, but at the top of the polytheistic ladder, there is one Supreme or High God. In addition, there is also a collection of many minor gods that often act as mediators between the High God and human beings.

Nearly all traditional African societies also assent to the belief that there is a world of spirits, invisible, but they still assert effects and affects on the visible world. Some of these spirits are ancestral spirits, and some are related to divination and magic. Most traditional African societies also believe in the efficacy of sacrifice. In most parts of Africa, these now involve the giving of food and drink to appease the gods or the spirit, and these sacrifices no longer involve animals.

In general, most traditional African societies have a collection of rituals related to rites of passage. In most places on the continent, there are five of these rites related to birth, becoming an adult, a marriage rite, a ritual related to becoming an elder, and a rite where one is accepted as an ancestral spirit.

Traditional African societies have views about how the universe began, as well as a description of the cosmology of reality, in which the levels of what is real are clearly delineated. This brings us to a discussion of some geographical considerations in discussing traditional African religions and how different areas of Africa are sometimes very different about how some of these theological matters are handled.

Geography and Indigenous Beliefs of Africa

For the most part, African religious beliefs have been divided by geographical regions for many centuries. Those people who spoke similar languages also had similar beliefs about religion. The Niger-Congo ethnolinguistic family of much of West Africa was substantially different from what became Islamic East Africa in places like Malawi, Tanzania, Somalia, the Sudan and Mozambique, for example.[884]

A century ago, three-quarters of all Africans practiced traditional African faiths, according to historical estimates from the *World*

Religion Database. In the year 1900, just 14 percent of those living in sub-Saharan Africa practiced Christianity. Today, however, Africa is overwhelmingly populated by believers in Islam and Christianity.[885] The Muslim population of sub-Saharan Africa has grown seventy-fold in that time, to the point that one in three believers is now a Muslim.[886]

Sub-Saharan Africa is now home to 20 percent of all Christians in the world, and one in seven Muslims in the world now live there, as well.[887] The statistical division of the United Nations has subdivided the African continent into five regions: North Africa; Central/Middle Africa, Southern Africa, East Africa, and West Africa. These regions tend to be very different from each other in terms of their cultures and religions.

North Africa, which includes Algeria, Egypt, Libya, Morocco, Sudan, Tunisia and Western Sahara, are all Islamic states. Central Africa, countries like Cameroon, Angola, Chad and the Congo Republic are mixed state combinations of Christianity, Islam and indigenous practices. Southern African countries, like Botswana and Namibia, for example, are 57 and 90 percent Christians. East Africa is a combination of Islamic nations and Christian countries, the holdover from Portuguese East Africa, with about 10 percent maintaining belief in traditional religion.[888]

West Africa is also a great mix. Senegal and Gambia are Islamic. Nigeria is a combination of Islam and Christianity. The Ivory Coast is a mix of Muslims, Catholics, Pentecostal and about 20 percent indigenous believers. Ghana is also a mixture of Christianity and Islam, and the same can be said of other West African nations.[889]

In terms of the indigenous African belief system, the five areas tend to share several beliefs. For the most part in Africa, there were no written scriptures. Beliefs spread for the most part, in an oral tradition handed down from one generation to the next. Folk tales, myths, symbols and rituals, as well as songs and festivals, developed about the unseen world. Most of the indigenous believers were polytheists, often separating the greater from the lesser gods. Often in these faiths, a High God, a supreme creator, is elevated above the rest, as we have shown earlier.[890]

In most indigenous African religious systems, we see a belief in ancestor worship, as well as other spirits who can affect and effect the living. The use of magic is also commonplace in indigenous African religion, as is traditional medicine in explaining some examples of evil and suffering.

For the most part, the metaphysical realm in indigenous African religions consists of:

- A unique supreme being, omniscient, omnipotent, creator of the universe.

- Intermediate deities or spirits who bridge the gap between the High God and human beings.

- Ancestral spirits who watch over their descendants.

- Other magical and spiritual forces that can influence the lives of the living.[891]

Many West African religions revolve around the belief in one High God, a single and distant deity credited with creating the universe and delegating other jobs to lesser deities. These minor deities serve as mediators between the High God and human beings. This supreme God is known by many names across Africa. The Dogon call him *Amma*.[892] The Supreme God of the Mende People is called *Ngewo*.[893]

The High God of the Bambara goes by the name of *Bamba* or *Ngala*. This god has four aspects—air, fire, water and earth. In many places of Nigeria, the Supreme God is called *Nupe*. He is said at once to be "far as well as near."[894] The Efik people call their High God *Abasi*. And most often, African societies have a supreme deity, as well.

The Western study of African ancestor worship goes back to the 1932 classic study *Hunger and Work in a Savage Tribe* by Audrey Richards.[895] Richards began writing about Bantu ancestral worship when she said:

> To begin with, we see at once that the whole core of ancestor worship among these peoples is centered in the cult of the immediate family gods. The ceremonies offered to the village or tribal deities grow out of the family rites, and are, in a sense, a replica of them.[896]

Regarding sacrifices made to the ancestors, Richards continues:

> The typical Bantu sacrifice consists in the offering of flour or
> beer to the ancestral spirits, or else the killing of an animal,
> and its division among the people according to fixed rules.
> The ancestor cult takes its root and being, first of all, in the
> ordinary occasions of family life.[897]

Richards tells us that sacrifices of food are made before eating and even before the cooking of the meal. The sacrifice of animals is only done on special occasions, often, for example, to mark rites of passage such as marriage, childbirth, initiation and death. Richards reports:

> Offerings are also made at any sign of sickness of any member
> of the household, or to ensure luck in the hunting fields—all
> events that affect the individual family member's group.[898]

Richards tells us that household shrines dedicated to the ancestors could usually be found in Bantu homes. The ancestors had to approve of marriages in order for them to be official. She remarks, "Without the offering of a sacrifice from the relatives of the bride to the ancestors of the groom's family, the marriage is in some cases incomplete."[899] In many African societies going back many years, the ancestral spirits were believed to behave like humans on Earth. They could feel emotions, including anger and jealousy, for example.

Audrey Isabel Richards (1899–1984) was a pioneering British social anthropologist. She produced many notable ethnographic studies, the most famous of which were initiation ceremonies for girls in Zambia. She also conducted field work in Uganda and other African nations, as well as work on family structure among the Bantu in Central Africa. She also published a study on "Land, Labour, and Diet" in Northern Rhodesia in the 1930s with Oxford University Press.[900]

In his book *Cultural Anthropology*, anthropologist William Haviland tells us this about the ancestor spirits:

> They even may participate in family and lineage affairs,
> and seats are provided for them, even though the spirits
> are invisible. If they are annoyed, they may send
> sickness or even death.[901]

Scholar Hilda Kuper did an ethnology study of the South African people called the *Swazi* in her book *Swazi: A South African Kingdom.*[902] She also wrote about the place of ancestor worship or veneration among the Swazi. She said:

> Ancestors have greater wisdom, foresight, and power than the rest of humanity; But no spirit of the deceased ever reached complete deification or is regarded as omnipotent, as was the High God. Swazi ancestors are approached as practical beings. There is no conflict between the ethics of the ancestral cult and the mundane desires of life.[903]

Dr. Kuper adds, "Each family propitiates its own ancestors at specific, domestic events like birth, marriage, death, and the building and moving of huts. In addition, the royal ancestors periodically receive public recognition."[904] Among the people in Northern Ghana known as the Tallensi, central to their religious beliefs is the veneration of the ancestors. In fact, there is a specified hierarchy of ancestors, as well as shrines dedicated to them. The ancestors may be direct and identifiable.[905]

One element that exists among the cult of the ancestors among the Tallensi is the "good destiny" shrine, a small household shrine formed and made from objects associated with specific people or events, such as success hunting or doing well as a farmer. In a chapter on the Tallensi for *The Oxford Handbook of the Archaeology of Ritual and Religion*, Timothy Insoll tells us this about the role of the good destiny shrine:

> Among the Tallensi, destiny is negotiated via the so-called "good destiny ancestors," who are ritually serviced and placated through regular sacrifices and libations at these shrines. The shrines are agents for unique ritual relationships between individuals whose destiny they control and unique configuration of ancestors.[906]

In his book *The Heathens: Primitive Man and His Religion*, published in 1962, Harvard anthropologist William Howells also wrote about the role of the ancestors in indigenous African religions. He observed:

> And here is the point of religious importance. Its members
> are knit almost as strongly in their feelings to the dead
> ancestors of the clan as they are to one another. It is all
> one clan, which marches through time like a parade, and
> the dead are simply those who have passed a point which
> the living are still approaching.[907]

Finally, a matrilineal people whose traditional homeland is in the Congo region of Africa tells us that each person belongs to the clan of the mother, and these matrilineal clans form the basis of the society. Among this group, the female ancestors are far more powerful and wise than the male ancestors. This society in the Congo is known as the Sakata people.[908]

The Sakata are also known as the Basakata people. They are one of the Bantu peoples of Central Africa, in the Democratic Republic of the Congo. They are indigenous to the Mai-Ndombe Province, formerly part of the Bandundu Province. They speak the Sakata language, as well as Lingala, the lingua franca of the region.[909]

Another source for some evil and suffering in African religious traditions is witchcraft and witches. In Africa, witchcraft has many faces. It may be conducted for the good or for healing, and it also may be negative and destructive. Our principal concern here is the witchcraft performed with evil intentions. Some magic performed by witches is to make people ill or even to cause people to die or go insane.[910]

In many African societies, witch doctors have the job of fighting the influences of witches and their magic. In modern countries like Kenya and Ghana, people are often accused of being witches. There are even "witch villages" in some places in Africa that act as sanctuaries for those who are often falsely accused of practicing witchcraft. Many scholars recently have argued that belief in witchcraft is on the decline in Africa.

In his article "The Cosmology of Witchcraft," Samuel Lumwe provides a case study of a witch doctor named Safari who "meets with five or six clients each week." His specialty is to help people overcome misfortunes caused by witches or other people. Lumwe also points out that those who visit witch doctors like Safari "do it with a belief that they will be treated and protected from any witch power."[911]

Many contemporary scholars on Africa have pointed out that beliefs about witches, witchcraft and witch doctors have diminished from the late twentieth century to the present. Some say the evidence for this phenomenon is the dual allegiance to traditional African religions and to Islam and Christianity. Others say witchcraft beliefs and practices are not disappearing. Whatever is true about these phenomena, as Lumwe puts the matter, "is largely about the changing views of the spirit world."[912]

Some point to E. E. Evans-Pritchard's study *Witchcraft, Oracles, and Magic among the Azande*, published in 1937, to be responsible for a reduction in appreciation of the value of magic and the activities of witches.[913] Others point to the work of Peter Pels, who believes that the lack of interest in these occult practices has overly concentrated on the negative aspects of witches and their activities.[914]

Thus, while invisible to humans, the spirit world of African religion is very real and present around them at all times. Ancestral spirits, natural spirits of the elements, and evil spirits related to witchcraft are never far away in the African mind. These powers try to influence the lives of those living on Earth. African tradition tells us that these negative spirits mostly operate at night, and many stories confirm this fact.

Among the Dogon people, it is forbidden to whistle or to make other noises for fear of attracting the attention of evil spirits at night.[915] Among the Igbo, one should never answer when he or she hears the call of his or her name, for it may be an unseen nighttime voice. Throughout all of West Africa, when weavers leave their looms at dusk and blacksmiths their forges, they hand back over those places to the denizens of the night.[916]

It remains the case in many societies in contemporary Africa that some unseen power causes all misfortunes. Most African societies have expressions used in such circumstances. The Swahili people of the Kenyan coast may say when someone is sick:

Kuna mkono wa mtu hapa.

This may be translated into English as, "There is someone's hand behind this," a version of the Free Will Defense.[917] This saying indicates that someone with ill intentions has decided to harm another. Therefore, according to the traditional African mindset, any misfortune or sickness is viewed as being caused by ancestral spirits, bad magic, sorcery or witchcraft. Lumwe points out, "This highly emotive issue may be the source of a lot of enmity, even among family members."[918]

In the indigenous African religions, "magic" was used to denote the management and control of forces, which, in moral terms, is thought to be neutral, but by the intentions of the practitioner may become evil or good. Among the Yoruba and the Ibo, illness was/is not attributed to germs and viruses. For them, illness can be caused by *ota*, or "enemies," that may include *aje* or "witchcraft;" *oso*, or "sorcery;" *orisa*, or "gods;" and *ebora*, or "ancestors." There are natural illnesses, or *aare*, and hereditary illnesses, or *aian idile*.

In his 1994 book, *The World of Ghosts and the Supernatural*, Richard Cavendish points out the difficulty Western religion sometimes has in the Yoruba and Igbo's rejection of germ theory. He relates that the Nigerian practices of witchcraft and sorcery "have a kind of fascination, and at the same time a feeling of being dangerous."[919]

This brings us to our case studies—the phenomena of evil and suffering among the Yoruba and the Igbo in West African society. We will begin with a short introduction, followed by sections on the origins of evil, the kinds of evil among the two Nigerian peoples, and the methods and theological responses for combating evil and suffering in modern Nigeria.

Introduction to Yoruba and Igbo Tribes in West Africa

Many of the African causes and responses to evil and suffering outlined in this tenth chapter may be seen as existing among the Yoruba and the Igbo of present-day Nigeria. This section of Chapter Ten should be seen as case studies in which many of the theological categories mentioned earlier are on display in Nigeria.

The Yoruba occupy most of the western region of Nigeria. They live in five states in the country: Lagos, Ogun, Oyo, Oshun and Ondo. Yoruba in these five states speak different dialects, but they all understand each other. The core of the extended family among the Yoruba is referred to as *Ebi*. It is a bond that is so strong that nothing may break it, either physical or metaphysical, except in very rare situations like sickness.

The Igbo people are native to South-Central and South-Eastern Nigeria, as well as Equatorial Guinea. Geographically, the Igbo are divided into two unequal sections, an eastern portion, which is the larger of the two, and a western section. The Igbo people are one of the largest contingents of African peoples.

The Igbo language is part of the Niger-Congo language family. In rural Nigeria, the Igbo work mostly as craftsmen, farmers and traders of goods. Their most important crop is the yam. Another staple crop among the Igbo is cassava, a starchy, tuberous root that looks like a carrot.

It is probably best to classify the Igbo people today as somewhere between a tribe and a nation. After the defeat of the Republic of Biafra in 1970, the Igbo are now sometimes referred to as a "stateless nation."[920] Traditional Igbo society has been based on a quasi-democratic, republican system of government. In very tight-knit and small communities, the Igbo system guaranteed equality, as opposed to a feudalist system with a king and his subjects as opposed.

In most Igbo villages, a council of elders ruled the community, and that was the situation when the Portuguese first arrived among the Igbo in the fifteenth century. Although these elders were respected for their accomplishments, they were never revered as gods. Among the Igbo, law and formality begin with the *Umunna*, or the male line. However, the distinction between males and females was very fluid, allowing women to become men and men to become women.[921]

The Igbo trade routes led to many European lands before 1900, but they also stretched as far as Mecca, Medina and Jeddah on the Arabian Peninsula. In the nineteenth century, the Igbo people began to shift away from trade to concentrate instead on homegrown goods. The Igbo also became enthusiastic in their embrace of Christianity, mostly from the influence of British rule in Nigeria. They also embraced the idea of Western education.

British colonial rule of the Yoruba and the Igbo was marked with open conflicts and much tension. Colonial rule transformed Igbo culture. This can be seen in the popular novel by Chinua Achebe, *Things Fall Apart*.[922] This was a 1958 novel that chronicles pre-colonial life in southeast Nigeria among the Igbo. Many see the book as the archetypal modern African novel in English. It is now a staple book in schools all over Africa. The hero of the book, a man named Okonkwo, is an Igbo man in a fictional Nigerian clan known in the book as the Umuofia. The novel is in three parts. The first is about the hero's family and personal history. The second and third sections are about the coming of the British and Christian missionaries and their relationships and influences on the hero's family.[923]

This brings us to the next section of this tenth chapter, in which we will examine the origins of evil in Yoruba and in Igbo cultures.

Origins of Evil in Yoruba and Igbo

There are several words in the Yoruba language to express evil and suffering. The normal word for "evil" is *ibi*, while *buburu* is "wickedness," *aidara* means "bad," and *aito* is employed to designate "unrighteousness." Among the Igbo, on the other hand, we also see a plethora of terms related to bad and evil. Among these are:

Ajo (bad)

Ajo (evil)

Mmehie (sin)

Ojoo (another word for evil)[924]

The term *omo* is another Yoruba word, which often designates something that is "evil" or "prohibited." The expression *ibi-omo* is also frequently employed to express the same idea in the Yoruba language. It refers to burying the placenta and umbilical cord because they believe it is risky to put it in any other place. Traditionally, they also have believed that if a dog eats the placenta, then either the dog or the baby will go mad.[925]

These Ibo terms are often seen as the opposites of words like *amala*, or "grace," *oma*, or "good," *ezigbo*, another word for "good," and the Igbo expression, *ka mma*, that is usually rendered "better" in

English. Two other Igbo words often employed in a moral context for the good are *ike* and *ike'*, the former means "ability," while the latter designates something close to "power" in English.[926]

One of the major sources of evil among the Yoruba is the god *Esu* who is also known as *Eshu*, *Exu* and *Echu*, depending on where among the Yoruba the name is employed. Among the early European missionaries to Nigeria, the god in question was translated as "Satan," or as the "Devil." In fact, Samuel Ajayi Crowther's *Vocabulary of the Yoruba*, published in 1842, translates the name in question just that way.[927]

Although the figure of Esu is believed to be the cause of much evil and suffering among the Yoruba people, he is actually a messenger oracle who is a trickster god, unpredictable, sly and fond of pranks that can cause disruption among humans. One tradition suggests that Esu became this way after he committed a trick on the High God. He stole yams from God's garden, he used the High God's slippers to make footprints in the garden and then claimed it was the High God who stole the fruit.[928] Nevertheless, the Yoruba people number the figure of Eshu among the causes of much evil and suffering in the world.

Scholar E. O. Oyelade, in his essay, "Evil in Yoruba Religion and Culture," suggests that the god Esu has two, separate sides to his make-up. "Esu causes evil by giving misleading suggestions that end in sadness and destruction. On the other hand, Esu is very close to Olodumare, an omnipotent High God for the Yoruba, Olodumare is responsible for the creation of the universe."[929]

The Yoruba also believe in a variety of supernatural powers. Among these are witches and the spirits of dead ancestors. What these two groups have in common is that they always pretend that they are being helpful, so that they may not be suspected of the evil they do. The Yoruba also believe that other human beings are sometimes the cause of some human evil. In this sense, the Yoruba people assent to a form of the Free Will Defense, as well as the Retributive Justice Theory.

In terms of Igbo society, we find three different causes of evil and suffering in the human world. First, some human evil is the consequence of moral evils committed by human beings. Humans are endowed with human freedom and its attendant moral responsibility. Again, this appears to be an application of the combining of the Free Will Defense with Retributive Justice Theory.[930]

Secondly, the Igbo link some human suffering not to the individual, but rather to the personal god of that individual. Among the Igbo, this personal god is called a *Chi*. The Chi is thought to bring both good things and bad things to his personal human being. In relation to the latter, one Igbo proverb tells us this:

Ebe onye dalu ka Chi ya kwatulu ya.[931]

This may be rendered into English, "When a person falls, his personal god has pushed him down."[932]

Thirdly, the Igbo people suggest a combination causal theory that links the personal god with the idea of destiny, or what we have called the Determinism Response to Evil and Suffering, as outlined in the opening chapter of this study on evil and suffering in the religions of the world. Scholar Abajide, in his essay, "The Concept of Evil in Yoruba and Igbo Thoughts," puts forth this summary of the three causes of evil and suffering in Igbo thought.[933]

This brings us to a discussion of the types or varieties of evil to be found in Yoruba and in Igbo philosophy, the topic of the next section of Chapter Ten.

Types of Evil in Yoruba and Igbo Thought

As E. O. Oyelade has shown, the people of Yoruba distinguished among four different types or kinds of evil. He summarizes these as:

1. Physical Evils
2. Moral Evils
3. Inflicted Evil
4. Predestined Evil[934]

Physical evil is nothing more than what we have called Natural Evil. Moral Evil is, of course, moral evil in our scheme from Chapter One. Inflicted Evil is metaphysical or psychological evil, and Predestined Evil is what we have called Determinism earlier in this study.

Oyerlade goes on to observe this about the first type:

The most disturbing manifestations of physical evil
include the destruction of houses, property, or persons
by lightning or thunder. The Yoruba regard this as the
function of Sango, historically a powerful Oyo King who
became a god after his death.[935]

According to the Yoruba people, Sango now resides in Heaven, where he became the hurler of thunderbolts. Another group of spirits believed to roam the Earth, either to protect humans or to cause mischief to them, is known as the *mmo.*[936] Often among the Yoruba, these wandering spirits are identified with the spirits of the dead ancestors. The Yoruban High God called *Chukwa* is believed to be in control of the Mmu. He also sends unwelcoming spirits to rebuke or to torment humans who have committed evil acts, or to protect those who are innocent.[937]

Another manifestation among the Yoruba is a god called *Sopona*, the god of smallpox. Among the Nigerians, smallpox was believed to be a disease foisted upon humans due to Sopono's "divine displeasure." Sopono's name is believed to be secret and taboo. One was not to invoke it, lest he would deliver you the disease. In 1907, the British banned the worshipping of Sopono in Nigeria. This mostly came after priests were discovered among the Yoruba to be giving and spreading the disease from scrapings of the skin of those infected.[938]

Another cause of evil among the Yoruba is a figure named *Orunmila*. One tradition says that Orunmila once lived on the Earth and aided mankind with his great wisdom. However, as a result of the actions of one of his sons, he was punished by the High God, Olorun. Oyelade tells us more about Orunmila:

> Orumila is the secret agent who discovered all the hidden behaviors and secrets of people and judges the justly. He is referred to as the "Retributor," who knows and judges the secrets of the heart.[939]

These secrets are often of the familial type. Any member of a family who reveals these thoughts about Orimila is a version of Retributive Justice Theory. The family may be severely punished and even ostracized from the extended family. Often the revealer of the secret is referred to as one who "has turned the world upside down."[940]

The category of "inflicted evil" among the Yoruba is that evil and suffering is caused by witches and medicine men. In fact, the Yoruba consider witches to be the most destructive and dreaded group of human beings. Many of the *Ifa* poems speak specifically about the power of the witches.[941]

The figure of Ifa is the Yoruba god of wisdom. He is also related to divination. The *Ifa Poems* mostly speak of this god in this latter context. In some Yoruba traditions, Ifa is identified as a "Grand Priest," who reveals the secrets of divinity and prophecy to selected human beings. In some places, the Yoruba call this god *Efa*, or *afa*. One who follows him is called a *Dibia*, one who specializes in herbs for healing and divination.[942]

In the theology of the Igbo people, they also make some distinctions among different kinds of evil. For the most part, these distinctions look very much like the three categories of evil outlined back in Chapter One. That is, when the Igbo speak about evil, it is as the product of human action or free will, what we have called "Moral Evil." Secondly, when the gods bring natural disasters and diseases like windstorms and smallpox, for example. And thirdly, when witches and medicine men bring moral pain and suffering to their fellow human beings. The second variety of evil we have labeled "Natural Evil," and the third kind as "Metaphysical Evil."[943]

This brings us to the next section of Chapter Ten in which we will describe and discuss what methods the Yoruba and the Igbo employ in dealing with evil, as well as the theological points of view that they use in regard to the phenomena of evil and suffering.

Methods and Responses to Evil and Suffering in Yoruba and Igbo Cultures

For the most part, Yoruba society believes that some evil may be under the control of humans, but much of it cannot be controlled. The Yoruba are active in the search for preventive methods to stave off evil. Among popular methods to do so are sermons, the medicine man, sacrifice, and even royalty.

All traditional Nigerian priests emphasize the results that come with evil deeds. The *Ifa Poems* preach a sanity and a good will that should follow evil acts. Those who commit evil acts should consider their punishment in the afterlife. One of the Ifa poems puts the matter this way:

Perpetuate no evil in this world
For Heaven's sake (repeated twice.)
For when you get to the Gate of Heaven,
You will give an account of your stewardship.[944]

The medicine man also preaches retribution. He informs his clients that a penalty is sure to come as a result of their wickedness. The medicine man in Yoruba culture is seen as the doctor of traditional African culture endowed by ancestral spirits with the power to counteract witchcraft. Hence, the medicine man is sometimes called the "witch doctor."[945]

Traditionally, Yoruba culture has used sacrifices to offer food and drink to the gods and the spirits to reciprocate to the living on Earth. In many places in Nigeria, even today, the practice of sacrifice is often accompanied by the pronouncements of oracles about the success of the sacrifice.[946]

Theologically speaking, we have seen several of our responses from the first chapter of this study at work among the Yoruba and the Igbo. For example, the Igbo accept the idea that if Good exists, it must coexist with Evil. There can be no such thing as Good unless there also is Evil. This clearly in an application of what we have called the Contrast Perspective back in Chapter One.

In both the Yoruba and the Igbo, we have also seen the tendency to blame some evil and suffering on human free will, or on the intentions of gods and spirits. In all of these situations, we see a version of the Free Will Defense and also Retributive Justice Theory. Although the figure of *Esu* in Nigeria, at least on first blush, appears to be related to the Influences of Demonic Forces Theory, most modern scholars don't see the figure that way.

The Igbo figure of *Ekwensu* is closer to a demonic force than is

the Yoruba Esu. In some traditions, the High God, *Chukwa*, designates
Ekwensu to be the "Testing Force" of the Igbo people. In this sense,
Ekwensu's job description is related to what we have called the Test
Perspective.[947] Ekwensu was numbered among the minor deities of the
Igbo. He ranks along with Ani, Amadj, Oha, Ikenga, Agwu, etc.[948] The
minor gods among the Igbo were/are called *Orishas*.[949] Other gods in
the Igbo pantheon included *Ala*, the goddess of the Earth; *Anyanwu*, the
god of the sun; and *Amadioha*, the god of thunder.

Among the Igbo, Ekwensu is also believed to become restless
during times of peace. But among the Igbo, there is no satan or devil
figure. There is also no traditional heaven or hell, nor are there angels
in Yoruba and Igbo cultures. When the colonial missionaries came to
Nigeria, and in their erroneous beliefs, anything that appeared to be
strange was called evil.

We also have seen so far in this tenth chapter that some evil
and suffering among the Yoruba and the Igbo are the result of divine
anger, even Olodumare himself. As Professor Oyelade related, "It is a
common saying that says:

> The Avenger will avenge, he cannot but avenge.
> He who queries will query, he cannot but query.
> This oracle to Orunmila made him get strict
> warning to his male and female children.[950]

The Yoruba believe if something that is taboo is done, then great
consequences will come to the person. The taboo is in great consonance
with the expressed injunction of a deity or deities, but the believer used
his free will to override the taboo. Thus, we should add the Free Will
Defense to our list of responses in this tenth chapter.

Finally, one of the key pillars of traditional African religions,
particularly among the Igbo and Yoruba, is the veneration of the dead,
or ancestor worship. For both Nigerian societies, the belief in ancestor
worship emanates from the worldview that the dead, whom they refer to
as the ancestors, have a direct impact on the living in their communities.
Consequently, they need respect from the living.

The worship of ancestors is a mutual relationship that helps both sides to keep their identity while also invariably strengthens the living. The acceptance of many Igbo to Christianity, however, in no way diminishes their belief in the potency of the dead. Among the Yoruba, the three most important and glorified ancestors are Sago, Orisa-Oko and Ayekla. All three were lauded humans on Earth and now reside in the heavens, where they are venerated by their descendants.[951]

The cult of the ancestors has long been recognized and studied, beginning with Bayard Taylor in 1871.[952] Taylor (1825–1878) was an American literary critic, translator, traveler and diplomat. He also founded a school in Pennsylvania. He is important for our purposes because he developed the first book-length study of ancestor worship, published in 1871.[953]

There is a tacit agreement among anthropologists and sociologists that ancestor worship is rooted in domestic, kinship and descent relations. As Meyer Fortes remarks about ancestor worship:

It is described by some as an extension of these relations to
the supernatural sphere, as a reflection of these relations,
and yet again as their ritual and symbolic expression.[954]

It should be clear that we mention ancestor worship among the Yoruba and the Igbo because in both places, the ancestors are/were regarded as agents that may harm as well as benefit, as the story of Sago has shown. Thus, we may add ancestor worship to our list of causes of, and responses to, the issues of evil and suffering.

The upshot of this section of Chapter Ten is that the two Nigerian peoples in this chapter—the peoples of Yoruba and the Igbo—appear to assent, or outright assert, the following theological responses in regard to the phenomena of evil and suffering:

1. The Contrast View
2. The Free Will Defense
3. Retributive Justice Theory
4. The Test View
5. The influence of Demonic Forces
6. Ancestor Worship
7. Determinism (Good Destiny)

This brings us to the final section of Chapter Ten, in which we will speak of how these two Nigerian societies are perfect case studies for representing the phenomena of evil and suffering in the continent of Africa.

Yoruba and Igbo as Exemplary African Examples to the Issues of Evil and Suffering.

Early in this chapter, we suggested a range of theological beliefs that African societies tend to share in common. In this final section, we will review those theological ideas and then show that the two Nigerian societies are exemplary examples of these African beliefs regarding the phenomena of evil and suffering.

Among those beliefs in traditional African religions, we have seen a belief in a High God; a dedication to a collection of minor deities; a belief in ancestral spirits; a strong belief in witches, witchcraft and medicine men, or witch doctors; the use of sacrifices; rites of passage; and many other philosophical and theological ideas.

It should be clear that both the Yoruba people and the Igbo have possessed the family resemblance characteristics for a traditional, religious African society. Both societies have High Gods. For the Igbo people, their High God is named *Chukwu*. In Yoruba, the chief god is known as *Olorun*. Both Nigerian societies also have a collection of minor gods. Among the Igbo, they are called *mmu*. Yoruba society also has a collection of minor gods, including *Olokun, Olosa, Shanlpanna, Shigidi*, as well as at least fifteen other minor deities.[955]

The veneration of the dead can also be seen in both Nigerian societies discussed in this chapter. Both the Yoruba and the Igbo also have strong beliefs about witches, witchcraft and medicine men in their societies. Both societies also engage in sacrifices, as we have shown, most often in the forms of food and drink in propitiation of the gods.

Both the Yoruba and the Igbo have rites of passage in their belief system. As we have suggested in the first section of this chapter, one aspect of traditional African religions is the idea of rites of passage. Most traditional African societies have rituals that mark these time periods in life, including a birth rite, a coming-of-age rite, a marriage rite, a rite in which one becomes an elder, and a death ritual, also known as a rite of becoming an ancestor.

The Igbo people also practice an additional rite of passage when a baby first receives its name. This is a solemn ceremony, and much thought and drama go into selecting a name. In Igbo culture, a male child is circumcised. The boy's mother buries the umbilical cord and placenta at the base of a tree specifically chosen for the ceremony. For the Igbo and the Yoruba, both societies put central emphasis on these rites of passage.[956] Other central, religious ideas also can be seen in both cultures.

Among these ideas are the following:

1. Divination
2. A Creation Myth
3. A Cosmology
4. Healing practices
5. Magic

And in each of these five ideas, as well, both the Igbo and the Yoruba engage in these practices (divination, healing practices and magic) or have substantial beliefs about how the universe began, and the levels of reality. Given the description of the dozen or so ideas and practices in traditional African religions introduced in the beginning of this tenth chapter, the conclusion to be made about the Igbo and the Yoruba should be clear. These two societies are very good representative examples of a traditional African society, as well as theological responses to the ideas of evil and suffering.

This brings us to the major conclusions we have made in this chapter. Chapter Eleven to follow is a summary chapter in which we will catalog the major conclusions we have made in this study on evil and suffering in the religions of the world. Following this material is a series of appendices in which we have outlined the foreign words and phrases utilized in this study.

Conclusions to Chapter Ten

We began this chapter by outlining and then discussing a series of beliefs and practices that traditional African religions have believed in and practiced. In that section, we made remarks about beliefs in a High

God, minor gods, spirits and a spirit world, the efficacy of sacrifice, the practice of rites of passage, the use of divination, magic, and an account of creation and the levels of reality.

In the second section of Chapter Ten, we continued our discussion of ideas and practices in traditional African religions, and discussed how geography has frequently made beliefs and practices in areas of Africa may be very different from another area of the continent.

In the third and central section of Chapter Ten, we gave a short introduction to the Yoruba and the Igbo tribes in West Africa. We spoke of the geography, languages, history and village life that existed among these two societies, mostly in Nigeria.

This material was followed by a description and discussion of what the Yoruba and the Igbo have had to say about the origin of evil. Indeed, we began that section with a summary of words in the Yoruba and Igbo languages relating to Good and Evil. We then cataloged many ways that the two West African societies responded to the phenomena of evil and suffering.

In the next section, we explored what the Yoruba and the Igbo have had to say about the kinds or types of evil in their societies. As we have shown, the Yoruba believe that there are four types or varieties of evil. These are physical evil, moral evil, inflicted evil and predestined evil.

On the other hand, the Igbo understand the phenomenon of evil to have three separate types—Natural, Moral, and Metaphysical evils—much like the distinctions among these three types introduced in Chapter One of this study.

In the fifth section of Chapter Ten, we discussed many methods and responses to the issues of evil and suffering found among the Yoruba and the Igbo. After showing how West African poetry and functionaries, such as medicine men or witch doctors, responded to the phenomena of evil and suffering, we then turned to a summary of theological responses to be found among the two Nigerian societies.

In that portion of the fifth section of Chapter Ten, we suggested that among the Yoruba and Igbo Peoples, evidence was found that their theologians and philosophers employed versions of the Contrast View; Free Will Defense; Retributive Justice Theory; Test View; Influences of

Demonic Forces, though most contemporary scholars are skeptical of this response to evil and suffering; Evil caused by Ancestral Spirits; and employment of the theory we called "Determinism" back in Chapter One. This last view may be seen, we have argued, in the West African idea of "Good Destiny."[957]

In the final section of Chapter Ten, we returned to the description of basic beliefs in traditional African religions enumerated in the opening section of the chapter. After reminding the reader of these practices and beliefs, we then showed that both Yoruba and Igbo societies might be seen as exemplary African examples of an African society concerning the issues of evil and suffering.

This brings us to Chapter Eleven, in which we summarize the major conclusions made in this study of evil and suffering in the religions of the world.

Chapter Eleven:
Some Conclusions of this Study

The idea of God is man's recognition of his own
longing to take his highest ideas seriously.

—Konstantin Kolenda, *Religion Without God*

If God were good, He would wish to make His creatures
perfectly happy. And if God were Almighty, He would be able
to do so. But His creatures are not always happy.

—C. S. Lewis, *The Problem of Pain*

It has been argued that the most complete, formal
solution of the problem of theodicy is the special
achievement of the Indian doctrine of Karma, the
so-called belief in the transmigration of the soul.

—Wendy Doniger, "Karma in Hindu Thought"

Introduction

The purpose of this final chapter is to sketch out the major conclusions
we made in this study of evil and suffering in the world's religious
traditions. We will divide this chapter into four sections. The first of
these is Chapter One, an introduction to the study of evil and suffering
in the religions of the world, in which we attempted to make sense of
concepts like "religion" and "evil" in Natural, Moral, and Metaphysical
forms after a discussion in Chapter One on the notion of a "definition" in
the West. Indeed, we discarded the Aristotle-Augustine understanding

of the nature of language in favor of the view of Ludwig Wittgenstein in his *Philosophical Investigations*.

In the second section of this summary, we will review the three oldest religions discussed in this study—Hinduism, Judaism and the dualistic religions Zoroastrianism, Mithraism and Manichaeism. In section three, we will review the four Far-East religions outlined in this study. That is Buddhism, Confucianism, Taoism and the Shinto faith. In the fourth and final section of this chapter, we will review the major conclusions developed in the chapters on Christianity and Islam—Chapters Eight and Nine. We begin our conclusive review, then, with a return to the ideas of evil and suffering, as well as the notion of a "religion," as these concepts were explored back in Chapter One.

Section One: Major Conclusions from Chapter One of this Study

In the opening chapter of this study on evil and suffering in the world's religious traditions, we have had four major goals. The first of these goals was to make some observations about the nature of a "definition" in the history of Western society. In that initial section, we pointed out that the standard understanding of a "definition" in Western society has been that of Aristotle and his idea of necessary and sufficient conditions for calling something by a specific name.[958] As we have shown, this is also the view of Augustine of Hippo regarding the nature of language at the beginning of his *Confessions*.

After discussing the approach of a definition in Aristotle, we then went on to show—using some philosophical development of Austrian philosopher Ludwig Wittgenstein—that Aristotle's approach to identity is an insufficient one. Indeed, using some observations from Wittgenstein's *Philosophical Investigations*, we suggested that his idea of "family resemblance" is a far better approach to understanding the nature and the uses of natural languages and the approach of Aristotle and Augustine of Hippo.[959] One of the ways we have shown the inadequacies of the Aristotle/Augustine view of a definition was by citing an example of a group of Egyptian boys playing a game in the 1980s.

Rather than employing Aristotle and Augustine's necessary and sufficient conditions for using words, we suggested that this approach be replaced with Wittgenstein's Family Resemblance Approach. Indeed, we have suggested at the beginning of Chapter One of this study that this Family Resemblance Approach is the best way to proceed when defining words like "evil" and "religion" concerning the use of language.

In the second section of the opening chapter, we introduced the concept of "evil." In traditional philosophy in the West there have been three separate kinds or versions of "evil." These are "Natural Evils," "Moral Evils" and "Metaphysical Evils."[960]

As we have shown, Natural Evils are those instances of evil and suffering that occur in the natural world, such as storms, floods and fatal diseases, for example. Moral Evils are those examples of evil that are caused by the actions of moral agent upon each other, such as rape, stealing, murder, etc. By "moral agent" in this study, we mean those creatures in reality who are subject to the idea of moral responsibility, such as humans and angels.

We stated in Chapter One that Metaphysical Evils are those examples of evil and suffering that primarily occur in the mind. We gave examples like dread, worry, fear and many other phenomena as instances of Metaphysical Evils, as are the intense suffering produced by many mental diseases and syndromes.

The second goal of our first chapter of this study was to apply Wittgenstein's notion of family resemblance to the idea of "religion" in the faiths of the world. In that section, we outlined ten separate characteristics for identifying something as a "religion." These family resemblance characteristics for a "religion" may be summarized this way:

1. A conception of ultimate reality.
2. A system of myths, symbols and rituals.
3. A distinction between sacred and profane.
4. Sacred persons, places and things.
5. A system of ethics sanctioned by the holy.
6. Responses to evil and suffering.
7. A notion of the self.
8. A view of survival after death.

9. Sacred scriptures.
10. An eschatology.[961]

These ten characteristics for a "religion" were adapted from scholar Huston Smith's book *The World's Religions*.[962] It is essential to point out, however, that all ten of these characteristics need not be present in order to call something a religion. Rather, Wittgenstein would say, we know something is a religion because of this loose network of family resemblance characteristics. For the Austrian philosopher, if a belief system has enough of these traits, then it begins to look and act like a religion.

After introducing and discussing each of these family resemblance characteristics of a "religion," we went on in Chapter One to our third goal of this initial chapter. That goal was to catalog the major ways in the religions of the world where they have attempted to answer, or to respond to, why there is so much evil in the world—natural, moral and metaphysical.

Indeed, in this final section, we introduced and discussed at some length eight traditional answers and responses, as well as several other supplemental views on evil and suffering in the world's religious traditions. These eight traditional views, as shown in Chapter One, can be summarized thusly:

1. Original Sin Theory
2. Free Will Defense
3. Retributive Justice Theory (Individual and Collective)
4. Influences of Demonic Forces View
5. Test Perspective
6. Moral Qualities Approach
7. Contrast View
8. Divine Plan Theory[963]

After explicating each of these eight perspectives, we then added several "supplemental theories" that often have been employed in the religions of the world to explain the phenomena of evil and suffering. These supplemental theories may be summarized this way:

9. The Karma-Samsara Approach
10. The Deprivation of the Good Theory
11. That God Permits Evil
12. The Principle of Plenitude Approach
13. The Best Possible Worlds Theory
14. Eschatological Verification Perspective
15. Limited God Theories
16. Ancestor Worship
17. The Hidden God Theory
18. Determinism[964]

After naming, explicating and discussing these supplemental theories that attempt to answer or to respond to the phenomena of evil and suffering in the world's religious traditions, we went on to an analysis of the three oldest religious faiths—Hinduism, Judaism and the dualistic approaches to evil and suffering: Zoroastrianism, Mithraism and Manichaeism. Indeed, these are the subject matter of the second section of this chapter.

Section Two: Evil and Suffering in the Oldest Faiths

As indicated in the above analysis, in the second section of this study, we introduced and discussed what are most likely the three oldest religious traditions—Hinduism, Judaism and the dualistic faiths of Zoroastrianism, Mithraism and Manichaeism. In fact, these faiths go back four thousand, three thousand, and twenty-five hundred years in the case of Zoroastrianism, the Persian dualistic faith.

We opened the second chapter with an analysis of Hinduism and with a series of preliminary remarks about ancient India and the world's "oldest faith." We pointed out that the word "Hindoo," or "Hindu," is a modern invention coined by Christian missionaries to India in the late seventeenth century.[965] We also indicated that Hinduism has no set founder, nor even when the Indian faith began. However, it does have specific sacred scriptures, including the Vedas, the Upanishads and the many Indian epics, which go back many centuries ago.[966]

In addition to these preliminary remarks, we indicated that even early on, the Hindu faith offered a variety of ways to salvation, that the faith is extremely diverse, that early Hinduism was polytheistic, and that the Hindu religion is very different from faiths in the Western world, such as Judaism, Christianity and Islam.

In the next section of chapter two, we described and discussed the major periods in the history of Indian religion, including the indigenous period, the Aryan and Vedic period, the epics and classical age, the medieval period, the pre-modern age, the British era of India, and independence of India.[967] We also indicated many of the theological and philosophical developments in each of these periods.

Next, in chapter two, we moved on to an introduction and a discussion of key concepts in the Hindu faith. Among these concepts were the following:

1. God and gods
2. Brahman
3. Atman
4. Karma
5. Samsara, Maya
6. Dharma
7. Bakhti
8. Moksha
9. Nirvana
10. The Caste System

As shown in Chapter Two, each of these ideas contributed to what the earliest Indian religious sources have had to say about the phenomena of evil and suffering in Hinduism. Among the most important of these central ideas in early Hinduism were its polytheism, the ideas of reincarnation, karma-samsara, nirvana, and the fact that Vedantic Hinduism was a Religion of Dissolution.

The central section of Chapter Two, of course, is what the Vedas and the Upanishads, as well as the Hindu epics, have related about how they understood the phenomena of evil and suffering in the early Hindu faith. To that end, we have seen that the ideas of karma and samsara predominated the early Hindu points of view, as did the fact that evil was seen as *Maya*, or "illusion," and thus Hinduism was a Religion of Dissolution.

In addition to this view, however, we have also seen versions of the Free Will Defense, Retributive Justice Theory, and the Influences of Demonic Influences in these earliest of Indian sources. In two subsequent sections of Chapter Two, we explored the philosophical views on evil and suffering of the two great medieval Hindu thinkers, Adi Shankara, from the eighth century; and twelfth-century Indian philosopher Ramanuja.[968]

When it came to responding to the issues of evil and suffering, what both of these Indian philosophers relied on was primarily the Karma-Samsara Response and that early Hinduism was a Religion of Dissolution, in that evil was seen as *Maya*. This section on these medieval Hindu perspectives was followed by a discussion of more modern Hindu voices regarding the same issues.

The perspectives of the modern Hindus we introduced were those of Tagore, Swami Vivekananda, Radhakrishna, and Mahatma Gandhi. Although these thinkers still relied very heavily on the Karma-Samsara Model, they also, particularly in the case of Radhakrishna, put forward Indian versions of the Free Will Defense, the Test Theory, as well as the Moral Qualities Point of View.[969] Still, the overall view on evil and suffering in the faith of Hinduism is that we have concluded that it is a Religion of Dissolution and that evil was seen as being illusory.

In our discussion in Chapter Three on evil and suffering in Judaism, we indicated that, at one time or another in the history of Judaism, one might find the assertion of all eight theories from Chapter One, as well the nine supplemental theories, with the exception of evil caused by ancestor worship.

We began Chapter Three with some preliminary remarks on Judaism. We spoke of the three portions of the Hebrew Scriptures—Torah, Prophets and the Writings. We also wrote about the concept of the *Berith*, or Covenant, and that the ancient Jews appeared to have borrowed the idea of the Covenant from the people known as the Hittites, neighbors of the ancient Jews in the second millennium BCE.[970] We also suggested that the category of the Covenant was the foundation for the earliest theological responses to evil and suffering in the ancient Jewish faith.

In the next section of Chapter Three, we examined how the three parts of Hebrew Scripture responded to the phenomena of evil and suffering and how responses in the Jewish faith came in and out of fashion in the history of the Jews. Indeed, in successive sections of Chapter Three, we have shown how important Jewish thinkers in the ancient world, the Middle Ages, and the modern period from the sixteenth century to the present have all responded to the phenomena of evil and suffering.[971]

As indicated earlier, important thinkers in the Jewish faith responded to the issues of evil and suffering by using the eight basic theories, as well as the supplemental views introduced and discussed back in the first chapter of this study. In fact, we have seen a heavy reliance on views like the Hidden God Theory and the view that God Permits Evil while not being responsible for it.[972] Among these medieval Jewish thinkers who wrote about evil and suffering, we mentioned Saadiah Gaon, Rashi, Moses Maimonides, Nachmanides, and several other Jewish philosophers and exegetes from the Middle Ages.

The final of our oldest religions of the world are three examples of Cosmic Dualism from the ancient world—Zoroastrianism, Mithraism and Manichaeism. In separate sections of Chapter Four, we indicated that each of these three faiths, as well as the metaphysics of ancient philosopher Plato and the Neo-Platonists of the medieval period, were all advocates of the Religions of Solution as outlined in the opening chapter of this study.[973]

For the most part, each of these four views responded to evil and suffering by blaming it on the bad god or an evil source that cannot be controlled by the Good. In a separate section of Chapter Four on Zoroastrianism, Mithraism and one on Manichaeism, as well as the section on Plato, we have shown why these four metaphysical views were Religions of Solution. In addition, we have also maintained that each of the four also employed several of our other responses introduced in Chapter One.

In Zoroastrianism, for example, we also found evidence for the use of the Free Will Defense, Retributive Justice Theory, the Influences of the Demonic God, Angra Mainya, as well as the employment of the Divine Plan Perspective. Additional views on evil and suffering also can be seen in Mithraism and Manichaeism, as well.

At the close of Chapter Four, we also indicated several modern thinkers where metaphysical dualism has made a comeback of a sort in figures such as John Stuart Mill, William James, E. S. Brightman, Charles Pierce, and what we have called the "Limited God" theorists that included Rabbi Harold Kushner and the process theologians. This brings us to the third section of this concluding chapter, in which we will speak of four faiths from the Far East—Buddhism, Confucianism, Taoism and the Shinto faith.

Section Three: Evil and Suffering in Religions of the Far East

We began the chapters of section three of this study with some comments on the faith of Buddhism in Chapter Five of this study. We opened the chapter with a short introduction to Buddhism, followed by the second section about the ideas of that faith that have been inherited from Hinduism. Among those ideas were: Karma-Samsara, the ideas of nirvana, dharma and maya, and the notion of demonic influences on human life, as well as other early ideas in Buddhism.

Indeed, we have shown that, with each of these ideas listed here, the early Buddhist faith changed and modified those ideas in unique ways. Rather than the atman, for example, Hinayana Buddhists posited the view that it was the *Skandas* that get reincarnated.[974] Whereas, nirvana in Hinduism was related to the expression, *Tat tvam asi*, or "That you are" in the Buddhist faith. It now involved the dissipation of the Skandas, to the point of nothingness.[975]

In the next section of Chapter Five, we introduced many early theological Buddhist ideas, including the Four Noble Truths and the Eight-Fold Path.[976] After that material, we turned our attention to ancestor worship as an early belief about the origins of some evil and the peculiar ways Buddhism understands other examples of evil as being related to the karmic cycle.[977]

In the final section of the chapter on Buddhism, we introduced and discussed the phenomenon of social justice and how some Buddhist schools deal with issues like the environment and suffering associated with it.

We also indicated in Chapter Five that various schools of Buddhism have assented to the uses of the Free Will Defense, The

Contrast Perspective, Ancestor Worship as a cause of Evil and Suffering, the Influences of Demonic Forces Theory, and the Karma-Samsara Rebirth Cycle, and that we also consider early Buddhism a Religion of Dissolution, like Vedantic Hinduism, as well.[978]

In Chapter Six of this study, we turned our attention to a second religion of the Far East—Confucianism. We began the chapter with a short section on the life and times of Confucius. This was followed by a description of the Confucian Scriptures, including the Four Books and the Five Classics, concentrating our attention on Confucius' *Analects*.[979] What followed next was a short section that describes sacred places and sacred persons in the Confucian faith.[980]

One of the most interesting facts about the belief system of Confucius, who lived around 500 BCE, is how many of the other founders of the religions in this study lived at the same time in what some historians call the "Axial Age." This includes Gautama Buddha, Zoroaster, Lao Tzu, and the major and minor prophets in Judaism.[981]

This expression *Achsenzeit*, or the "Axial Age," was coined by German philosopher Karl Jaspers to refer to a "pivotal age" characterized by a period in ancient history from about 700 BCE until around 300 BCE. This idea of Jaspers first appeared in his book *Vom Ursprung und Ziel der Geschichte*, or *The Origin and Goal of History*.[982]

All of this material in Chapter Six was followed by a section on the principal ideas in the Confucian faith, many of which have been shared with Buddhism, as we have shown. Next, we analyzed and discussed many of the places in the *Analects* where the issues of evil and suffering arise in that belief system. This was followed by a summary in which we have maintained that the *Analects* mentions, or outright endorses Retributive Justice Theory, the Contrast View, the Test Perspective, Ancestor Worship, the Influences of Demonic Forces Theory as explanations for evil and suffering in Confucian thought.[983]

In the final part of sections of Chapter Six, we articulated many of the views about the nature and extent of Moral Goodness in Confucian thought, as well as a section on more modern Confucian perspectives on evil and suffering.[984] Indeed, in these views from modern Confucianism, we have seen a reliance on the earlier ideas established in the *Analects*. In Chapter Seven of this study, we concentrated on our final two Far

East religions—Taoism and Japanese Shintoism. Indeed, we split the chapter by first discussing Taoism, followed by the perspectives on evil and suffering to be found in Shintoism.[985]

Much of the material on Taoism in Chapter Seven came from the two great Taoist philosophers Lao Tzu, who died around 500 BCE, and Chuang Tzu, who dies in 286 BCE. We found that these two thinkers mention or endorsed the Free Will Defense, the Contrast View, the Divine Plan Theory, and the Influences of Demonic Forces Theory. We also have seen that Lao Tzu makes some deep and cogent comments about Natural Evils and their causes and meaning in the world of the senses.[986]

As indicated earlier, the second half of Chapter Seven was taken up with how the Japanese religion Shintoism in its history responded to the phenomena of evil and suffering in the world. As we have shown, the Shinto faith is based on the idea of *Kami*, a Japanese term that means a variety of things.[987]

From this material on the Shinto faith, we maintained that traces of the following theories about evil and suffering might be found in this traditional Japanese faith: Evil caused by Ancestor Worship, Divine Plan Theory, Retributive Justice Perspective, Divine Plan Theory, and Evil and Suffering caused by the influence of Demonic Forces in Shinto thought. This brings us to the fourth and final section of this tenth chapter, where we will discuss the two youngest religions in this study, Christianity and Islam.

Section Four: Evil and Suffering in the Most Recent Religions

In the fourth section of this chapter, we will end by suggesting the conclusions made in the two most recent religions in this study—Christianity and Islam.

The main focus of Chapter Eight is Christianity and its history. We began the chapter with a summary of how the phenomena of evil and suffering have been responded to or explained in the books of the New Testament. In this material, we see that nearly all of our theories outlined in Chapter One were employed, in one way or another, in the twenty-seven books of the New Testament.

In the second section of Chapter Eight, we explored many of the thinkers in the ancient and medieval churches where evil and suffering became subject matters for theological discourse in those periods. Among the most significant of these thinkers in the Christian tradition were Augustine of Hippo and Italian philosopher Thomas Aquinas. In these two prominent Christian thinkers we saw the endorsement of, or the assenting to, nearly all of our eight basic theories, as well as most of the supplemental theories outlined in Chapter One of this study.

What we have maintained about the thought of Augustine of Hippo on the issues of evil and suffering, the bishop endorses or outright assents to ten different approaches. These include the Free Will Defense, the Contrast View, Original Sin Theory, Retributive Justice Approach, the Influences of Demonic Forces Theory, the Deprivation of the Good Approach, the Leibnizian Best of All Possible Worlds Theory, the Divine Plan Perspective, and the Test View.[988]

Many of these same responses to the issues of evil and suffering were present in the theological views of Thomas Aquinas, as well, and he even employed a few approaches not found in the Bishop of Hippo. In the nine major works of Aquinas that we consulted for this study, we found evidence that the Italian endorsed Retributive Justice Theory, the Influences of Demonic Forces Theory, the Original Sin Perspective, the Free Will Defense, the Deprivation of the Good Perspective, the Contrast View, The Test Theory, the Moral Qualities View, and the Divine Plan Perspective. Two other theories for explaining evil and suffering of Thomas Aquinas that were not found in Augustine were the Principle of Plenitude and Eschatological Verification Theory.[989] By the High Middle Ages, then, we have seen in Thomas Aquinas as full and as in-depth a treatment to evil and suffering that we have seen in this entire study, and particularly in the Christian tradition.

In the second section to Chapter Eight, we explored the perspectives on evil and suffering from two of the major Reformation thinkers in the Christian Church—Martin Luther (1483–1546) and John Calvin (1509–1564). As with Augustine and Aquinas, the views of Luther and Calvin on the questions at hand were extensive.[990]

What we saw in our analysis of these two Reformation thinkers is that both men employed retributive Justice Theory, the Moral Qualities View, the Test Perspective, Eschatological Verification Theory, the

Influences of Demonic Forces Perspective, Original Sin Theory, and the Divine Plan View.[991]

In the theological works of the two Reformers, we also saw a rejection of the Free Will Approach theory, primarily because neither reformer favored salvation by works, while both were in favor of the idea of being saved by the Grace of God. More specifically, through what they called "Irresistible Grace."[992] In addition, we see that in a few places in his *Institutes*, Calvin endorses the view we have called the "Permission Theory." That is, that God "permits" evil, but He does not cause it.[993]

In the next section on Chapter Eight, we explored three representative thinkers in the Christian tradition in the early modern period in the eighteenth and nineteenth centuries. In that section, we introduced and discussed the works of G. W. Leibniz, Immanuel Kant, and poet and painter William Blake on the phenomena of evil and suffering. We found that Leibniz invented the word "Theodicy," as well as the view that this is the "Best of All Possible Worlds."[994]

As we have shown, the German philosopher Immanuel Kant wrote extensively on evil and suffering in a major essay on theodicy, as well as two essays on natural disasters, and a concept of his that he referred to as "Radical Evil." Kant's comments on evil and suffering are philosophically subtle and complicated, rarely discussed in most evaluations of his philosophical work.[995]

One final representative in the early modern Christian period who has written a great deal about evil and suffering was Romantic poet and artist William Blake. As we have shown, Blake had a life-long fascination with the Book of Job.[996] He also completed a series of prints in 1825 on the Man From Uz and his book.[997]

In the final section of Chapter Eight, we explored the theological works of three modern representative Christian thinkers in the contemporary period: American philosopher William James; cleric John Henry Newman; and poet, essayist, and novelist G. K. Chesterton. Each of these three thinkers wrote about evil and suffering, as well as about the Book of Job.

James wrote extensively about Job in many of his major works.[998] John Henry Newman constructed and published many sermons on the book,[999] and Chesterton completed an English version of the Man From Uz and his book, as well as an extensive, theological essay on the biblical book, in which, among other things he calls Job "The first Existentialist."[1000] This brings us to the major conclusions about our final world religion discussed in Chapter Nine of this study—the faith of Islam.

We began Chapter Nine on evil and suffering in the Islamic faith with a summary of classical Arabic vocabulary on evil, suffering and words connected to Moral Goodness in the Muslim faith. This was followed by the first section of Chapter Nine that acted as a short introduction to the faith of Islam. In this introduction, we spoke of the religion's founder, its Holy Book, *Al-Qur'an*, brought by the Angel, Jibril, as well as its Six Basic Beliefs and Islam's five major moral requirements.[1001]

These six pillars of faith were *Tawhid*, or the Oneness of Allah; belief in the *Mala'ika*, or "Angels;" the belief in Sacred Scriptures; belief in the Prophets; belief in the Day of Judgment; and belief in *Al-Qadar*, or the "Decrees of Allah." The five moral requirements were the *Shahadah*, or the "Profession of Faith;" *Salat*, or five daily prayers; *Zakat*, or the giving of Alms; *Sawm*, or Fasting, especially during the month of Ramadan; and the *Hajj*, or the "Pilgrimage" at least once in the believer's lifetime, if able.

This material was followed in Chapter Nine by the two central sections of the chapter, one on evil and suffering in the Muslim Holy Book and the other on evil and suffering in traditional Hadith literature. In the former, we have provided twenty-five examples of where the subjects of evil and suffering have appeared in *Al-Qur'an*. In the latter, we have shown traditions from many of the traditional collectors of Hadith, both Sunni and Shiite.[1002] Among these *Ahadith*—the plural form—we have provided examples from Sahih Hurayra, Sa'id Al-Khudri, Abu Bukhari, Sahih Muslim, and philosopher Jafar Al-Tabari, among other Muslim thinkers.[1003]

In the next section of Chapter Nine, we introduced and discussed many ways that noted figures in medieval Islamic philosophy dealt with the phenomena of evil and suffering. Among these noted medieval Muslim thinkers we introduced and discussed were The Mu'tazila thinkers and those of the Ashariyah School, Al-Ghazali, Ibn Sina, Ibn Arabi, Al-Razi, Ibn Taymiyyah, Al-Qayyim, and the Persian poet and mystic Rumi, who wished to turn Islam into a Religion of Dissolution.[1004]

This material was followed in Chapter Nine by a description of how many philosophical thinkers in modern Islam have responded to the issues of evil and suffering. Among the modern thinkers mentioned and discussed were Mulla Sadra; Muhammad Abduh; Jamal Afghani; Sa'id Nursi; the radical thinker, Sayyid Qutb; and the only female philosopher in our analysis, Tubanur Ozkan.[1005]

We indicated that of these modern thinkers, Mulla Sadra and Sa'id Nursi were the most significant figures in contributing to the Muslim literature on the phenomena of evil and suffering. We also indicated the work of Pakistani philosopher Muhammad Iqbal, who, in his poetry and philosophical works, has written a great deal about the issues of evil and suffering, much more so than any other modern Islamic thinker.[1006]

From the work of Iqbal, we have seen rejections of some philosophical perspectives on the phenomena of evil and suffering and the adopting of another approach. Among the discarded views on Iqbal's part were Original Sin Theory; the Influences of Demonic Forces View; the Monism, or Religion of Dissolution of Hinayana Buddhism; and the Deprivation of the Good Theory. In the work of Muhammad Iqbal, we have also seen the adoption of the western philosophical movement that has come to be known as "Panentheism," as borrowed from Western thinker Charles Sanders Peirce."[1007]

Muhammad Iqbal has also compared the account in the Qur'an of the Fall of Adam and Eve to the biblical version at Genesis three. He points out that in Islam, Adam and Eve eat the fruit together, whereas, in Genesis, Eve eats first and then offers it to Adam. In Genesis, the Earth is cursed for Adam's transgression, while there is nothing comparable in the Qur'an.[1008] The Qur'an specifies that the tree is the "Tree of Eternity," while in the Bible it is the "tree of the knowledge of good and evil."

Finally, in Chapter Ten of this study, we began by enumerating several traditional beliefs found in indigenous African religions. This was followed by a summary of the Yoruba and Igbo peoples of Western Africa. This was followed by separate sections of Chapter Ten on the causes of evil, the varieties of evil, and the methods and responses employed by the Yoruba and the Igbo in their metaphysical ruminations.

In that section, we maintained that the two Nigerian tribes used versions of several of the theological responses to evil and suffering sketched out in Chapter One of this study. Among those responses were the following: the Contrast View; the Free Will Defense; the Retributive Justice Theory; the Test View; the possible influences of Demonic Forces Theory; Evil caused by Ancestor Worship, and the view that we called Determinism in Chapter One.

Following this chapter, we have included several appendices that catalog the many foreign words and phrases in the many languages employed in this study that have included Sanskrit, Pali, Classical Hebrew, Mandarin Chinese, Ancient Persian, Greek, Latin, as well as several modern languages.

Appendix A:
Words and Phrases in Ancient Sanskrit/Pali

Advata School - non-dualism

Agamas - scripture

Agni - god of fire

Ahimsa - non-violence

Ajiva - matter

Antar-yamin - immortal one

Aparagrapha - few possessions

Ashuras - demons

Asvamedha parva - horse sacrifice

Ateya - no stealing

Atman - soul

Avarna - no caste

Bhagavad Gita - Hindu epic

Bhakti - devotion

Brahma - Divine principle

Brahmanas - Hindu writings

Brahmin - top caste

Brahmacharya - celibacy

Brihadararanyaka - one of Upanishads

Dharma - law

Dukkha - suffering in Buddhism

Dyaus - god of the sky

Guru Granth Sahib - Scripture (Sikh religion)

Homa - sacrifice

Indra - god of war

Jiva - soul

Kami - Japanese ancestors

Kara - Pali demon

Karma - rebirth

Khansha - Sanskrit word for Skandas

Kshatriya - second caste

Magga - the path that frees (Buddhist)

Maya - illusion

Mahabharata - Hindu epic

Mitar - father

Mitra - god of night

Moksha - release from rebirth wheel

Mukti - synonym for *Moksha*

Namucci - destroyer god (India)

Narayana - Hindu god

Nikaya - order of monks (Buddhism)

Nirhodha - end of suffering (Buddhism)

Nirvana - salvation

Pitar - father

Puranas - Hindu Scripture

Pushan - god of nourishment

Rayarana - way of the diamond (Buddhism)

Rig - one of the Vedas

Rta - cosmic order

Samhitas - Scripture

Samsara - wheel of life

Samtnra Dharma - eternal law

Samudya - cause of suffering (Buddhism)

Satya - truthfulness

Shudra - lowest caste

Skanda - nature of self in Buddhism

Smrti - good customs

Sri or *Laksmi* - consort of Vishnu

Suttas - texts

Tat tvam asi - "That you are."

Tipatika - three baskets (Buddhism)

Upanishads - Hindu Scripture

Vaisyas - third caste

varnas - untouchables

Varuna - Hindu god

Vaishnava Alvars - twelve sages

Vedas - Hindu Scripture

Vidya - a kind of *maya*

Vishnu - Hindi god

Yajna - sacrifice

Yatudhans - mythological beasts

Appendix B:
Words and Phrases in Classical Hebrew

Berith - Covenant

El - God

Elohim - God

Kethuvim - writings

Nacah - to test

Nabim - prophets

Natash - to permit

Rashyon - permission

Tam - blameless

Torah - first five books of the Hebrew Bible

Yashar - upright

Yawheh - The God of Israel

Yetzer - imagination or inclination

Yetzer hara - evil imagination

yetzer tov - good imagination

Appendix C:
Words and Phrases in Ancient Persian

Angra - angry

Angra Mainya - evil god in Zoroastrianism

Ahura - honorable

Ahura Mazda - good god in Zoroastrianism

Asha - truth

Daevas - Devils

Devas - Persian for devils

Divs - devils

Faravahar - symbol

Sindus - beyond the Indus

Vendidad - Persian Scripture

Visperad - Scriptures

Yashts - Persian Scripture

Yasnas-Gathas - Scripture in Zoroastrians

Zend-Avesta - Zoroastrian Writings

Appendix D:
Words and Phrases in Swahili,
Yoruba and Igbo Languages

Aidrara - bad (Yoruba)

Aje - witchcraft

Ajo - bad (Yoruba)

Aito - unrighteous (Yoruba)

Aja-Oshu - goddess of the moon (Igbo)

Ajo' - evil (Yoruba)

Ala - goddess of the Earth (Igbo)

Amadioha - god of thunder (Igbo)

Amala - grace (Igbo)

Burburu - wickedness (Yoruba)

Ebe onye dalu ka Chi ya Kwatulu ya - When a person falls, his personal god pushed him. (Yoruba)

Ebi - extended family (Yoruba)

Ebora - ancestors

Ekwensu - evil god (Igbo)

Eshu, Exu, or *Echu* - god of evil (Yoruba)

Ezigbo - good (Igbo)

Ibi - evil (Yoruba)

Ibi-omo - evil or prohibited (Yoruba)

Ike - good (Igbo)

Ike' - good (Igbo)

Ka mma - better (Igbo)

Kuna mkono wa mtu hapa - There is someone's hand behind this. (Swahili)

Mmehle - sin (Yoruba)

ojoo - evil (Yoruba)

Olokun - god of the sea

Oke - god of hills and mountains (Igbo)

Olosa - goddess of Lagos Lagoon (Igbo)

oma - good (Igbo)

omo - evil or prohibited (Yoruba)

orisa - minor gods

Orun - the sun god (Igbo)

Osanhin - god of medicine (Igbo)

Oshosi - god of hunters (Igbo)

Oso - sorcery

Oshimare - rainbow god and god of underworld (Igbo)

Oto - enemy

Oye - god of wind (Igbo)

Shankpanna - god of smallpox (Igbo)

Shuigidi - god of evil (Igbo)

Appendix E:
Words and Phrases in Classical Chinese

Baigujing - figure from Chinese mythology

Chung Yung - doctrine of the mean

Chun Tzu - gentleman

De - Chinese virtue

Fengshen Yanyi - fictional character in Ming Dynasty

Kong Li - Son of Confucius

Kung Fu Tzu - Confucius

Li - Chinese virtue

Lin yu - The Analects of Confucius

Lu - state in China

Meng Tzu - Book of Mencius

Qufu - city in China

Ren - Chinese virtue

Ta hsueth - the Great Learning

Tao - the Way

Tao Te Ching - Book of Changes

Tian - Heaven

Wen - Chinese virtue

Wu Jing - five classics

Xiao - Chinese virtue

Xin - Chinese virtue

Yang - Chinese force

Yi - Chinese virtue

Yin - Chinese force

Yong - Chinese virtue

Zhong - Chinese virtue

Zhou - Chinese dynasty

Appendix F:
Words and Phrases in Greek and Latin

Ab origine - at the beginning (Latin)

Amima/animus - soul (Greek and Latin)

Axis mundi - the center of the Earth (Latin)

Corax - raven (Latin)

Deus - God (Greek)

Eschata - last thing (Greek)

Heliodromus - Sun-runner (Greek)

Hennotheism - form of polytheism (Greek)

Homo religious - religious man (Latin)

Illo tempore - outside of time (Latin)

Kaos - chaos (Greek)

Leo - lion (Latin)

Logos - the Word (Greek)

Mater - mother (Latin)

Miles - soldier (Latin)

Mithras - God in Mithraism (Greek)

Nymphus - bridegroom (Greek)

Pater - father (Latin)

Peres - Persian (Latin)

Privation boni - deprivation of the good (Latin)

Tauroctony - Killing of the bull in the Mithraite faith.

Appendix G:
Words and Phrases in Classical Arabic

Al-uqul al-khalisa - those who have been actualized

Ayat - verse of Al-Qur'an or a sign

Ayyub - Job

Barzakh - intermediate state

Dajjal - Antichrist

Eid al-Adha - ritual of sacrifice

Hayyal - sly

Hajj - pilgrimage

Hijra - New Year's Day

Iblis - Satan

Israa - The Night Journey

Isa - Jesus

Jahiliyyah - period of ignorance before Islam

Israfil - angel who blows trumpet

Jannah - Heaven

Jhannam - Hell

Ka'bah - sacred cube in Mecca

Kharab - bad

Khayir - good

Mutter - mother (German)

Muskritun - Those who practiced Shirk

Nabim - prophets

Nafs - soul

Ruh - spirit

Salah - virtue

Sabahah - companions to Prophet Muhammad

Shaytan - Satan

Sharr - evil

Shirk - unforgivable sin

Sur - trumpet or horn

Tayyib - good

Zakat - alms

Zenayah - virtue

Appendix H:
Other Foreign Words and Phrases

Anatnam - no soul (Buddhism)

Ayacanna Suttra - the request (Buddhism)

Ba - soul (ancient Egyptian)

Butsudan - Buddhist prayer altar

Deo - devil (Urdu)

Dhamma - Buddhist word for dharma

Div - devil (Turkish)

Edzil - soul that survives death (ancient Egyptian)

Hayagriva - Buddhist demon

Hirma - male soul (Mbua people)

I Ching - Taoist Scripture (Chinese)

Jinkiniki - Japanese Scripture

Ka - soul (ancient Egyptian)

Kage no yama - shadow sickness (Japanese)

Kami - gods or spirits (Shinto)

Kiryo - sickness demon (Japan)

Kiva - Pueblo ritual site

Kojiki - Scriptures (Japanese)

Kubera - Buddhist demon

Mara - God of underworld (Buddhism)

Mitima - gentle spirit (Shinto)

Mutsubi - sacredness of all living things (Japan)

Nee - personality (Mbua People)

Niem - conscience (ancient Egyptian)

Nihon Shoki - chronicles of Japan (Shinto)

Oni - Japanese demon

Rakshasas - Japanese demon

Sangha - community (Buddhism)

Sigla - soul (Mbua people)

Seo - soul (Old Saxon)

Shimenawa - symbol of purity (Shinto)

Sipapu - hole in ground where ancestors emerge

Tengu Kanji - mythological dog (Japanese)

Tipitak - Scripture (Chinese)

Tule - female soul (Mbua people)

Yomi - Japanese Land of the Dead (Shinto)

Endnotes

1   Aristotle, *The Metaphysics* (New York: Dover Books, 2018); *Posterior Analytics*, ed. Hugh Treddenick (London: Loeb Classics, 1960); *History of Animals*, ed. A. L. Peck (London: Loeb Classics, 1970).

2   *The Metaphysics*, Book Z, 92a.

3   *Posterior Analytics*, 96b.

4   *History of Animals*. p. 57.

5   Augustine, *Confessions* (Oxford: Oxford World Classics, 2009), I, 8.

6   Ludwig Wittgenstein, *Philosophical Investigations* (Oxford: Wiley-Blackwell, 2009).

7   Ibid., section I.

8   Ibid.

9   Immanuel Kant, *Religion Within the Limits of Reason Alone* (Cambridge: Cambridge University Press, 2009), 33.

10   Ibid.

11   Ibid., 34.

12   Philosophical Egoism is the theory that one's self is, or should be, the motivational goal of one's own actions. It may be prescriptive or normative. The descriptive version conceives of egoism as a factual description. The normative version says that people should be so motivated.

13   Kant, 35.

14   The idea of the *yetzer ha ra*, or the Evil Imagination or Inclination, first appears in the Hebrew Bible, or Old Testament, after the flood at Genesis 6:5 and 8:21.

15   Hanna Arendt, *The Origins of Totalitarianism* (New York: Harvest Books, 1973); *Eichmann in Jerusalem: A Report on the Banality of Evil* (New York: Harcourt Brace, 2006).

16   Arendt, *Origins*, 119.

17   Richard J. Bernstein, *Why Read Hannah Arendt Now?* (New York: Polity Books, 2018).

18   Henry E. Allison, "On the Very Idea of a Propensity to Evil," *Journal of Value Inquiry* 36, no. 1 (2002): 337–348.

19   Huston Smith, *The World's Religions* (San Francisco: Harpers, 2011), 7–17.

20   The expression *Tat tvam asi* appears in the Vedas, as well as the
      Upanishads. It also appears in some of the Paranas.

21   Plato, *Timaeus* (New York: Hackett Books, 2000). Plato's god
      called the Demiurge attempts to order the universe out of a
      pre-existent *Kaos*, or Matter, but he is unable to order all of the
      Kaos. Thus, in his view, there is god and the unordered parts of
      Kaos; thereby, the Athenian is a believer in Dualism.

22   John Waterhouse, *Zoroastrianism* (New York: Book Tree,
      2006), 14–16. For more on Zoroastrianism, see: Peter Clark,
      Zoroastrianism (London: Sussex Academic, 1998); and Jenny
      Rose, *Zoroastrianism* (London: Bloomsburg Academic, 2019).

23   Waterhouse, 16.

24   Manfred Clauss, *The Roman Cult of Mithras* (Oxford:
      Routledge, 2001).

25   Ibid., 21–22.

26   Michel Tardieu, *Manichaeism* (Chicago: University of Illinois
      Press, 2001).

27   Stephen Vicchio, *The Voice from the Whirlwind: The Problem
      of Evil in the Modern World* (Westminster: Christian Classics,
      1989), 14–16.

28   Ibid., 17.

29   Philip Wilkinson, *Myths and Legends* (New York: Dk, 2003),
      11–12.

30   Ibid., 13.

31   For more on the Kota people and their beliefs, see: David
      Mandelbaum, *Society in India* (Los Angeles: University of
      California Press, 1971), vol. 1; and Richard Kent Wolf, "The
      Kotas," https://bit.ly/3m2yIam.

32   In the Islamic tradition, the son for sacrifice of Ibrahim
      (Abraham) is not Isaac, but Ishmael.

33   Mircea Eliade, *The Sacred and the Profane* (New York: Harcourt
      Brace, 1957), 8–19.

34   Ibid.

35   Ibid., 22–25.

36   For more on the *95 Theses*, see: Martin Luther, *95 Theses*
      (Minneapolis: Fortress Press, 2015).

37   Eliade, 24.

38   Ibid.

39   Gilbert R. Wenger, *The Story of Mesa Verde National Park*, https://bit.ly/2Jlinuq. Also see: F. Waters, *Book of the Hopi* (New York: Penguin Books, 1963).

40   Ibid.

41   Ibid.

42   The Ten Commandments may be found at Exodus 20:2–17 and the Book of Deuteronomy 5:6–21.

43   Confucius, *The Analects* (New York: Penguin Books, 1979).

44   Anonymous, *The Zend-Avesta* (London: Forgotten Books, 2008).

45   Diana Gordan, *Hiroshima: A Morality Play* (New York: D. Gordan, 2013).

46   Immanuel Kant has the most famous Deontological System of Ethics, while John Stuart Mill produced the most famous Teleological Ethical System. Kant's theory is related to what he calls the "Categorical Imperative." Mill's to what he calls "Rule Utilitarianism."

47   The Holy Qur'an, Surah 17:22–37 (author's translation).

48   Al-Bayhaqi, *Hadith* (Islamabad: Sheikhy Press, 2018), vol. 1, hadith no. 1420. Imam Al-Bayhaqi (994–1066) was the final Sunni collector of Hadith literature.

49   Ibn Hajar, *Hadith* (Karachi: Islamosaic Press, 2007), hadith number 7073. Ibn Hajar (1372–1449) was a medieval Egyptian scholar.

50   Agustín Pániker, *Jainism* (Delhi: Motilal Press, 2010).

51   Shalu Sharma, *Hinduism Made Easy* (Delhi: Amazon Digital Services, 2019), 32.

52   Ibid., 34.

53   D. T. Suzuki and Carl Jung, *An Introduction to Zen Buddhism* (New York: Grove Books, 1994), 51–52.

54   Materialism is the philosophical view that maintains that all that exists in reality are material entities.

55   Sharma, 39.

56   Resurrection of the Body is a metaphysical belief first found in the Hebrew Bible, or Old Testament, see: The Book of Daniel 12:1–3.

57   Transmigration of the Soul is a metaphysical belief that is also called Reincarnation and Rebirth in the Indian religions.

58   Henri Frankfurt, *Ancient Egyptian Religion: An Interpretation*

(New York: Dover Books, 2011), 19–21.

59   Louis Perrois, *Fang: Vision of Africa Series* (London: 5
     Continents, 2008), 11.

60   Darlene Sadlier, *Brazil Imagined* (Austin: University of Texas
     Press, 2008), 72–74.

61   The Mossi, or Mosse, people are a West African ethnic group,
     primarily in the Volta River Basin. For more on the Mossi, see:
     Elliott P. Skinner, *The Mossi of the Upper Volta* (Palo Alto:
     Stanford University Press, 1989).

62   *Nefesh* and *ruah* are employed in the Hebrew Bible, or Old
     Testament, at Genesis 2:7, Job 12:7–10, Leviticus 17:11, and
     Psalm 33:6, as well as many other places.

63   The nouns *nafs* and *ruh* are used many times in Al-Qur'an,
     see: Surah 2:54 and 17:85, for example. Sometimes they are
     employed as words for the "Self," such as at 7:205.

64   The Sanskrit word *jiva*, a living being imbued with a life force,
     comes from the root JIV, which means "to breathe" or "to live."
     The word also appears in the Bhagavad Gita and the Upanishads.
     See the entry on "Jiva" in W. J. Johnson, *A Dictionary of
     Hinduism* (Oxford: Oxford University Press, 2009).

65   See Note 54. For more on Materialism, see: Terry Eagleton,
     Materialism (New Haven: Yale University Press, 2016),
     particularly chapter one.

66   The collection of texts known in Islam as the *Hadith* are the
     words and activities of the Prophet Muhammad recorded by his
     followers called his "Companions," known as the *Sabahah*.

67   *Kojiki: An Account of Ancient Wisdom*, ed. Ō no Yasumaro (New
     York: Columbia University Press, 2014), particularly Book I.

68   Donald Lopez, *Buddhist Scriptures* (New York: Penguin Books,
     2004).

69   There are two versions of the Talmud. They are the Babylonian
     Talmud and the Jerusalem Talmud.

70   The *Agamas* is an Indian form of spiritual literature and practice.
     They are a kind of collection of guides for various aspects of
     living including paths to salvation, holy places, principles of the
     universe, etc. See: https://bit.ly/3oGZR4r.

71   *The Vedas*, ed. Job Fergus (New York: Create Space, 2017). *The
     Upanishads*, ed. Eknath Eashwaran (Bombay: Nilgiri Press,

2007).

72   *The Zend Avesta* (London: Forgotten Books, 2008).

73   *The I Ching*, ed. and trans. Brian B. Walker (New York: Saint Martin's Press, 1991).

74   Confucius, *The Analects* (New York: Penguin Books, 1979).

75   *Guru Granth Sahib* (London: Forgotten Books, 2007).

76   Baha'u'llah, *The Seven Valleys and Four Valleys* (London: Bahá'í Publishing Trust, 1945).

77   The Kota people are an ethnic group in the Nilgiris Hill Range in India's southern-most state, the Tamil Nadu Region. The language of the Kotas is among the oldest on Earth. They practice fraternal polygyny.

78   The English word "eschatology" comes from the classical Greek *Eschaton,* which means "the end." The first use of the word in the *Oxford English Dictionary* comes from 1931.

79   For more on the Arabic word *Dajjal*, see: Stephen Vicchio, *Biblical Figures in the Islamic Faith* (Eugene: Wipf and Stock, 2008), 197–222.

80   Fergus, 199.

81   Lopez, 43–44.

82   Zechariah 14:1–21 (NRSV).

83   Ludwig Wittgenstein, *The Philosophical Investigations* (Oxford: Wiley Blackwell, 2009).

84   Vicchio, *The Voice from the Whirlwind*, 5–44.

85   Stephen Vicchio, *Job in the Ancient World* (Eugene: Wipf and Stock, 2006), 2–4.

86   Vicchio, *The Voice from the Whirlwind*, 102–113.

87   Ibid., 104–105.

88   Stephen Vicchio, *Theodicy in the Christian Tradition* (Pittsburgh: Rose Dog Books, 2020), 18.

89   Ibid., 18–19.

90   Ibid.

91   Ibid., 19.

92   Ibid.

93   Ibid., 19–21.

94   Ibid.

95   Ibid., 20–23.

96   Vicchio, *The Voice from the Whirlwind*, 8 and 27.

97 Ibid.

98 Ibid., 102–103.

99 For more on the Antecedent and Consequent Wills, see: Thomas Aquinas, *Summa Theologica*, part I, question 19, articles 1, 2, and 3.

100 Arthur Lovejoy, *The Great Chain of Being* (Cambridge: Harvard University Press, 1976).

101 G. W. Leibniz, *Theodicy* (New York: Open Court Press, 1986). Also see: Vicchio, *Theodicy in the Christian Tradition*, 296–304.

102 Ibid.

103 John Hick, *Evil and the God of Love* (London: Macmillan, 1966). Also see: Vicchio, *The Voice from the Whirlwind*, 138–153. For more on Hick's theodicy, see: Vicchio, *Theodicy in the Christian Tradition*, 497–529.

104 See: Sunder Willet, "Evil and Theodicy in Hinduism," *Denison Journal of Religion* 14 (2015): 40–53. The determinist view is on p. 48.

105 Ibid.

106 For more on the determinism of Marx and Freud, see: Valentin Voloshinov, *Freudianism: A Marxist Critique* (Moscow: N. P., 1927).

107 J. B. Watson and R. Raynor, "Conditioned Emotional Reactions," *Journal of Experimental Psychology* 3, no. 1 (1920): 1–14; B. F. Skinner, *Beyond Freedom and Dignity* (New York: Knopf, 1971). Also see: Skinner's novel, *Walden Two* (New York: Macmillan, 1948).

108 Baruch Spinoza, *Ethics* (New York: Penguin Classics, 2005). Other determinists in the nineteenth century included the Baron d'Holbach, Pierre Simon Laplace, Niels Bohr, Ralph Waldo Emerson, and more recently, Daniel Dennett. See Dennett's *Breaking the Spell: Religion as a Natural Phenomenon* (New York: Penguin Books, 2007). For more on Spinoza's view of theodicy, see: Vicchio, *Theodicy in the Christian Tradition*, 287–296.

109 The Hidden God Theory may be seen in the Old Testament, for example, at: Deuteronomy 31:17–18 and 32:20, Micah 3:4, Ezekiel 39:23–24, Isaiah 54:8, and Psalm 30:7.

110 For more on ancestor worship, see: Aladokun, *Ancestor Paths:*

Honoring Our Ancestors and Guardian Spirits Through Prayers, Rituals, and Offerings (Tokyo: Oba Ilari Books, 2012).

111 *The Bhagavad Gita* (New York: St. Martin's Press, 2019); *Mahabharata*, ed. John D. Smith (New York: Penguin Books, 2009); *The Ramanaya*, ed. Ramesh Menon (New York: North Point Press, 2019).

112 "Hindoo" in the *Oxford English Dictionary*, ed. E. S. C. Weiner (Oxford: Oxford University Press, 1991).

113 William Jones (1746–1794) was an Anglo-Welsh philologist and a member of the Bengal Supreme Court in British India. He also wrote poetry in English and Bengali.

114 Ram Mohan Roy (1772–1833) was born into a Brahmin family in British Bengal. Like his father, Ramkanto Roy, he became a scholar of Sanskrit, Persian and English languages. He also knew Arabic, Greek and Latin.

115 "Henotheism" is a metaphysical view that comes from the German *henotheismus*, which in turn comes from the Greek *heno* or "one," and *theos* or "god." It involves the belief in one prominent god while not denying the existence of the other gods.

116 Asko Parpola, *The Roots of Hinduism* (Oxford: Oxford University Press, 2015), 3–34.

117 Ibid., 21–23.

118 *Mohenjo-Daro* (Boston: Charles River Editions, 2015), 12.

119 Ibid.

120 Ibid., 13.

121 Scott Clem, *Harappa* (Boston: Charles River Editions, 2019), 19–20.

122 Mortimer Wheeler, *Civilization in the Indus Valley* (London: Thames and Hudson, 1966), 14–18.

123 Kenneth Kennedy, "Have Aryans Been Identified in the Prehistoric Skeletal Record from South Asia?" in *The Rise and Fall of the Indus Civilization*, ed. Nayanjot Lahiri (New Delhi: Permanent Black, 2000), 5–111.

124 The term "Dravidian" refers to the early inhabitants of the Indian sub-continent. It is most often used in the context of a group of languages in Southern India spoken by about 250 million Indians today.

125 Elly Van Gelderen, *A History of the English Language*

(Philadelphia: John Benjamin Publishers, 2006), 34.

126 Kennedy, 97–98.

127 The *Ashvamedha,* or "horse sacrifice," followed by the Śrauta tradition of Vedic religion, was used by the ancient Indians to prove their imperial sovereignty. For more on this idea, see: K. M. Ganguli, https://bit.ly/379KjQE.

128 Ibid.

129 *The Rig Veda,* ed. Wendy Doniger (New York: Penguin Books, 2005), 10.86.14 and 8.43.11.

130 The Sanskrit word *Devas* usually refers to a goddess: "a woman who has delicate limbs and soft looks."

131 The Sanskrit word *homo,* or *humos,* for example, are the origins of the English *homo,* or "man," as well as "humus," or soil.

132 For more on the concept of the *Devas*, see: Madhu Khanna, *Saktapramodah of Deva Nandan Singh* (New Delhi: D. K. Print World, 2013).

133 For more on the Fire god *Agni,* see: James Kalomiris, *The Many Faces of Agni* (New Delhi: Balboa Press, 2014).

134 In the *Rig Veda, Rudra* is a wind or storm deity. He is called the "mightiest of the mighty."

135 In Sanskrit, the word *rta,* or "Cosmic Order," is used throughout the Vedas. Varuna was believed to be the ruler of this realm.

136 The goddess *Mitra* is mentioned on the monuments in Commagene, a small and independent Arminian kingdom formed in 162 BCE. This was a period when the Seleucid Empire was beginning to crumble, and those at Commagene took advantage of it.

137 For more on the god Vishnu, see: Anonymous, *Hindu Supreme Lord, Vishnu* (Bombay: Handicraft Store, 1998).

138 See Note 111.

139 The Gupta Empire existed from the mid-third century CE until 543 CE. This period is considered by many to be the golden age of India.

140 The god *Devi* is also known as Mahadevi, or the "Great Goddess." In the Vedic period, she was assimilated into the Hindu pantheon and came to represent female energy or *Shakti,* one of the Sanskrit words for "Power."

141 The Sanskrit word *Bhakti* literally means "attachment,"

particularly in relation to the devotion to a deity in the Vedas.

142 The Amarnath Temple is in the Jammu region of Kashmir. It is a cave at an altitude of 4,000 meters and is one of the fifty-one Shakti Peethas temples throughout South Asia.

143 For more on the *Vaishnava Alvars*, see: S. Robertson, *Bhakti Tradition of Vaisnava Alvars and Theology of Religions* (Bombay: Punthi Pustak, 2006).

144 The Sanskrit word *Advaita* refers to a branch of Hindu theology. See: Swami Bhaskrananda, *Journey from the Many to the One* (New Delhi: Viveka Press, 2009).

145 Madhvacarya, or Madva, (1238–1317) was a Hindu philosopher and the chief proponent of the school called *Dvaita*, a Sanskrit word that means "duality" or "dualism." In this sense, Madva and his followers were advocates of a religion of solution as introduced in Chapter One of this study.

146 Emperor Akhbar (1542–1605) was the third Mughal emperor who reigned from 1556 to 1605. Akhbar gradually increased the size of the empire until it included nearly all of the Indian subcontinent. Akhbar had a library of more than 24,000 volumes.

147 For more on Akhbar the Great, see: "Akbar the Great," https://bit.ly/3qQsY7h.

148 The "Sant tradition" or the "Sant Mat" was a spiritual movement in India in the thirteenth century CE. They consisted of two groups, the northern group in the Punjab region and a southern group known as the Marathi. They later came to be called the Sikhs. For more on the Sikh tradition, see: Elenore Nesbitt, *Sikhism* (Oxford: Oxford University Press, 2016).

149 The Battle of Plassey was fought on June 23, 1757. Robert Clive was supported from a very unlikely quarter, the Armenians, a trading community who had fled persecution in Persia and later settled in India.

150 For more on Clive and the Battle of Plassey, see: Sudeep Chakravarti, *Plassey: The Battle that Changed the Course of Indian History* (London: Aleph Books, 2020).

151 The *Brahmo Samaj* is the societal component of Brahmoism, which began as a monotheistic reformist movement. See: J. N. Farquhar, *Modern Religious Movements of India*, https://bit.ly/37UMEOr, p. 29.

152   The *Santana Dharma* is a Sanskrit term to denote the "eternal" or "absolute" set of duties incumbent of all Hindus. This is contrasted with the *Svadharma*, or the "individual duty," according to his or her *varna*, or "caste."

153   Swami Narasingha, *The Universal Teacher* (Calcutta: Devavision, 1998).

154   Sri Ramakrishna (1836–1886) was one of the great Hindu sages in the nineteenth century. The Ramakrishna-Vivekananda Center of New York is dedicated to his name.

155   Mahatma Gandhi, *The Story of My Experiments with Truth* (New York: Create Space, 2016).

156   Vaibhav Vats, "Witness to Destruction: Remembering the Babri Mosque Demolition," *Al-Jazeera*, Dec. 6, 2019.

157   Subhamoy Das, "The Spiritual Quest of George Harrison in Hinduism," *Indian Arts and Culture*, March 5, 2019.

158   Christopher Vince Gonzales, *The Twelve Laws of Karma* (Bombay: Lulucom, 2018).

159   For more on Samsara, see: Gavin D. Floyd, *An Introduction to Hinduism* (Cambridge: Cambridge University Press, 1966), 82–86.

160   A variety of Greek philosophers assented to different versions of reincarnation, including Plato, Pythagoras, Meander and Lucian. Pythagoras, for example, believed that his last life was during the Trojan wars.

161   For more on moksha, see: Floyd, 154.

162   Ibid.

163   For more on *Tat tvam asi*, see: Edwin Raphael, *The Pathway of Non-Duality* (Asparsin: Philosophy Series, 2010), 100–107.

164   Ajnana is one of the *Nastika*, or "traditional schools," of heterodox Hinduism. It was a major rival of Buddhism.

165   For more on the notion of Maya, see: Gavin Floyd, "Nirvana," in *Oxford Dictionary of World Religions*, ed. John Bowker (Oxford: Oxford University Press, 2014).

166   For more on Dharma, see: Floyd, *An Introduction to Hinduism*, 11–12 and 17.

167   See Floyd, "Nirvana," 131.

168   Ibid., 17.

169   Raphael, 106–107.

170 Ibid., 107.

171 Floyd, "Nirvana," 132.

172 *Manusmriti*, ed., Bribhat Prakashan (New Delhi, N. P., 2018).

173 Ibid., 99.

174 Ibid.

175 Ibid., 100.

176 Ibid.

177 Doniger, 10.22.6.

178 *The Purusha Sukta* (London: Forgotten Books, 2017).

179 B. K. Matilal, *Hindu Logic and Epistemology* (Boston: Springer, 1982), 53–54.

180 *Katha Upanishad*, ed., Eknath Eshwaren (New Dehli: Nigiri Press, 2007), 288–290.

181 John Bowker, *Problems of Suffering in the Religions of the World*, 14.

182 Ibid., 14–15.

183 Vicchio, *The Voice from the Whirlwind*, 15.

184 Floyd, *An Introduction to Hinduism*, 85.

185 Raphael, 106.

186 Floyd, *An Introduction to Hinduism*, 17.

187 Doniger, 188.

188 Vicchio, *The Voice from the Whirlwind*, 95–102.

189 "The Kali Purana" in F. E. Pargiter, *The Purana Texts of the Dynasties of the Kali Age* (London: Biblio-Life, 2009), 17–28.

190 Ibid., 25.

191 For more on the demonic in Hinduism, see: Michael Stephen, *Desire, Divine, and Demonic* (Honolulu: University of Hawaii Press, 2005).

192 Ibid., 200–209.

193 Ibid., 200.

194 This war is known as the *Kurukshetra Conflict*. Some scholars date the conflict to 3000 BCE.

195 *The Mahabharata*, ed. John D. Smith (New York: Penguin Books, 2009), 99–103.

196 Stephen, 11–13.

197 Ibid., 14–16.

198 Ibid., 16.

199 The Sanskrit word *Asura* was a class of beings related to the

more benevolent Devas. They battle constantly with the Devas. They are powerful, super-human demigods. See: Edward Hale Wash, *Asura in Early Vedic Religion* (New Delhi: Motilal Barnasidass Press, 1999), 5–11, 22 and 99–102.

200 Emperor Aurangzeb, also known as Muhi-ud-Din-Muhammad, (1618–1707) one of the greatest Mughal emperors.

201 For more on Adi Shankara, see: Parvan Kuarma, *Adi Shankara: India's Greatest Philosopher* (Delhi: Tanquesbar, 2018).

202 Ibid., 22.

203 Ibid.

204 Ibid., 25–27.

205 Ibid., 26.

206 Will Durant, "The System of Shankara," kamakoti.org/souv/2-6.html.

207 Kaurma, 30.

208 Ibid.

209 Ibid., 31–32.

210 Ibid., 32.

211 Ibid., 33–34.

212 Doniger, 10.190.3.

213 Adi Shankara, "Atma Shatkam" is a poem consisting of six verses, or *slokas*. The poem summarizes the basic teachings of Hinduism.

214 Anselm, *Cur Deus Homo* (London: Pantianos Classics, 2010), 51–52.

215 For more on Ramanuja, see: Julius Lipner, *The Face of Truth* (New York: SUNY Press, 1986), 9–10.

216 Ibid., 11.

217 Ibid., 12–13.

218 Ibid., 13.

219 Ibid., 14.

220 Ibid., 9–10.

221 Ibid., 51.

222 Ibid.

223 Ibid.

224 Ibid., 52–53.

225 Ibid.

226 Ibid., 54–55.

227 Ibid., 55.
228 For more on the *agamas*, see: Sadhu Vivekjinadas, *Hinduism: Sacred Texts* (New Delhi: Shaminayara, 2017).
229 Ibid., 226.
230 Ibid.
231 Ramanuja, "Hinduism at a Glance," https://brewminate.com/hinduism-at-a-glance/, 20.
232 Ibid., 251–252.
233 Ibid., 25.
234 Ibid., 36.
235 Ibid.
236 For more on Ram Mohan Roy, see: William Adam, *A Lecture on the Life and Labors of Rammohan Roy* (London: Kessinger, 2010).
237 For more on Tagore, see: Rabindranath Tagore, *The Essential Tagore* (Cambridge: Belnap Press, 2017).
238 Ibid., 5–39.
239 For more on Radhakrishnan, see: S. Radhakrishnan, *The Hindu View of Life* (San Francisco: Harpers, 2015).
240 Ibid., 59–60.
241 William Cenker, *Evil and the Response of World Religion* (St. Paul: Paragon Books, 1997), 136.
242 Bill Arnold, *Introduction to the Old Testament* (Cambridge: Cambridge University Press, 2014), 1–14.
243 For more on the Hittites, see: Joanne Williamson, *Hittite Warrior* (London: Living History Library, 1999).
244 Ibid., 121.
245 Ibid.
246 Ibid.
247 Ibid., 122.
248 Ibid.
249 Ibid., 124–125.
250 First Samuel 10:10 (NRSV).
251 Jeremiah 12:1–3.
252 See: Deuteronomy 31:21, for example.
253 Job 38:5–6.
254 See, for example, Psalm 33:11.
255 Eruchin 6b.

256   See Ta'an 11a, for example.

257   See Vicchio, *Job in the Ancient World* (Eugene: Wipf and Stock, 2006), 158–176.

258   Babylonian Talmud 16a.

259   Ibid.

260   Ibid.

261   Vicchio, *Job in the Ancient World*, 139–158.

262   Ibid., 143.

263   Ibid., 145.

264   Ibid.

265   Ibid., 146.

266   Ibid.

267   Ibid.

268   Ibid., 147.

269   Ibid.

270   Ibid., 148.

271   Oliver Leaman, *Evil and Suffering in Jewish Philosophy* (Cambridge: Cambridge University Press, 1995), 37.

272   Ibid.

273   Ibid., 35–36.

274   Ibid., 36.

275   See: Stephen Vicchio, *Job in the Medieval World* (Wipf and Stock: 2006), chapters 15 and 16.

276   Ibid., chapter 15, 101–102.

277   Ibid., 88–97.

278   Ibid., 90–91.

279   Ibid., 93–94.

280   Ibid., 95.

281   Ibid., 95–96.

282   Ibid., 96.

283   Ibid., 99–101.

284   Ibid., 99.

285   Ibid., 100.

286   Ibid., 101.

287   Sanhedrin 108a.

288   Rashi quoted in Vicchio, *Job in the Medieval World*, 101–102.

289   Moses Maimonides quoted in Vicchio, *Job in the Medieval World*, 106–115.

290 Ibid., 106–107.
291 Ibid., 114–115.
292 Ibid., 115.
293 Ibid., 112–113.
294 Ibid., 113.
295 Ibid.
296 Ibid., 93.
297 Ibid.
298 Ibid.
299 Ibid., 110–111.
300 Ibid., 111.
301 Ibid.
302 Ibid.
303 Ibid., 112.
304 Ibid.
305 Ibid.
306 Ibid., 113.
307 Ibid.
308 Ibid.
309 Ibid., 114.
310 Ibid., 115.
311 Gersonides quoted in Ibid., 116–123.
312 Ibid., 117–118.
313 Ibid., 119.
314 Ibid.
315 Ibid., 120–121.
316 Ibid., 121.
317 Ibid., 122–123.
318 Ibid.
319 Ibid., 123.
320 Ibid.
321 Ibid.
322 Michael Zank, "Hermann Cohen on the Figure of Job,"
     November 10, 2019, http://bit.ly/3rbbjaA.
323 Hermann Cohen, *Der Begriff der Religion im System der
     Philosophie* (Berlin: Bruno Cassirer, 1915).
324 Herman Cohen, *Religion of Reason* (Berlin: Bruno Cassieer,
     1922), 184.

325   Martin Buber, *I and Thou* (New York: Touchstone Books, 1971).

326   Martin Buber, *Images of Good and Evil* (Oxford: Routledge, 1952), 69.

327   Martin Buber, *Imitatio Dei: The Eclipse of God* (Princeton: Princeton University Press, 2015), 81.

328   Abraham Heschel, *God in Search of Man* (New York: Farrar, Straus, and Giroux, 1976), 78–79.

329   Mordecai Kaplan, *The Problem of God* (New York: Jewish Reconstruction Foundation, 1947).

330   Robert Gordis, *The Book of God and Man* (Chicago: University of Chicago Press, 1978).

331   Ibid., 156.

332   Ibid.

333   Ibid., 157.

334   Plato, *Timaeus* (New York: Hackett Books, 2000).

335   Pierre Bayle, *Historical and Critical Dictionary* (New York: Hackett Books, 1991).

336   For more on the Cathars, see: Sean Martin, *The Cathars* (New York: Shelter Harbor Press, 2013).

337   Bayle, 71.

338   Ibid.

339   Ibid., 177.

340   Plato, 27d.

341   Ibid.

342   Plato, *The Republic*, Book IV.

343   Ibid., Book IX.

344   Plato, *Phaedo*, 69e to 84b.

345   Ibid.

346   Ibid.

347   *The Republic*, 613a.

348   *The Laws*, X 903b and c.

349   Ibid.

350   For more on an introduction to Zoroastrianism, see: Peter Clarke, *Zoroastrianism* (Sussex: Sussex Academics, 1998).

351   Ibid., 9–11.

352   *The Gathas* are seventeen hymns believed to have been written by Zoroaster.

353   Clarke, 20–21.

354 Ibid., 21.

355 For more on Cyrus the Great, see: Stephen Dando-Collins, *Cyrus the Great* (London: Turner Books, 2020).

356 Ibid., 111.

357 Clarke, 50.

358 For more on the Parsees, see: Arthur Henry Bleeck, *Avesta: The Religious Books of the Parsees*, vol. 1 (New York: Adamant Books, 2001), 43.

359 Ibid., 7.

360 Clarke, 30.

361 Ibid., 31.

362 For more on sky burial, see: Fatemeh Askarieh, "Sky Burial: Ancient Tradition of Iran's Zoroastrians," http://bit.ly/38tciKp.

363 Ibid.

364 Friedrich Nietzsche, *Thus Spoke Zarathustra* (New York: Modern Library Editions, 1995).

365 The expression "God is dead" first appeared in Nietzsche's *The Gay Science*, ed. Walter Kaufmann (New York: Vintage Books, 1974), sec. 125.

366 Clarke, 42–43.

367 Ibid., 43.

368 *The Yasnas*, XXX, 1–2.

369 Ibid.

370 Ibid., XLV, 2.

371 Ibid., 2–3.

372 Ibid.

373 Stephen Vicchio, *The Voice from the Whirlwind*, 14–16.

374 Clarke, 73–74.

375 For more on the Daevas, see: Kat Ross, *The Midnight Sea* (New York: Acorn Books, 2016).

376 Clarke, 80.

377 Ibid.

378 *The Yasnas*, XXX, 8–9.

379 Albert Bailey, "Zarathushtrian Theodicy," http://bit.ly/3pgkZie.

380 Ibid.

381 Ibid.

382 Ibid.

383 Alfred North Whitehead, *Process and Reality* (New York: Free

Press, 1929), reprinted in 1979.

384   Griffin, quoted in Vicchio, *The Voice from the Whirlwind*, 24–25.

385   Ibid.

386   For more on Mithraism, see: Minou Reeves, *Deus Sol Invictus: The Persian Sun God Mithras and the Conquering God of Rome* (New York: Garnet Publishing, 2020).

387   Ibid., 109–110.

388   Ibid., 110.

389   Ibid., 27–29.

390   Ibid., 30.

391   Ibid., 116–118.

392   Ibid., 116.

393   Ibid.

394   Ibid., 117.

395   Ibid.

396   Ibid., 118.

397   Ibid.

398   Ibid.

399   Ibid., 9–11.

400   The *Cologne Mani-Codex* is a parchment codex dated to the fifth century BCE. It is written in Greek and the author is unknown. It was originally sold by a Cairo agent. It is now owned by the University of Cologne in Germany.

401   For more on the life of Mani, see: Duncan Greenlees, *The Gospel of the Prophet Mani* (London: Book Tree, 2007).

402   Ibid., 22.

403   Ibid.

404   Ibid., 247.

405   Ibid., 25.

406   Ibid., 25–26.

407   Ibid., 26.

408   Ibid.

409   Ibid., 27–28.

410   Ibid., 28.

411   Augustine, *The Confessions*, ed. Henry Chadwick (Oxford: Oxford University Press, 2007), 5.10:18–19. He also says similar things at 3.4:6–8 and 10, as well as at 3.6:10.

412   Ibid.

413 Greenlees, 24.

414 Ibid.

415 Ibid., 25–26.

416 Ibid., 26.

417 Ibid.

418 Ibid.

419 Ibid., 25.

420 Ibid., 27–28.

421 David Hume, *Dialogues Concerning Natural Religion* (New York: Hackett, 1998).

422 David Hume, *Enquiry Concerning Human Understanding* (New York: Hackett, 1993).

423 Rabbi Harold Kushner, *When Bad Things Happen to Good People* (New York: Anchor Books, 2004).

424 Hartshorne, quoted in Vicchio, *The Voice from the Whirlwind*, 23–24.

425 Ibid.

426 Ibid., 24.

427 Ibid.

428 Brightman, quoted in Stephen Vicchio, *Theodicy in the Christian Tradition*, (Pittsburgh: RoseDog Books, 2020), 487.

429 Ibid.

430 Ibid., 484.

431 Ibid.

432 Ibid., 487.

433 Ibid.

434 John Stuart Mill, *Three Essays on Religion* (New York: Prometheus Books, 1998).

435 See: Vicchio, *Theodicy in the Christian Tradition*, 484–488.

436 William James, *The Dilemma of Determinism* (London: Kessinger, 2010).

437 Ibid., 41.

438 Ibid., 41–42.

439 Ibid., 42.

440 Ibid.

441 William James, *The Varieties of Religious Experiences* (New York: Independently Published, 2017).

442 Ibid., 106.

443 William James, *A Pluralistic Universe* (New York: Dover Books, 1995), 222.

444 Rashdall Hastings, *The Theory of Good and Evil* (London: Wentworth Press, 2019).

445 Ibid., 143.

446 Ibid.

447 Ibid., 199.

448 Ibid.

449 Ibid., 201–203.

450 Ibid., 2–3.

451 Kushner, Ibid.

452 See, for example, Kyle Butt, "The Wrong Way to Deal with the Problem of Pain," *Apologetic Press*, 2015, http://bit.ly/3nCTrmF.

453 Heather Sanche, *The Life of the Buddha* (New York: Bala Kids, 2020).

454 Ibid., 2–3.

455 Ibid., 4.

456 Ibid., 5–6.

457 Ibid., 6.

458 Ibid., 8.

459 Ibid., 9–10.

460 Ibid., 10.

461 For more on the Four Noble Truths, see: Dalai Lama, *The Four Noble Truths* (London: Thorsons, 1998).

462 Ibid., 9–11.

463 Ibid., 11.

464 Dalai Lama, *The Eight-Fold Path* (London: Thorsons, 1996).

465 Ibid., 19–21.

466 Ibid., 21.

467 Ibid.

468 Matthew Meghaprasara, *New Guide to the Tipitaka* (New York: Sangha Books, 2013).

469 Ibid., 21–22.

470 Ibid., 22.

471 Ibid., 25–26.

472 Ibid., 28.

473 Ibid.

474 Gautama Buddha, *The Numerical Discourses of the Buddha*

(London: Wisdom Books, 2010).

475 Ibid., 444.
476 Ibid.
477 Ibid., 704.
478 Ibid.
479 Ibid., 1113–1114.
480 Ibid., 1114.
481 Ibid.
482 Ibid., 1115–1116.
483 Ibid., 1116.
484 Ibid.
485 Walpola Rahula, *What the Buddha Taught* (New York: Grove Press, 1974), 63.
486 John Daido Loori, *On Karma in Buddhism* (London: Sangha Press, 1981), 49.
487 Ibid.
488 Chogyam Rinpoche, *The Art of Taking Action* (London: To Do Institute Books, 2014), 54.
489 For more on *Dhamma*, or Dharma in Buddhism, see: Sauche, 29–31.
490 Ibid., 31.
491 Ibid.
492 What is Dharma, http://bit.ly/2WHD0ty.
493 *The Bhagavad Gita*, ed. Edward Viljolen (New York: St. Martin's Press, 2019) 186.
494 Rahula, 70.
495 Sauche, 21.
496 Rahula, 71.
497 Ibid.
498 Ibid.
499 Ibid., 75.
500 Dalai Lama, *The Eight-Fold Path*, 41.
501 Ibid.
502 Ibid., 42–43.
503 Sauche, 22.
504 Dalai Lama, *The Eight-Fold Path*, 45.
505 Meghaprasara, 30–31.
506 Ibid., 31.

507 Ibid.
508 Dalai Lama, *The Eight-Fold Path*, 46.
509 Ibid.
510 Aristotle, *Nicomachean Ethics* (London: SDE Classics, 2019).
511 Rinpoche, 55–56.
512 Ibid.
513 For more on ancestor worship in China, the classic work is still R. S. Gundry, *Ancestor Worship in China* (London; Fortnightly Review, 1895).
514 Ibid., 120.
515 Ibid.
516 Ibid., 121–122.
517 Ibid., 122.
518 Ibid.
519 Ibid.
520 Ibid., 200.
521 Ibid., 212.
522 Ibid.
523 Gail Hinich Sutherland, "Demons and the Demonic in Buddhism," *Oxford Bibliographies*, April 24, 2013, http://bit.ly/2WFWjTT.
524 Ibid.
525 Ibid.
526 Ibid.
527 Ibid.
528 Ibid.
529 Ibid.
530 Ibid.
531 Ibid.
532 Ibid.
533 Ibid.
534 Ibid.
535 Ibid.
536 Dale DeBakcsy, "The Dark Side of Buddhism," *New Humanist*, January 23, 2013, n.p.n., https://bit.ly/3azrHM9.
537 Ibid.
538 Ibid.
539 Ibid.

540 Ibid.
541 Quoted in Rahula, 77.
542 Monima Chadha and Nick Trakakis, "Karma and the Problem of Evil," *Philosophy; East and West*, (2007).
543 Ibid.
544 Ibid.
545 Dalai Lama, *The Four Noble Truths*, 73.
546 Ibid.
547 Ibid., 90.
548 Ibid.
549 Dalai Lama, *The Eight-Fold Path*, 62.
550 Ibid.
551 Geshe Phelgye, "Planting Seeds in the Minds of Children," Buddhist Institute, Spokane, Washington. Geshe was born in 1956 and is a Tibetan Monk.
552 Ibid.
553 Ibid.
554 Dalai Lama, *The Eight-Fold Path*, 46.
555 Gautama Buddha, *The Numerical Discourses of the Buddha*, 100.
556 Ibid.
557 Ibid., 102–103.
558 Ibid., 103.
559 Ibid.
560 The first use of the word "Confucianism" in the *Oxford English Dictionary* comes from 1762.
561 Confucius, *The Analects*, trans. James Legge, (New York: Penguin Books, 1979) 4–7.
562 Ibid., 7.
563 Anne Davison, *A Short History of China* (New York: Amazon Digital Services, 2019), 5–27.
564 *The Analects*, 10–12.
565 Ibid., 12.
566 Davison, 25–26.
567 Ibid.
568 Robert Eno, https://bit.ly/3mGy8iQ.
569 *The Analects*, 10.
570 Ibid.

571   Ibid., 21–25.

572   Ibid., 24.

573   Ibid.

574   The Kong family cemetery and temple contains the graves of Confucius and 100,000 of his relatives. It is in the state of Lu near the city of Nanjing.

575   Qu Ying Jie, *A Brief History of the Confucian Temple* (Beijing: Social Science Academic Press, 2011).

576   Robert Cornuke, *Temple* (London: Koinonis House, 2017).

577   See Note 576.

578   Davison, 26.

579   Ibid.

580   *The Analects*, 17–18.

581   Ibid., 18.

582   Ibid., 20.

583   Ibid.

584   Ibid., 21–22.

585   Ibid., 22.

586   Ibid., 23.

587   Ibid.

588   Ibid., 25–26.

589   Ibid., 26.

590   Ibid.

591   Ibid., 27.

592   Ibid.

593   Ibid., 28.

594   Ibid. 30–31.

595   Ibid., 32.

596   Ibid.

597   Ibid., 33.

598   Ibid.

599   Ibid., 35.

600   Ibid., 36.

601   Ibid.

602   Ibid., 37–38.

603   Ibid., 38.

604   Ibid.

605   Ibid., 119.

606 Ibid., 121.
607 Ibid.
608 Ibid., 125.
609 Ibid.
610 Ibid., 130–131.
611 Ibid., 131.
612 Ibid., 134.
613 Ibid.
614 Ibid., 159.
615 *Hua Po* is a collection of poems about demonic spirits. It has only survived in oral traditions.
616 *The Analects*, 161.
617 William Jennings, "On Filial Piety," https://www.tota.world/article/888/.
618 Thomas A. Wilson, "Spirit and Soul in Confucian Ritual Discourse," *Journal of Chinese Religions*, 41, no. 1 (2014): 185–212.
619 Ibid., 187–188.
620 *The Analects*, 164–166.
621 Ibid., 165.
622 Ibid., 166.
623 Ibid., 168–169.
624 Ibid., 169.
625 Ibid., 171.
626 Ibid., 172–173.
627 Ibid., 173.
628 Davison, 27.
629 Aristotle, *Ethics* (New York: Penguin Classics, 1979).
630 Ti Hwang (1501–1570) was one of the two most prominent Korean philosophers during the Joseon Dynasty. The other was his younger contemporary Yi I, also called Yulgok. Hwang's most important work was his *To Become a Sage*. Hwang also wrote in four languages.
631 Ti Hwang, *To Become a Sage: The Ten Diagrams on Sage Learning*, p. 66.
632 Ibid., 68.
633 Yong Huang, *Evil In Neo-Confucian Thought* (Oxford: Routledge, 2018).

634 Ibid., 11–13.

635 Sachiko Murata, "The Passions of the Soul in the Ministrations of Becoming," in *Good and Evil in Islam and Neo-Confucianism.*

636 For more on the Kong family cemetery, see: http://bit.ly/37R7JLb.

637 Xun Zi (300–235 BCE) was a Chinese philosopher who lived during the Warring States period. For more on him, see: John H. Knoblock, "The Chronology of Xun Zi's Works," *Early China*, 8 (1982–83).

638 Ibid.

639 Ibid.

640 Lao Tzu, *Tao Te Ching*, ed. Stephen Mitchell (San Francisco: Harpers, 2006).

641 For more on Stoicism, see: Ward Farnsworth, *The Practicing Stoic* (Boston: David Godine Books, 2018).

642 The concept of *wu wei* in Taoism has been variously translated as "effortless action," "no action," "without action," and many other ways.

643 The three treasures, or *San-Bao* in Mandarin Chinese, are the *Tao,* the *Jing* and the *Shi*. In some Chinese traditions they are called the "Three Pure Ones."

644 In fact, the earliest Chinese sources that mention ancestor worship we have so far are from the sixth century CE.

645 Emperor Xuanzong is sometimes called Li Yi or Li Chen. He was considered the last capable emperor of the Tang Dynasty.

646 See: Pei Ting Yu, *Tang Dynasty Emperor Xuanzong* (Beijing: Book DNA, 2013).

647 Sima Qian, quoted in Jennifer Jay, *The Grand Scribe's Records Written by Sima Qian* (Cambridge: Cambridge University Press, 1952), 48.

648 Mitchell, 5–6.

649 Ibid., 6.

650 Ibid., 111.

651 See the article on Laozi published in the *Stanford Encyclopedia of Philosophy* (December 15, 2001).

652 Mitchell., 7–9.

653 The *Songs of Chu* in an anthology of ancient Chinese poetry

by Qu Yuan and others. Columbia University Press published an edition of the work in 2017, edited and translated by Gopal Sikhu.

654 All of these Chinese ideas and virtues may be found in Sarah Allan, *The Way of Water and the Sprouts of Virtue* (Albany: SUNY Press, 1997).

655 Mitchell, 17.

656 Ibid.

657 Ibid., 92.

658 Chuang Tzu, *The Book of Chuang Tzu*, ed. Martin Palmer (New York: Penguin Books, 2007), 10–11.

659 Ibid., 11.

660 Ibid., 22.

661 Ibid., 79.

662 Skepticism is a philosophical movement first identified with the Eleatics and Heraclitus.

663 Hui Shih (380–310 BCE) was a philosopher during the Warring States period. He represented what was called the "School of Names" and was famous for his twelve paradoxes similar to Zeno's paradoxes in the West.

664 For more on the *Yuen Sun*, see: Derek M. C. Yuen, *Deciphering Sun Tzu* (Oxford: Oxford University Press, 2014).

665 Mitchell, 195.

666 Mojtaba Zarvani, "Evil in Taoism," *Religious Inquiries* 5, no. 10 (2016): 35–47.

667 Ibid., 40.

668 Mitchell, 73.

669 Ibid., 74–75.

670 Ibid., 75.

671 Zervani, 41.

672 Ibid., 42–43.

673 Ibid.

674 Chuang Tzu, 88.

675 Ibid.

676 Mitchell, 100.

677 Mitchell, 11–12.

678 Ibid., 105.

679 Ibid., 93.

680   Ibid., 94–95.

681   Fred W. Drake, *China Charts the World: Hsu Chi-yu and His Geography of 1848* (Cambridge: Harvard University Press, 1975).

682   Ibid.

683   Ibid.

684   Ibid., 57.

685   Ibid.

686   Ibid., 59–60.

687   Ibid., 63.

688   Mitchell, 141.

689   Drake, 142.

690   The word *Fashi* in China is also known as the *Hangtou daoishi*, which also means "Red-headed."

691   For more on the monsters and demons discussed here, see: Jacob Dalton, *The Taming of the Demons: Violence and Liberation in Tibetan Buddhism* (New Haven: Yale University Press, 2013).

692   The Japanese expression *Kami no michi* means "The way of the Kami." It corresponds to the Mandarin *Shen-tao* as the designation for the indigenous religion of Japan. See: *The Concise Oxford Dictionary of World Religions*.

693   Ibid.

694   For more on the *Magatsuhi*, see: Brian Bocking, *A Popular Dictionary of Shinto* (Richmond: Curzan Books, 1995).

695   "Matsuri" in Ibid.

696   Ibid.

697   The *Yayoi* period was at the beginning of the Neolithic Age and continued through the Bronze Age. Carbon dating evidence suggests this society was much older than initially believed, even as early as the tenth century BCE.

698   Both the *Kojiki* and the *Nihon Shoki* have recently been published in new editions by Forgotten Books in 2008. They both use the Basil Hall Chamberlain (1850–1935) translations from the early twentieth century.

699   Ibid.

700   Ibid.

701   The Meiji Era was a forty-four-year period from 1868 until 1912 when Japan was ruled by Emperor Mutsuhito, who was the first

emperor with any real power for generations.

702 This occurred when Japan officially surrendered on September 2, 1945.

703 The word *Bunrei* refers to the entreating of a deity enshrined in one location to depart so that it might then reside in another place. For more, see: Nishioka Kazuhiko, "Benrei," *Encyclopedia of Shinto* (March 31, 2007), http://21coe.kokugakuin.ac.jp/.

704 The word *mutsubi* in modern Japanese designates a form of energy that exists in all believers of the Shinto faith. It literally comes from the verb "to tie." It is a reference to the binds of close relationships.

705 The word *Aki* is as close as one can come in Japanese to a natural disaster, or some great natural evil.

706 The *Shimenawa* is a "sacred rope" that identifies a place as a Shinto shrine.

707 See: Bocking, "Shinto," *A Popular Dictionary of Shinto*.

708 Motoori Norinaga (1730–1801) was perhaps the greatest of Shinto thinkers in the modern era. Most of his major works are translated into German, but not, as yet, in English.

709 Most of the quotations from Norinaga come from a MA thesis Delia Ursulesch completed on Norinaga at Liberty Baptist University, Virginia, in April of 2010.

710 Ibid.

711 Ibid.

712 See Note 706.

713 Norinaga.

714 Ibid.

715 Urabe Kanetomo, *A Study of Shinto* (London: Routledge, 1926), 126.

716 Taishi Kato, interview July 24, 2016, http://bit.ly/3rxzb8a.

717 For more on the Tengu, see: Roald Knutsen, *Tengu* (Leiden: Brill, 2011).

718 Ibid., 99–102.

719 Ibid., 57–60.

720 Ibid., 11–13.

721 Ibid., 64–65.

722 Ibid., 65.

723   Ibid., 70.
724   Ibid., 65.
725   Ibid.
726   Ibid., 104–105.
727   For more on Japanese Noh Masks, see: Friedrich Perzynski, *Japanese No-Masks* (New York: Dover Art Books, 2005).
728   *The Great Wave of Kanagawa by Hokusai*, Metropolitan Museum of Art, Acc. No. JP1847.
729   Ibid.
730   The Japanese word *Horishi* is used for both wood carvers and tattoo artists in Japan.
731   See Note 653.
732   See Note 696.
733   Luke 13:4.
734   John 9:1–12.
735   *The Adnationes* quoted in Vicchio, *Job in the Medieval World*, 150–152.
736   *Adnationes*, Comment on Job 1:20–22.
737   Ibid.
738   Ibid., on Job 2:6.
739   *On Genesis* 22:1.
740   *The City of God*, book XI, chapter 17.
741   Thomas Aquinas, *Summa Contra Gentiles* (Casper: Coyote Canyon Press, 2011); *Summa Theologica* (Casper: Coyote Canyon Press, 2010).
742   Commentary on Book of Job, on Job 2:6–12.
743   Arthur Lovejoy, *The Great Chain of Being* (Cambridge: Harvard University Press, 1936), 57–60.
744   Martin Luther, *On the Bondage of the Will* (Ada: Baker Academic 2012).
745   Ibid., p. 63.
746   Erasmus, *The Battle over Free Will* (New York: Hackett, 2012).
747   Ibid., p. 5.
748   Luther, *On the Bondage of the Will*.
749   Erasmus, 10–22.
750   Luther, *Letters* (July 9, 1537).
751   Erasmus, 19.
752   Ibid.

753 Luther, *On the Bondage of the Will*, 37.
754 Ibid.
755 Ibid., 38–39.
756 Ibid., 39.
757 Ibid., 43.
758 Ibid., 59.
759 Ibid.
760 Ibid., 66.
761 Ibid.
762 John Calvin, *The Institutes of the Christian Religion*, vol. 3.
763 Immanuel Kant, "On the Failure of All Attempted Philosophical Theodicies," in Michel Despland, *Kant on History and Religion* (Canberra: McGill Queens, 1973), 47–59.
764 G. W. Leibniz, *Theodicy* (New York: Open Court, 1986).
765 Kant, "On the Failure of All Attempted Philosophical Theodicies," speaks of Job and his book, 36–41.
766 Ibid.
767 Ibid.
768 Immanuel Kant, "On Natural Disasters" (Konigsberg, 1762).
769 Ibid.
770 Immanuel Kant, "On Earthquakes" (Konigsberg, 1755).
771 Ibid.
772 Immanuel Kant, "On Wind" (Konigsberg, 1758).
773 Immanuel Kant, "On the Comet of July 23, 1762" (Konigsberg, 1762).
774 Immanuel Kant, "On the Volcanoes on the Moon" (Konigsberg, 1963).
775 Immanuel Kant, "On Weather" (Konigsberg, 1794).
776 "On Failure," 113–114.
777 Immanuel Kant, *Bereitstellung und Pflege von Kants Gesarmmelten Werken in Elektronisher* (Cambridge: Cambridge University Press, 2008).
778 William Blake, *Illustrations of the Book of Job* (London: UPNE, 1966).
779 Ibid.
780 Ibid.
781 William Blake, *Songs of Innocence* (New York: Dover Books, 1971).

782 William Blake, "Job Protesting His Innocence," 1792.

783 John Henry Newman, *Parochial and Plain Sermons* (San Francisco: Ignatius Press, 1997).

784 G. K. Chesterton, Essay on the Book of Job, https://www. chesterton.org/introduction-to-job/.

785 Ibid.

786 Ibid.

787 Ibid.

788 G. K. Chesterton, *The Man Who Was Thursday* (London: Chesterton Books, 2017).

789 Anwar Cara, *5 Pillars of Islam* (London: Islamic Foundation, 2015).

790 For more on the Angel *Jibril*, see: Ibn Kathir, *Allah's Angels* (Islamabad: Dar-Islam, 2017).

791 For more on the prophets recorded in Al-Qur'an, see: Irfan Alli, *25 Prophets in Islam* (New York: Independently Published, 2017).

792 Ibid.

793 The seven levels of Hell in Islam are: *al naraka* (place of punishment), *al-Nar* (the Fire), *Jahim* (Blazing Fire), *Hutamah* (that which breaks to pieces), *Hawayah* (The Abyss), *Ladtha* (the Blaze), and *Saqar* (the Worst).

794 For more on the concept of *Qadar*, see: Saeed Sieny, *Fate: Al-Qadaa Wa Qadar* (Karachi: Al-Attique, 2000).

795 For more on the five requirements of Islam, see: Idries Shah, *Seeker After Truth* (Karachi: ISF Publishing, 2018).

796 Ibid., 11–12.

797 Ibid., 13.

798 Ibid., 15.

799 Ibid., 16.

800 Ibid., 18.

801 Ibid., 20.

802 For more on survival after death in Islam, see: Katherine Boo, *Behind the Beautiful Forevers* (New York: Random House, 2014).

803 For more on the idea of *Barzakh*, see: Muhammad Ibn Mustafa, *Life in al-Barzakh: From Death until Resurrection* (Karachi: Al-Kitaab & as-Sunnah Publishing, 2013).

804 For the ninety-nine names for Allah in Isla, see: Daniel Thomas Dyer, *The 99 Names of God Contemplation* (Montpelier: Chickpea Press, 2019).

805 For more on the ideas of the *Dajjal* in Islam, see: Ahmad Thomson, *Al-Dajjal* (London: Ta Ha Publishing, 1997).

806 For more on the idea of the *Mahdi*, the Arabic word for the "Messiah," see: Sayyid Muneer Alkhabbaz, *The Mahdi* (New York: The Mainstay Foundation, 2018). For more on *Israfil*, see: Stephen Burge, *Angels in Islam: Culture and Civilization in the Middle East* (London: Routledge, 2019), also see: Stephen Vicchio's *The Mala'ika: Angels in Islam* (Minneapolis: Wisdom Editions, 2020).

807 The seven levels of Heaven in Islam are *Jannah* (Residence), *Firdaus* (The Garden), *Jannah an-Naeem* (The Garden of Delight), *Jannah Mawah* (The Garden of Refuge), *Dar-ul Khuld* (The Garden of Immortality), *Dar-us-Maqaam* (The Mansion of Eternity), and *Dar-Al-Salaam* (The Abode of Peace).

808 For more on the idea of *Shirk* in Al-Qur'an, see: 26:89, 72:5, 30:17, 38:3 and 19:46.

809 For more on the *Ka'ba*, see: Terry Nelson, *Ka Ab Ba: Building the Lighted Temple* (Mattapan, MA: Academy of Kemetic Education & Wellness, 2000).

810 This traveling to Jerusalem by Jibril and Muhammad is known as the *Night Journey* in traditional Islam. See: Kathryn Lacky, *The Night Journey* (London: Puffin Books, 2005).

811 The city of Karbala in Iraq is important in Islam because it is the site of one of the early Great Battles of Islam that took place on October 11, 680.

812 The "Grand Mufti" is only used in Sunni Islam.

813 The "Grand Ayatollah" is only used in Shiite Islam.

814 The Holy Qur'an 5:100. Unless otherwise stated, all Arabic translations are those of the author.

815 The Holy Qur'an 65:93.

816 The Battle of Uhud appears in Al-Qur'an at 3:121–123.

817 A'id Al-Khudri, *Hadith*, No. 666.6.

818 Sahih Bukhari, *Hadith*, bk. 70, no. 545.

819 Ibid., no. 548.

820 Sahih Muslim, *Hadith*, bk. 26, no. 5432.

821 Bukhari, bk. 70, no. 550.

822 Abu Daud, *Hadith*, no. 121.

823 Abu Hurayra, *Hadith*, bk. 4, no. 4345.

824 Ibid.

825 Jafar Al-Tabari, *Hadith*, no. 492.

826 Hurayra, bk. 4, no. 53.

827 For more on the *Mu'tazila*, see: Matthew Martin, *The Mu'tazila* (New York: Google Digital Services, 2013).

828 Ibid.

829 For more on the Asharites, see: Faruq Hamadah, *The Asharites* (Damascus: Dar al-Qalam, 2014).

830 Ibid., 107.

831 Hamid Al-Ghazali, *The Alchemy of Happiness* (London: Martino Fine, 2017), 163.

832 Edoardo Albert, *Ibn Sina: A Concise Life* (London: Kube Books, 2013), 53–54.

833 Fakhr al-Din al-Razi, *Rizi's Traditional Psychology*, trans. A. J. Arberry (London: Kazi Publications, 2013), 96.

834 Jon Hoover, *Ibn Taymiyya* (Islamabad: Oneworld Academic, 2020), 59–61.

835 Ibid., 61.

836 Ibn Qayyim, *Purification of the Heart and Soul* (Karachi: Darussalam, 2019), 277.

837 Jalal Ibn Rumi, *The Essential Rumi* (San Francisco: Harpers, 1983), 129.

838 Ibid., 130–131.

839 Ibid., 131.

840 Tubanur Ozkan, *A Muslim's Response to Evil: Said Nursi on Theodicy* (London: Routledge, 2018).

841 Ibid., 189–195.

842 Ibid., 93–116.

843 Abdul Hakim, *The Political Struggle of Sayid Jamal al-Din Afghani* (Cairo: Bailahi, 1977).

844 Muhammad Abduh, *The Theology of Unity* (London: George Allen & Unwin, 1966), 49–53.

845 Ibid., 29–43.

846 Sayyid Ibrahim Qutb, *Milestones* (Cairo: Islamic Book Service, 2006).

847 Ibid.
848 The report from the American 9-11 Commission, for example, mentioned Sayyid Qutb as a philosophical source for Osama bin Laden.
849 Mulla Sadra, *The Wisdom of the Throne* (Princeton: Princeton University Press, 1983).
850 Ibid., 217.
851 Ibid.
852 Ibid., 220.
853 Ibid.
854 Ibid., 221.
855 Ibid.
856 Ibid., 222.
857 Said Nursi, *The Words* (Istanbul: Tughra Books, 2010), 66.
858 Ibid.
859 Ibid., 70–71.
860 Ibid., 71.
861 Ibid.
862 Ibid., 72–73.
863 Ibid., 73.
864 Ibid., 74–75.
865 Ibid., 75.
866 Ibid.
867 Ibid., 76–77.
868 Ibid., 77.
869 The Holy Qur'an 25:77, author's translation.
870 Nursi, *The Words*, 811–82.
871 Muhammad Iqbal, *The Development of Metaphysics* (Lahore, 1908), re-issued by Tughra books in 1980.
872 Muhammad Iqbal, *Tulip in the Desert* (Canberra: McGill-Queens University Press, 1980), 53.
873 Ibid., 67.
874 Muhammad Iqbal, "Omniscience and Human Freedom," *The Muslim World* 95, no. 1 (2005).
875 Muhammad Iqbal, *The Reconstruction of Religious Thought in Islam* (New York: CreateSpace, 2016).
876 Ibid., 81.
877 Ibid., 82–83.

878 Ibid., 83–84.

879 Ibid.

880 Ibid., 121–123.

881 Ibid., 123.

882 Ibid., 81–83.

883 Ibid.

884 All of these countries mentioned here are Islamic lands, although there are many Catholics in Mozambique.

885 World Religion Database (2015).

886 Ibid., 163.

887 United Nations Statistical Division, "The Religions of Africa," (2018).

888 Ibid.

889 Ibid.

890 Ibid.

891 E. O. Oyelade, "Evil in Yoruba Religion and Culture," in *Evil and the Responses of the World's Religions*, ed. William Cenker (Saint Paul: Paragon Books, 1997), 157–169.

892 See the article written by Laird Scranton in *Encyclopedia Britannica*.

893 For more on West African high gods, see: Charles H. Long's "The West-African High God: History and Religious Experience," *History of Religions* 3, no. 2 (Winter, 1964): 328–342.

894 For more on the High God in African religion, see: "High God" by the editors of *Encyclopedia Britannica*, as well as Charles H. Long, "The West African High God," *History of Religions* 3, no. 2 (Winter, 1964): 328–342.

895 Audrey Richards, *Hunger and Work in a Savage Tribe* (New York: Psychology Press, 2004). The original study was published in 1932.

896 Ibid., 17.

897 Ibid., 22.

898 Ibid., 25.

899 Ibid.

900 Ibid.

901 William Haviland, *Cultural Anthropology* (Independence: Cengage Learning, 2016), 62.

902 Hilda Kuper, *Swazi: A South African Kingdom* (New York: Rinehart and Winston, 1963), 79.

903 Ibid.

904 Ibid., p. 80.

905 For more on the Tallensi, see: Meyer Fortes, *The Dynamics of Clanship Among the Tallensi* (London: Routledge, 2020).

906 "The Tallensi," in *The Oxford Handbook of the Archaeology of Ritual and Religion*, ed. Timothy Insoll (Oxford: Oxford University Press), 43–47.

907 William Howells, *The Heathens: Primitive Man and His Religion* (New York: Doubleday, 1962), 57–58.

908 For more on the Sakata People, see: Eric Bylin, *Basakata: Le peuple du pays de l'entre-fleuves Lukenie-Kasai* (Paris: NP, 1966). Also see: Lisa Colldén, *Trésors de la tradition orale Sakata* (Uppsala: Studies in Cultural Anthropology, 1979).

909 Ibid., Colldén, 56.

910 For more on witches in Kenya and Ghana, see: James Howard Smith, *Bewitching Development* (Chicago: University of Chicago Press, 2009).

911 Samuel Lumwe, "The Cosmology of Witchcraft," *Journal of Adventist Studies* 13, no. 1 (2017): 83–97.

912 Ibid.

913 E. E. Evans-Pritchard, *Witchcraft, Oracles, and Magic among the Azande* (Oxford: Oxford University Press, 1976).

914 Peter Pels, *Magic and Modernity* (Palo Alto: Stanford University Press, 2003).

915 See the article on the Dogon people written by the editors of the *Encyclopedia Britannica*.

916 See https://www.igboguide.org/HT-chapter6.htm.

917 Author's translation.

918 Lumwe, 94.

919 Richard Cavendish, *The World of Ghosts and the Supernatural* (New York: Facts on File, 1994), 104.

920 The expression "stateless nation" was used in Africa throughout the 1970s.

921 The word *Umunna* in the Igbo language means "of the same clan or family." See the Umunna Cultural Association of Manitoba for more meanings of the term.

922 Chunua Achebe, *Things Fall Apart* (New York: Penguin Books, 1994).

923 Ibid.

924 Author's analysis.

925 Ibid.

926 Author's translations.

927 Samuel Ajayi Crowther, *Vocabulary of the Yoruba* (Amazon Digital Services, 2014).

928 Ibid., entry on Esu.

929 Ibid.

930 Ibid.

931 Ibid.

932 Author's translation.

933 Wande Abimbola, *Ifá Divination Poetry* (Lagos: NOK Press, 1977), 173–174.

934 Oyelade, 160.

935 Ibid.

936 For more on the *mmo*, see the article in *Encyclopedia.com*.

937 For more on the name Chukwa, see: Edmund Egboh, "A Reassessment of the Concept of Chukwa in the Igbo Tradition," in *Chukwa: Myth, History, and Society* (Lagos: Africa World Press, 2006).

938 For more on the god *Sopona*, see: David J. Sencer, "Shapona: The Yoruba God of Smallpox," Center for Disease Control and Prevention.

939 Oyelade, 160–161.

940 Ibid.

941 Ibid.

942 The word *dibia* or *dibia aja* are two terms for diviner or medicine man in the Yoruban language.

943 The last category is what the Igbo would call "Metaphysical Evil," which is psychological pain or distress.

944 Wande Abimbola, *Ifá Divination Poetry* (Lagos: NOK Press, 1977), 77.

945 The witch doctor in Nigeria was originally a type of healer who treated ailments believed to be caused by witchcraft. Now it is more often used to describe a healer. The first mention of "witch doctor" in the *Oxford English Dictionary* was in 1842.

946 For more on Igbo Oracles, see: Simon Ottenberg, "Ibo Oracles and Intergroup Relations," *Southwestern Journal of Anthropology* 14, no. 3 (Autumn, 1958): 295–317.

947 For more on Ekwensu, see: Damian Opata, *Ekwensu in the Igbo Imagination: A Heroic Deity or Christian Devil* (Nsukka: Great AP Express, 2005).

948 For more on these minor gods, see: Mildred Amadiegwu, "The Power of the Alusi," *The Guardian*, August 6, 2004.

949 For more on the Orishas, see: Lilith Dorsey, *Orishas, Goddesses, and Voodoo Queens* (London: Weiser Books, 2020). Among the most significant of the Orishas are:
   1. *Olokun,* god of the sea
   2. *Olosa,* goddess of the Lagos Lagoon
   3. *Shankpanna,* smallpox god
   4. *Shigidi,* personifies hate
   5. *Olarosa,* god of houses
   6. *Dada,* god of newborns
   7. *Oya,* goddess of the Niger
   8. *Oshun,* goddess of the River Oshun
   9. *Oba,* goddess of the River Oba
   10. *Aje Shaluga,* god of wealth
   11. *Orisra Oko,* god of vegetation and farming
   12. *Osanhin,* god of medicine
   13. *Aroni,* god of the forest
   14. *Aja,* god of the vine
   15. *Oye,* god of the wind
   16. *Ibeji,* god of twins
   17. *Oshumare,* rainbow god
   18. *Oke,* god of hills and mountains
   19. *Oshosi,* god of hunters
   20. *Orun,* god of the sun
   21. *Aja-Oshu,* goddess of the moon

950 E. O. Oyelade, "Evil in Yoruba Religion and Culture," in *Evil and the Responses of the World's Religions*, ed. William Cenker (Saint Paul: Paragon Books, 1997), 161.

951 Of these three, Orisa-Oko is the most noteworthy. She is the defender of the laws of the Earth according to the Yoruba language.

952   Bayard Taylor, *Ancestor Worship* (New York: NP, 1871).

953   A collection of Taylor's articles was published in two volumes as *Views Afoot; Or, Europe Seen with Knapsack and Staff* published in 1859.

954   Meyer Fortes, "Some Reflections on Ancestor Worship in Africa" in *African Systems of Thought* (Oxford: Oxford University Press, 1985), 121. Meyer Fortes (1906–1983) was a South African-born anthropologist. He taught at the University of Cambridge from 1950 until 1973 as a Professor of Anthropology.

955   See Note 947.

956   For more on rites of passage in West African societies, see: Anonymous, "Rites of Passage: African Rites," in *Encyclopedia. com* and Shankwan Winddrow, *Initiations* (New York: Borders Publishing, 2005).

957   This Determinist View is related to what is known as "Good Destiny" in many places in West Africa. For more on the concept in Igbo culture, see: Nelson Urokhuwamedua, "The Ontology of Destiny and Freedom in the Igbo African" in *Idea* (2016): 272–286.

958   Aristotle discusses the idea of a definition several places. The most important of these is the "Posterior Analytics," in *Metaphysics* (New York: Dover Books, 2018), bk. Z, 992a–96b. Aristotle also discusses the nature of human identity in his *De Anima*, or "On the Soul," at bk. I.5; bk. III.4, where he says a human is a "featherless biped."

959   Ludwig Wittgenstein, *Philosophical Investigations* (Oxford: Wiley-Blackwell, 2009). Augustine's example of how he learned language could be found in his *Confessions* (Oxford: Oxford University Press, 2009), I.8. For more on Wittgenstein's Family Resemblance Approach, see: Eric Mueller, *Family Resemblance* (London: Daylight Books, 2020). Also see: Stephen Vicchio, *The Voice from the Whirlwind: The Problem of Evil in the Modern World* (Westminster: Christian Classics, 1989), 238–242.

960   Ibid., 69–71.

961   Aristotle was the first thinker in the West to suggest when someone is fully morally responsible for his or her behavior. He says one is responsible for evil if the person, 1. Intended to

do evil, 2. Knew it was evil, 3. Understands the circumstances under which it is done, and 4. If the person had the "ability to do otherwise." The Greek philosopher makes these claims in his *Nicomachean Ethics*, bk. II, 6–9. For more on his view, see: Susan Sauve Meyer, *Aristotle on Moral Responsibility* (Oxford: Oxford University Press, 2012).

962 Huston Smith, *The World's Religions* (London: Harpers, 2009), 9–11. Smith sketches out these characteristics for a "religion" in the opening of the book. Also see: O. M. Mathew, *Introduction to the World's Religions* (New York: Create Space, 2016), 6–11; and John Bowker, *Problems of Suffering in the Religions of the World* (Cambridge: Cambridge University Press, 1970), 1–4.

963 Vicchio, 85–152.

964 Stephen Vicchio, *Theodicy in the Christian Tradition: A History* (Pittsburgh: RoseDog Books, 2020), 23–25.

965 The first mention of the word "Hindoo" in *The Oxford English Dictionary* was in 1671.

966 A. L. Basham, *The Origins and Development of Early Hinduism* (Oxford: Oxford University Press, 1989), 1–20. Also see: Asko Parpoli, *The Roots of Hinduism: Early Aryan and Indus Civilization* (Oxford: Oxford University Press, 2015).

967 Ibid., 24–26.

968 For more on Shankara and Ramanuja, see: Swami Adivivananda, *Sri Ramanuja Bhasya* (Delhi: Ramakrishnan Math, 2009).

969 Ibid., 121.

970 For more on the concept of *Berith*, see: Bernard Lamborelle, *The Covenant: On the Origins of the Abrahamic Faith by Means of Deification* (New York: CreateSpace, 2017).

971 For more on the three parts of Hebrew scriptures, see: Robert Alter, *The Hebrew Scriptures* (New York: Norton, 2018), 17–21. Also see: the BBC's "Sacred Scripture" www.bbc.co.uk.

972 The Hidden God view may be seen at Micah 4:4; Ezekiel 39:23–24; Psalm 44:24, 88:14, and 10:1, for example. The Permission Theory can be found at Isaiah 45:7, Proverbs 16:4, Second Chronicles 18:22, and the Book of Job 2:10. For more on Dualism, see: Matt Stefon, "Dualism," britannica.com/topic/dualism-religion.

973 Vicchio, *The Voice from the Whirlwind*, 18–20.

974 For more on the idea of the *Skandas*, see: *The Skanda Purana*, (Dehli: Motilal Books, 2007).

975 For more on reincarnation in Buddhism, see: Takashi Tsuji, "Reincarnation," https://bit.ly/2N18f14. Also see: Lati Rinbochay and Jeffrey Hopkins, *Death, Intermediate State and Rebirth in Tibetan Buddhism*, (Boulder: Snow Lion Books, 1981).

976 For more on the Four Noble Truths and the Eight-Fold Path, see: Judith Yandell, *Buddhism for Beginners* (New York: Independently Published, 2012), particularly 30–53.

977 Ibid., 54–73.

978 Vicchio, 126–129.

979 Confucius, *The Analects* (New York: Penguin Classics, 1979). For more on the *Analects*, see: The various editions edited by James Legge, The Skylight edition of 2011, and the Digireads edition of 2017.

980 Daniel Gardner, *Confucianism* (Oxford: Oxford University Press, 2014).

981 The Axial Age was an expression invented by German philosopher and psychologist Karl Jaspers (1883–1969).

982 Karl Jaspers, *The Origin and Goal of History* (New Haven: Yale University Press, 1949). Jaspers also uses the same term in his *The Ways to Wisdom* (New Haven: Yale University Press, 1951).

983 Gardner, 16–23.

984 Ibid.

985 For more in the Shinto faith, see: Sokyo Ono, *Shinto: The Kami Way* (San Francisco: Tuttle Publishing, 2004). Also see: O. M. Mathew, *Introduction to World's Religions* (New York; Create Space, 2016), 37–54.

986 For more on Taoism, see: Alan Watts, *The Tao* (New York: Pantheon Books, 1977). Also see: Eva Wong, *Lieh-Tzu: A Taoist Guide to Practical Living* (Boulder: Shambhala Books, 2001).

987 Ono, 9–13.

988 Vicchio, 138–153.

989 Ibid., 85–152.

990 Stephen Vicchio, *Theodicy in the Christian Tradition* (Pittsburgh: Rose Dog Books, 2020), 195–203.

991 Ibid., 229–256.

992 For more on irresistible grace, go to: http://bit.ly/35zqFMz.

993 John Calvin, *The Institutes of the Christian Religion* (New York: Independently Published, 2017), 252–254. In John Calvin's famous TULIP formulation, of course, the I stands for "Irresistible Grace."

994 G. W. Leibniz, *Theodicy* (New York: Open Court, 1986). For more on Leibniz's views on the problem of evil and theodicy, see: Vicchio, *Theodicy in the Christian Tradition*, 296–304.

995 For more on Kant's idea of "radical evil," see the article by Erik Hanson on radical evil in the *International Encyclopedia of Philosophy*. For more on Kant's views on theodicy, see: Vicchio, *Theodicy in the Christian Tradition*, 401–433.

996 William Blake, *Illustrations of the Book of Job* (Richmond: Virginia Museum of Fine Arts, 2004). For more on Blake's views on evil, suffering, and the Book of Job, see: Vicchio, Stephen Vicchio, *Job in the Ancient World*, 100–115.

997 G. K. Chesterton, "An Essay on the Book of Job," in *Heretics and Orthodoxy* (London: Lexam Books, 2017). Chesterton also dealt with the issues of evil and suffering in his novel *The Man Who Was Thursday* (London: Chesterton Books, 2017). For more on Chesterton's view on evil, see: Stephen Vicchio, *Job in the Modern World* (Eugene: Wipf and Stock, 2006), 186–188.

998 Among these books of William James were *The Varieties of Religious Experience*, *Pragmatism*, *The Will to Believe*, *The Principles of Psychology*, and *A Pluralistic Universe*, for example. For more on his view of the Book of Job, see: Vicchio, *Job in the Ancient World*, 178–179.

999 John Henry Newman, *Parochial and Plain Sermons* (London: Rivingtons, 1875). For more on Newman's views on the Book of Job, see: Vicchio, *Job in the Ancient World*, 177–178.

1000 G. K. Chesterton, *The Book of Job* (London: Classic Reprints, 2017). Also see: Vicchio, *Job in the Ancient World,* 187–189.

1001 Anwar Cara, *5 Pillars of Islam* (London: Islamic Foundation, 2015). For more on the Five Pillars of Islam, see: Musharraf Hussain, *The Five Pillars of Islam* (Karachi: Kube Publishing, 2012), and Isam Ahmad, *Five Pillars of Islam* (Makkah: Al-Makahranna, 2013).

1002 Charles Le Gai Eaton, *The Book of Hadith* (London: Book

Foundation, 2008). For more on traditional Hadith literature, consult Jonathan A. C. Brown, *Hadith* (Islamabad: Oneworld Publications, 2017), second edition.

1003 Ibid., 100–105.

1004 Khaled Rouhyleb, *Islamic Philosophy* (Oxford: Oxford University Press, 2019). For more on these Islamic philosophers, see: Peter Adamson, *Philosophy in the Islamic World* (Oxford: Oxford University Press, 2014), and Seyyed Hossein Nasr, *Islamic Philosophy from Its Origin to the Present: Philosophy in the Land of Prophecy* (Albany: SUNY Press, 2006).

1005 Tubanur Ozkan, *A Muslim Response to Evil: Said Nursi on the Theodicy* (London: Routledge, 2018).

1006 Rouhyleb, 173–202.

1007 For more on Panentheism, see: anonymous article on "Panentheism," in Encyclopedia.com, July 17, 2020. Also see: David Ray Griffin, *Panentheism and Scientific Naturalism* (Claremont: Process Century Press, 2014).

1008 Muhammad Iqbal, *The Reconstruction of Religious Thought in Islam* (Lahore: Muhammad Ashraf, 1982), 81–83. Also see: Adnan Aslan, "The Fall and Overcoming Evil and Suffering in Islam," in *The Origin and the Overcoming of Evil and Suffering in the World Religions*, ed. Peter Koslowski (Dordrecht: Klower Academic Publishers, 2001), 24–47.

Index

About the Author

Before his retirement in 2016, Stephen Vicchio taught for more than forty years at the University of Maryland, Johns Hopkins, St. Mary's Seminary in Baltimore, and other universities in Britain and the United States. He has authored over three dozen books, as well as essays and plays, mostly about the Bible, philosophy and theology. Among his books since 2000 is his interpretation of the Book of Job, *The Antichrist: A History*; *Biblical Figures in the Islamic Faith* and books about the religions of American presidents George Washington, Thomas Jefferson and Abraham Lincoln, including *Ronald Reagan's Religious Beliefs*.

Made in the USA
Middletown, DE
22 August 2021